New Perspectives on the Black
Intellectual Tradition

New Perspectives on the Black Intellectual Tradition

✦

Edited by Keisha N. Blain,
Christopher Cameron,
and Ashley D. Farmer

NORTHWESTERN UNIVERSITY PRESS
EVANSTON, ILLINOIS

Northwestern University Press
www.nupress.northwestern.edu

Printed in the United States of America

10 9 8 7 6 5 4 3 2 1

Library of Congress Cataloging-in-Publication Data
Names: African American Intellectual History Society. Annual Conference (1st :
    2016 : Chapel Hill, N.C.) | Blain, Keisha N., 1985– editor. | Cameron, Christopher,
    1983– editor. | Farmer, Ashley D., editor.
Title: New perspectives on the Black intellectual tradition / edited by Keisha N. Blain,
    Christopher Cameron, and Ashley D. Farmer.
Description: Evanston, Illinois : Northwestern University Press, 2018. | Includes
    index. | "In March 2016 we organized the inaugural conference of the African
    American Intellectual History Society (AAIHS), a scholarly organization founded
    in 2014 to foster dialogue about researching, writing, and teaching black thought
    and culture."
Identifiers: LCCN 2018023769 | ISBN 9780810138124 (pbk. : alk. paper) | ISBN
    9780810138131 (cloth : alk. paper) | ISBN 9780810138148 (ebook)
Subjects: LCSH: African Americans—Intellectual life—Congresses. | African
    Americans—Social conditions—Congresses. | African diaspora—Congresses.
Classification: LCC E185.89.I56 A37 2016 | DDC 305.55208996073—dc23
LC record available at https://lccn.loc.gov/2018023769

CONTENTS

Part III. Racial Politics and Struggles for Social Justice

Part IV. Black Radicalism

New Perspectives on the Black
Intellectual Tradition

The Contours of Black Intellectual History

Keisha N. Blain, Christopher Cameron, and Ashley D. Farmer

In March 2016 we organized the inaugural conference of the African American Intellectual History Society (AAIHS), a scholarly organization founded in 2014 to foster dialogue about researching, writing, and teaching black thought and culture. Since its debut AAIHS has quickly become one of the leading organizations, and its blog, *Black Perspectives*, has become the leading online platform for public scholarship on the black intellectual tradition. With the inaugural conference, we set out to advance these online conversations in person and foster new and innovative ideas about race and intellectual history. The conference exceeded our expectations; it brought together hundreds of scholars from across the nation and the globe who grappled with the significance and varied meanings of black intellectual history, a growing and thriving subfield in US and African diaspora history. As the diverse papers at the conference revealed, black intellectual history is by no means monolithic, and there are varied approaches to the study of black thought.

At its core the general field of intellectual history deals with the ideas and symbols that people use to make sense of the world.[1] A guiding assumption of this field is that human beings depend upon the use of language, which gives meaning to individual lives. Another common assumption is that human beings cannot live in the world without theorizing about what they are doing. These theories may be explicit or implicit, but they are always present and make up our cultural construction of reality, which depends upon symbols and language. Intellectual history, then, is not about what people did, necessarily, but more about what they thought about what they were doing. This is not to suggest that intellectual history is entirely divorced from other fields of history, including social and cultural history. To the contrary, intellectual history helps to deepen our understanding of social and cultural history, forcing us to investigate the ideas that undergird political and social life and grapple with the theories and ideologies that inform historical actors.

Within the field of intellectual history, the study of black thought and culture remains underrepresented and people of African descent are often marginalized, if not excluded entirely from historical narratives.[2] Despite the critical role black intellectuals have played—and continue to play—in shaping US and global political thought, they are often relegated to the sidelines and sharply criticized by those who fail to take seriously their ideas and contributions.[3] *New Perspectives on the Black Intellectual Tradition* provides an important corrective to this exclusionary framework, building on a body of work that centers the historical and contemporary contributions of black intellectuals in the United States and in other parts of the globe.[4]

This volume highlights the individual and group contributions of black intellectuals to national and global politics, racial ideologies, social justice movements, and popular culture. Drawing insights from diverse fields, including history, African American studies, feminist theory, religion, and cultural studies, the essays in this collection foreground the ideas and activities of black intellectuals in the United States and other parts of the globe from the early nineteenth century to the 1970s. They draw on several methodological approaches and primary sources to capture the black intellectual tradition, which the historian Manning Marable aptly describes as "the critical thought and perspectives of intellectuals of African descent and scholars of black America, and Africa, and the black diaspora."[5] By foregrounding the ideas of black men and women in various locales and working in different social and economic contexts, this volume debunks the myth of a monolithic black intellectual tradition, highlighting the varied lines of black thought. Indeed it captures the range and depth of the ideological and social traditions upon which black intellectuals drew in their efforts to address key issues in black communities.

New Perspectives on the Black Intellectual Tradition extends the scholarship on the black intellectual tradition along the lines of historiography, place and space, and methods and methodologies. Whereas much of the literature in the field centers on the ideas or life of an intellectual—often a member of the black middle-class or elite—this volume broadens the scholarly discourse both on what counts as black intellectual history and who counts as an intellectual.[6] While some chapters explore the ideas and theories of one or a group of black intellectuals, others instead grapple with the varied ways certain ideas spread in nontraditional arenas. Still others examine the ideological interrelationship among various black social movements.

Many of the essays highlight the ideas and activities of ordinary men and women, representing a key departure from traditional approaches to black intellectual history—which has privileged the voices of well-known (male) figures such as W. E. B. Du Bois, Booker T. Washington, and C. L. R. James. While this volume does not overlook these key historical persons, it broadens the field by centering the ideas and political visions of an array of black men and women, including members of the working class and those who had little or no formal education. Indeed *New Perspectives on the Black Intellectual Tradition* highlights the crucial, yet often overlooked, ways that black people, of all walks of life, contributed to US and global history as key producers of knowledge. As the essays reveal, these men and women did not simply act on a whim; they carefully thought about their actions and they carefully devised strategies and tactics. They proposed solutions, they offered critiques, and they challenged others—all the while resisting many of their contemporaries who dismissed their contributions often on account of their education and social standing.[7]

Reflecting older trends, recent scholarship has centered on the black intellectual tradition in the United States, often exploring the contributions of black intellectuals during the twentieth century. One of our goals in this volume is to not only capture the *longue durée* of black intellectual thought but to extend its geographical focus. Essays in this volume offer perspectives on the black intellectual tradition in various locales across the African diaspora from the early nineteenth century to the 1970s. They also grapple with the diverse transnational connections and networks forged among black intellectuals and highlight the diffusion of ideas among people of African descent in various parts of the globe. Significantly this volume highlights the wide range of methods and methodologies—including new approaches and sources—that scholars utilize in the study of black intellectual history. To that end the essays draw on traditional primary sources and methods as well as unconventional ones—in some cases, examining written texts as critical sites of intellectual production and integrating personal historical accounts of intellectualism. Drawing on an array of innovative and untapped primary and secondary sources, such as underutilized historical newspapers, editorials, organizational records, and oral histories, this anthology critically engages with the ideas of a diverse group of black men and women and offers new insights on black thought formation and dissemination from the era of slavery to the civil rights and Black Power era.

A Brief Historical Overview

Black cultural and intellectual production has been a critical component of US and global history for centuries. In the United States black intellectuals and activists—Phillis Wheatley, Richard Allen, Kelly Miller, and Absalom Jones, among them—played key roles in shaping early political thought, including ideologies of republicanism, liberalism, democracy, and natural rights.[8] During the era of slavery, courageous black men and women such as David Walker, Maria Stewart, Frederick Douglass, Harriet Jacobs, and Sojourner Truth used their writings and speeches to call for the end of the "peculiar institution" and demanded the rights and dignity of black people in the United States and other parts of the globe.[9] Utilizing autobiographies and slave narratives, popular genres of the period, several black men and women, including Nigerian-born Olaudah Equiano and Mary Prince, an enslaved woman from Bermuda, helped fuel abolitionist movements by exposing the pain and suffering that enslaved men and women endured under slavery.

While these early black intellectuals skillfully used autobiographies and slave narratives as mediums to condemn slavery, others created pamphlets and booklets in a collective effort to wage an assault on the institution of slavery. In his 1829 treatise, "An Appeal to the Coloured Citizens of the World," David Walker, an abolitionist residing in Boston, shook the nation to its core by calling for a violent overthrow of slavery. Reflecting the revolutionary spirit of Toussaint Louverture and the other freedom fighters in Haiti who created the first black republic in 1802, Walker called on black men and women to "kill or be killed."[10] Recognizing that freedom would be attained only by force, Walker articulated a militant response to white supremacy that would lay the foundations of black nationalist thought and activism in the United States for centuries to come.

Walker's "Appeal" captured the essence of "black revolutionary liberalism," a "radical political movement that took seriously the abstract principles of freedom, equality, and universality," and used these ideals to challenge mainstream racial hierarchies of the period.[11] Like Walker, Maria Stewart endorsed "black revolutionary liberalism," and in the aftermath of Walker's mysterious death in 1830, she emerged as one of America's first black women political writers and one of the first women to publicly speak before an interracial audience.[12] In her public speeches and writings, Stewart not only criticized white society for racism and segregation but also critiqued free blacks for their passivity concerning slavery. Significantly Stewart also denounced those who denied black women access to education and economic advancement. She argued that black women needed to fully participate in the women's rights movement and abolitionist movement because they were "doubly oppressed" on account of their dual struggle to combat racism and sexism. Other black intellectuals and activists, including Sojourner Truth, Frederick Douglass, and Frances Ellen Watkins Harper, also articulated a commitment to abolishing slavery and obtaining equal rights for women.[13]

The central concerns that animated early black intellectuals extended well into the twentieth century. In the United States the Great Migration of the early twentieth century was a crucial turning point in the lives of black men and women. From 1915 to 1925 more than 300,000 African Americans migrated from the South to the Northeast, and another 350,000 migrated to the Midwest. The influx of southern migrants into northern cities set the stage for collaborative efforts between black northerners and their southern counterparts and provided fertile ground for the Harlem Renaissance, or "New Negro Movement," a period of prolific black artistic and cultural expression in poetry, literature, and music. A diverse group of black intellectuals, artists, and writers, such as Langston Hughes, Alain Locke, Nella Larsen, W. E. B. Du Bois, and Zora Neale Hurston, were the driving forces behind the Harlem Renaissance.[14]

The Afro-Caribbean black nationalist leader Marcus Garvey and several other black intellectuals, including Amy Jacques Garvey, Hubert Harrison, and Amy Ashwood Garvey, played central roles in the Harlem Renaissance—popularizing the ideas of black pride, African heritage, and self-determination.

Some of the most well-known artists and intellectuals of the period, among them Claude McKay, John Edward Bruce, and T. Thomas Fortune, were associated with Garvey's Universal Negro Improvement Association (UNIA).[15] Moreover the organization's official periodical, the *Negro World*, provided a crucial platform for black artistic expression. In addition to fueling the growth of the Harlem Renaissance, the UNIA helped to initiate a resurgence of black nationalism and black radical politics in the United States and across the world, building on the ideas of a diverse group of Afro-diasporic thinkers, including the founder of the Tuskegee Institute, Booker T. Washington; the African American journalist Martin Delany; the Liberian politician Edward Blyden; and the Egyptian journalist Duse Mohamed Ali. Garveyism, a global political movement, also fanned the flames of Pan-Africanist consciousness in Africa and throughout the African diaspora.[16]

An insurgent political response to global white supremacy, Pan-Africanism has taken on different forms and manifestations at various historical moments. Expressions of Pan-Africanism could be found in various religious and social movements during the eighteenth and nineteenth centuries, including emigrationist efforts in the United States and the rise of Ethiopianism in South Africa. During the twentieth century Du Bois, often referred to as the father of Pan-Africanism, attended the first Pan-African Convention, in London in 1900, organized by the Trinidadian Henry Sylvester Williams. From 1919 to 1945 Du Bois played a fundamental role in organizing a series of Pan-African congresses to call for an end to colonialism and white imperial control. Meanwhile, during the 1930s and 1940s, a group of young black intellectuals in France—the Martiniquan poet Aimé Césaire, the Senegalese Léopold Senghor, and the Martiniquan writer Paulette Nardal, among them—developed négritude, a literary and cultural movement that brought together French-speaking black intellectuals from France's colonies in Africa and the Caribbean. Reflecting the ideological underpinning of Pan-Africanism, négritude leaders converged around issues of black identity, racial pride, black solidarity, and political self-determination.

All of these issues were at the forefront of discussions at the Fifth Pan-African Congress, arguably the most influential gathering of black intellectuals of the twentieth century. Held in Manchester, England, in 1945, the congress brought together a diverse group of black intellectuals and activists from various parts of the African diaspora, including the West Indian Marxist George Padmore, the Kenyan leader Jomo Kenyatta, and the Pan-Africanist feminist Amy Ashwood Garvey. From the outset leaders of the Fifth Pan-African Congress emphasized their unwavering commitment to African liberation: "We look with jealous pride upon these [imperialist] nations and regard them as symbols of realization of the political hopes and aspirations of African people still under imperialist domination."[17] This new realization exemplified a radical shift that was taking place in the minds of people of African descent during World War II.[18]

In the decades to follow, many of the seeds that these intellectuals planted at the Fifth Pan-African Congress informed the political ideas of black intellectuals and activists in the diaspora. During the 1950s and 1960s black intellectuals and activists—Ella Baker, Martin Luther King Jr., Fannie Lou Hamer, Robert F. Williams, Mabel Williams, Malcolm X, James Baldwin, Paul Robeson, Eslanda Robeson, and Stokely Carmichael, among them—led the way in shaping black thinking about the struggle for civil rights and human rights in the twentieth century.[19] Utilizing the media, these men and women waged an assault on racism, discrimination, and white supremacy. Significantly black intellectuals and activists during this period linked the fight for civil rights in the United States with the struggle for African decolonization and other anti-imperialist movements abroad. Throughout the diaspora Steve Biko, Nelson Mandela, Winnie Mandela, Walter Rodney, and other black intellectuals and activists articulated global visions of freedom and employed a range of strategies and tactics intent on improving the lives of people of color worldwide.[20]

Over the past several decades, black intellectuals have continued to leave an indelible mark on global black politics, shaping policy debates on some of the most pressing issues facing black communities. In the United States black feminists such as Flo Kennedy, Angela Davis, and Shirley Chisholm forced black men and women to reassess the ties among race, gender, and state power. During the 1980s and 1990s African American thinkers such as Supreme Court Justice Clarence Thomas and the syndicated columnist Star Parker made important contributions to conservative political thought, addressing a range of key issues, including affirmative action, welfare, and education.

While all of these examples underscore the ubiquity and influence of blacks in all realms of US and global intellectual history, the study of black thought and culture is still an underrepresented aspect of this broader field. This edited volume makes a significant intervention in the field of intellectual history by centering the ideas and experiences of people of African descent in the United States and other parts of the globe. It assembles some of the best new scholarly works in the field of global black history and captures the significance and the depth and complexity of black intellectual thought.

Overview

This volume is organized into four thematic sections that explore the depth and richness of black intellectual history in the United States and across the African diaspora. Part I, "Black Internationalism," contains three essays that analyze the global racial consciousness of black intellectuals during the twentieth century. A central aspect of the black intellectual tradition, black internationalism shaped the political ideas and praxis of black men and women throughout the diaspora. In "'Every Wide-Awake Negro Teacher of French Should Know: The Pedagogies of Black Internationalism in the Early Twentieth Century," Celeste Day Moore examines the role and significance of the French language among African American writers, musicians, artists, students, and scholars. Drawing on a range of primary and secondary sources, including archival material and textbooks, Moore explores the instruction of French at historically black colleges and universities—Howard University and Atlanta University, in particular—during the 1930s. In so doing she effectively shows how the French language provided a key vehicle for black men and women in the United States to forge networks and collaborations with other people of African descent in the diaspora, especially those residing in France and in French colonies during this period. In her essay a diverse group of black intellectuals, including Mercer Cook, Jane Nardal, and Paulette Nardal, take center stage as Moore demonstrates how these men and women creatively and strategically utilized French as a means of "forging diaspora."[21] "Through their work," Moore argues, "the language of colonialism was transformed into a critical tool with which allegiances were built, for even linguistic failures and mistranslations offered a heuristic for understanding the possibilities and limitations in claiming racial identities."

Reena Goldthree's essay similarly explores the global racial consciousness of black intellectuals during the twentieth century. In "Afro-Cuban Intellectuals and the New Negro Renaissance: Bernardo Ruiz Suárez's *The Color Question in the Two Americas*," Goldthree analyzes the writings of Ruiz Suárez, an Afro-Cuban intellectual residing in Harlem during the 1920s, who published *The Color Question in the Two Americas*—a comparative study of race relations in the United States and Cuba in 1922. Goldthree shows how Suárez, a largely unknown figure in the literature, was a key black intellectual during the Harlem Renaissance who skillfully used his writings to challenge antiblack racism. Black intellectuals like Ruiz Suárez, who traveled extensively between Anglophone and Spanish-speaking black communities during the 1920s, "contributed firsthand knowledge about the global modalities of racism, bringing attention to antiblack violence and marginalization beyond the Anglophone world." By placing Ruiz Suárez's writings in conversation with other Spanish-language writings of the period, Goldthree shows how he engaged a series of debates on race and relations during the period and articulated a vision of black internationalism that stood in stark contrast to many of his contemporaries. In his conception of black internationalism, Goldthree argues, Ruiz Suárez "decentered three central tropes of diasporic thought: Africa (as a site of origin and displacement), chattel slavery, and notions of transnational black culture." Exploring the ways in which Ruiz Suárez's writings were similar to yet often different from the writings of other black intellectuals in Harlem and in other parts of the globe, Goldthree significantly captures the complexities and indeed contradictions of black thought and praxis during the twentieth century.

These contradictions and complexities are further explored in Brandon R. Byrd's essay, "'To Start Something to Help These People': African American

Women and the Occupation of Haiti, 1915–1934," which examines black women's engagement with Haiti during the early twentieth century. Centered on the years of the US occupation (1915–34), Byrd's essay captures the tensions in middle-class and elite black women's views on Haiti and their complex engagement with Haitians during these pivotal years. Drawing on a wide array of primary sources, including archival material and historical newspapers, Byrd argues that African American women—Margaret Murray Washington, Addie Hunton, and Nannie Helen Burroughs, among them—worked to bring greater awareness of Haitian history and culture while endorsing racial uplift policies and civilizationist views that sought to deny Haitian agency. "The schools and philanthropic groups they created in Haiti," Byrd points out, "emerged from imperialist discourses and sometimes relied upon the ideological structures of the US occupation to fulfill their mission: the uplift of the Haitian masses from material and moral poverty to Victorian respectability." Byrd's essay underscores how the ideas and social activities of black intellectuals during the twentieth century were often shaped by classism as well as a Western conception of modernity that at times accommodated rather than challenged imperialism.

Part II, "Religion and Spirituality," offers three essays that highlight both the centrality of religion and challenges to Christianity for the black intellectual tradition. As was the case for nineteenth-century black intellectuals, religion remained a primary marker of identity for many twentieth-century black thinkers. In "Isolated Believer: Alain Locke, Baha'i Secularist," David Weinfeld explores the ties between religion and secularism in the life of the philosopher and writer. Tracing Locke's religious ideas from his time at Harvard in the early 1900s to the 1940s, Weinfeld argues that "Locke should be acknowledged as a major secularist among African Americans." Scholars have been slow to explore Locke's secularism for two main reasons. First, Locke was not outspoken about his lack of belief in a deity. In fact, he did not publicize his religious beliefs at all. He embraced the Baha'i faith around 1918 yet wrote little about it except in private correspondence. His membership in the Baha'i Church is the second major reason why few scholars have explored his secularism in depth. As Weinfeld argues, however, this membership did not mean Locke was traditionally religious but rather that he found a spiritual outlet in which to express his secular ideals. Chief among these secular ideals was his belief in cultural pluralism, a forerunner to modern multiculturalism and a philosophy that squared nicely with Baha'i notions of the unity of God and all humanity. While Locke's formal membership with the Baha'i Church in Washington, D.C., lapsed in 1941, he remained an "isolated believer" and a Baha'i secularist for the remainder of his life.

Christopher Cameron's "The New Negro Renaissance and African American Secularism" moves beyond a traditional focus on religion to explore the growth of freethought among black writers of the 1920s. Focusing on two well-known writers of the era—Langston Hughes and Nella Larsen—

Cameron argues that the New Negro renaissance provided fertile ground for the development of black atheism, agnosticism, and secular humanism. The Great Migration of the 1920s brought together hundreds of thousands of blacks in Detroit, Chicago, New York, and other northern cities, a situation that initiated significant changes in black religious life but also led many to question religion altogether. Hughes began to question the tenets of religion while still a teenager and used poems such as "Song for a Dark Girl" and "Who but the Lord?" to argue that black people must look to themselves, and not to God, to solve their earthly problems. Hughes's contemporary in Harlem, Larsen, likewise produced a critical examination of religion in her 1928 novella, *Quicksand*. In this autobiographical work, Larsen displayed what she believed to be the many destructive aspects of religion, including its ties to patriarchy and stifling of opportunities for women. Cameron notes that Larsen and Hughes were joined by many other secular thinkers, including Claude McKay, Zora Neale Hurston, and Hubert Harrison, and that their writings inaugurated an important yet unrecognized tradition of black freethought.

The final essay in this section speaks to some of the key themes in both Weinfeld's and Cameron's pieces. LeRhonda Manigault-Bryant's essay, "'I Had a Praying Grandmother': Religion, Prophetic Witness, and Black Women's Herstories," speaks to the significance of religion in constructions of black female identity during the mid- to late twentieth century. While many scholars have recently begun paying attention to the critical role of black motherhood in passing down knowledge, including ideas about religion, Manigault-Bryant argues that grandmothers often serve the same function within black communities. Drawing on literature, music, and personal experience, this chapter positions testimony as a critical rhetorical form in cultural transmission. The chapter likewise argues for a recognition of four forms of knowledge—perspective knowledge, experiential knowledge, faith knowledge, and conjure knowledge—that are just as valid as archival sources and should be utilized by intellectual historians to better understand black women's religious "herstories."

In part III, three authors explore the theme of racial politics and struggles for social justice. The first essay, "Historical Ventriloquy: Black Thought and Sexual Politics in the Interracial Marriage of Frederick Douglass" by Guy Emerson Mount, examines the racial politics and historical writing surrounding Douglass's interracial marriage to Helen Pitts in 1884. Analyzing a range of primary sources, including historical newspapers, Mount demonstrates how various historians have written about this controversial interracial marriage since the late nineteenth century. "By juxtaposing the limited professional scholarship that exists on this topic against the actual reactions of everyday black people in 1884," he argues, "it becomes clear that what black people thought about interracial marriage in 1884 bears almost no resemblance to what scholars today think they thought about it." Significantly

Mount highlights Douglass's own views on the marriage, analyzing the abolitionist's statements in various newspapers of the period. He also analyzes how leading black journalists and race leaders viewed Douglass's decision to marry a white woman during a period that the historian Rayford Logan described as the "nadir" of race relations in the United States.[22] By offering these multiple perspectives, Mount not only captures the distinctions of the black intellectual tradition, but he also reveals the ever changing dynamics of black intellectual history.

The second essay in this section similarly challenges the "prevailing historiography" on antiracist and assimilationist ideas during the twentieth century. In "Reigning Assimilationists and Defiant Black Power: The Struggle to Define and Regulate Racist Ideas," Ibram X. Kendi charts the intellectual history of antiracism in the United States, revealing how beliefs in "pathological black masculinity and femininity" informed assimilationists' definition of racism even as they claimed to challenge eugenicist ideas of the past. Analyzing several key historical texts by assimilationists of the period—including Ruth Benedict's *Race: Science and Politics* (1940) and Gunnar Myrdal's *An American Dilemma* (1944)—Kendi highlights this complex racial discourse and then examines the myriad ways Black Power intellectuals "waged an intellectual struggle to redefine racist ideas" ideas during the 1960s. Through their writings, key figures such as Malcolm X and Frances Beal challenged "America's domineering assimilationist ideas" and pointed out the underlying racism of assimilationists of the period. By charting this history, Kendi "offers a new perspective on the history of racist ideas and builds on the black intellectual tradition, which, like Black Power, has consistently rewritten the modern story of race and racism."

Ashley Farmer explores the theme of racial politics and struggles for racial justice by examining the political ideas of black women in cultural nationalist groups of the 1960s and 1970s. Like Kendi and Mount, Farmer challenges the historiography in several key ways in "Becoming African Women: Women's Cultural Nationalist Theorizing in the US Organization and the Committee for Unified Newark." First, she centers the ideas of women activists who are often marginalized in Black Power scholarship. Second, she demonstrates how these women effectively challenged patriarchy in cultural nationalist groups of the period. Through the practice of Kawaida, "a cultural nationalist philosophy based on the idea that culture was the 'crucible in which black liberation takes form,'" these women enacted the ideal of the "African Woman," which Farmer describes as "a political identity based on a set of core cultural nationalist beliefs." During the 1960s and 1970s these women produced an array of essays in which they engaged in lively discourse on gender roles in nationalist movements, challenging masculinist and patriarchal views that sought to limit women's leadership opportunities. Farmer highlights the various ways black women, of various social backgrounds and in various locales, shaped twentieth-century black intellectual history.

The chapters in part IV, "Black Radicalism," offer a unique survey of insurgent strains of black political thought in three temporal moments and locales. The essays speak to the ways in which women and men across the African diaspora articulated and acted on ideals that transformed the meanings of freedom, community, and rebellion in their times. In "Runaways, Rescuers, and the Politics of Breaking the Law," Christopher Bonner foregrounds how enslaved and free people contributed to black thought in their efforts to combat fugitive slave legislation in antebellum America. Bonner documents what he calls the "politics of lawbreaking," or the ways in which free communities and fugitive slaves "declared to lawmakers that they were unwilling to comply with the legal instruments that upheld slavery." Highlighting the lives of enslaved people like William Dixon and Adam Crosswhite, Bonner reveals the lengths to which free communities went in order to protect runaway slaves. He also argues that their efforts were more than simply heroic acts; they were manifestations of shared ideas about emancipation that formed a key part of the black intellectual tradition. Operating within the contested meanings of slavery and freedom in the nineteenth century, these men and women articulated new conceptions about personal and collective liberty and used them to push for legal changes to fugitive slave laws. Through this analysis Bonner expands the historiography and documents how enslaved and freed people attempted to radicalize contemporaneous ideas about freedom through their willingness to break the law.

Gregory Childs also analyzes enslaved and freed people's forms of insurgency in his essay, "Conspiracies, Seditions, Rebellions: Concepts and Categories in the Study of Slave Resistance." Focusing on the Tailors' Conspiracy—a supposed plot among freed and enslaved people to overthrow slavery and Portuguese rule in 1798 in Bahia, Brazil—he reveals the need to reexamine such incidents as examples of seditious acts and public articulations of black political thought. Childs argues that historians' preoccupation with secrecy and violence has overshadowed black people's open declarations of resistance ingrained in their rebellions against the institution of slavery and the crown. Ultimately his chapter captures the collective articulation of political thought and action among enslaved and freed people in Cuba and Brazil in the late eighteenth and early nineteenth century. It also warns against the individualist conceptions of black thought, black thinkers, and black radicalism in the Age of Revolutions.

In the final essay, "African American Expats, Guyana, and the Pan-African Ideal in the 1970s," Russell Rickford explores how black radical activists came to view "Guyana as a kind of sanctuary from unraveling mass movements" in the United States. Drawing on various primary sources, including archival material and historical newspapers, Rickford documents how a group of black activists from the United States, including Una Mulzac, John Henrik Clarke, and Odetta, relocated to Guyana during the 1960s and 1970s in their effort to advance black nationalist and Pan-Africanist ideals. As

Rickford demonstrates, these men and women pursued relocation to Guyana in their quest for self-government and social belonging during a period of political upheaval in the United States. While historians generally focus on emigrationist movements to Liberia and Ghana, Rickford shows how Guyana became a critical site for black nationalist and Pan-African politics. His incisive analysis offers insight into the contours of late twentieth-century black radical and Pan-African thought and the ideological interrelationship between African American and African liberation struggles. Rickford's chapter illustrates the potentialities of radical organizing across borders and foregrounds the important lessons that activists learned when attempting to translate political ideologies into radical action.

Together the twelve essays included in this volume capture the depth and complexity of black intellectual thought in the United States and across the African diaspora. They explore black men's and women's roles as activists and as producers of knowledge—paying careful attention to the diverse vehicles they utilized to popularize their ideas and the varied strategies and tactics they employed to resist race, class, and gender oppression.

Notes

1. Christopher Cameron, "Five Approaches to Intellectual History," *Black Perspectives*, April 5, 2016, http://www.aaihs.org/approaches-to-black-intellectual-history/.

2. Major scholarly works contain few pieces written by or about black intellectuals, while major journals, such as the *Journal of the History of Ideas*, publish few articles on the topic. On the literature, see David A. Hollinger and Charles Capper, eds., *The American Intellectual Tradition* (New York: Oxford University Press, 2015); Samuel Moyn and Andrew Satori, eds., *Global Intellectual History* (New York: Columbia University Press, 2016).

3. On the challenges facing black intellectuals in the United States, see Jonathan Scott Holloway, "The Black Intellectual and the 'Crisis Canon' in the Twentieth Century," *Black Scholar* 31, no. 1 (2001): 2–13; Lewis R. Gordon, "Africana Philosophy and Philosophy in Black," *Black Scholar* 43, no. 4 (2013): 46.

4. The literature on black intellectual history is extensive. Key works include Harold Cruse, *The Crisis of the Negro Intellectual* (New York: New York Review of Books, 1967); Earl Thorpe, *The Mind of the Negro: An Intellectual History of Afro-Americans* (Westport, Conn.: Negro Universities Press, 1970); August Meier, *Negro Thought in America, 1880–1915* (Ann Arbor: University of Michigan Press, 1995); William M. Banks, *Black Intellectuals: Race and Responsibility in American Life* (New York: Norton, 1996). New works include Mia E. Bay, Farah J. Griffin, Martha S. Jones, and Barbara D. Savage, eds., *Toward an Intellectual History of Black Women* (Chapel Hill: University of North Carolina Press, 2015); Brian D. Behnken, Gregory D. Smithers, and Simon Wendt, eds., *Black Intellectual Thought in Modern America: A Historical Perspective* (Jackson: University Press of Mississippi, 2017); Cornelius L. Bynum and Derrick P. Alridge,

eds., *The Black Intellectual Tradition in the United States in the Twentieth Century* (Urbana: University of Illinois Press, forthcoming).

5. Manning Marable, ed., *Dispatches from the Ebony Tower: Intellectuals Confront the African American Experience* (New York: Columbia University Press, 2000), 1.

6. On earlier scholarship that centers on the ideas or life of an intellectual, see, for example, V. P. Franklin, *Living Our Stories, Telling Our Truths: Autobiography and the Making of the African-American Intellectual Tradition* (New York: Oxford University Press, 1996); Martin Kilson, *Transformation of the African American Intelligentsia, 1880–2012* (Cambridge, Mass.: Harvard University Press, 2014); David Levering Lewis, *W. E. B. Du Bois: Biography of a Race* (New York: Henry Holt, 1993); John D'Emillio, *Lost Prophet: The Life and Times of Bayard Rustin* (Chicago: University of Chicago Press, 2004); Jacqueline Johnson, *Stokely Carmichael: The Story of Black Power* (Englewood Cliffs, N.J.: Silver Burdett Press, 1990).

7. Keisha N. Blain, "Writing Black Women's Intellectual History," *Black Perspectives*, November 21, 2016, http://www.aaihs.org/writing-black-womens-intellectual-history/.

8. For an excellent overview of early black intellectual history, see Mia Bay, *The White Image in the Black Mind: African-American Ideas about White People, 1830–1925* (New York: Oxford University Press, 2000).

9. Kenneth Stampp, *The Peculiar Institution: Slavery in the Antebellum South* (New York: Knopf, 1956).

10. David Walker, *Walker's Appeal, in Four Articles; Together with a Preamble, to the Coloured Citizens of the World, but in Particular, and Very Expressly, to Those of the United States of America* (Boston: Revised and published by David Walker, 1830).

11. Kristin Waters, "Past as Prologue: Intersectional Analysis from the Nineteenth Century to the Twenty-first," in *Why Race and Gender Still Matter: An Intersectional Approach*, edited by Namita Goswami, Maeve M. O'Donovan, and Lisa Yount (London: Pickering & Chatto, 2014), 35.

12. Kristin Waters, "Crying Out for Liberty: Maria W. Stewart and David Walker's Black Revolutionary Liberalism," *Philosophia Africana: Analysis of Philosophy and Ideas in Africa and the Black Diaspora* 15, no. 1 (2003): 35–60.

13. Christopher Cameron ties both Walker and Stewart to the tradition of the black jeremiad that began with early black thinkers such as Phillis Wheatley and Prince Hall. See Cameron's *To Plead Our Own Cause: African Americans in Massachusetts and the Making of the Antislavery Movement* (Kent, OH: Kent State University Press, 2014), chapter 7.

14. David Levering Lewis, *When Harlem Was in Vogue* (New York: Oxford University Press, 1979).

15. See Ronald J. Stephens and Adam Ewing, eds., *Global Garveyism: Diasporic Aspirations and Utopian Dreams* (Gainesville: University Press of Florida, forthcoming); Adam Ewing, *The Age of Garvey: How a Jamaican Activist Created a Mass Movement and Changed Global Black Politics* (Princeton, N.J.: Princeton University Press, 2014); Robert Trent Vinson, *The Americans Are Coming! Dreams of African American Liberation in Segregationist South Africa* (Athens:

Ohio State University Press, 2012); Ramla Bandele, *Black Star: African American Activism in the International Political Economy* (Urbana: University of Illinois Press, 2008); Mary G. Rolinson, *Grassroots Garveyism: The Universal Negro Improvement Association in the Rural South, 1920–1927* (Chapel Hill: University of North Carolina Press, 2007); Claudrena N. Harold, *The Rise and Fall of the Garvey Movement in the Urban South, 1918–1942* (New York: Routledge, 2007). On women in black nationalist movements, see Ula Y. Taylor, *The Veiled Garvey: The Life and Times of Amy Jacques Garvey* (Chapel Hill: University of North Carolina Press, 2002); Keisha N. Blain, *Set the World on Fire: Black Nationalist Women and the Global Struggle for Freedom* (Philadelphia: University of Pennsylvania Press, 2018).

16. In this book we define Pan-Africanism as the belief that peoples of African descent throughout the continent and in the diaspora share a common past and destiny. This shared understanding of the past and future informs how people of African descent mobilize against racial discrimination, colonialism, and economic, political, social, and cultural oppression.

17. George Padmore, *Pan-Africanism or Communism? The Coming Struggle for Africa* (London: Dennis Dobson, 1956), 168.

18. Penny Von Eschen, *Race against Empire: Black Americans and Anticolonialism, 1937–1957* (Ithaca, N.Y.: Cornell University Press, 1997); James Meriwether, *Proudly We Can Be Africans: Black Americans and Africa, 1935–1961* (Chapel Hill: University of North Carolina Press, 2002); Lindsey R. Swindall, *The Path to the Greater, Freer, Truer World: Southern Civil Rights and Anticolonialism, 1937–1955* (Gainesville: University Press of Florida, 2014); Carol Anderson, *Bourgeois Radicals: The NAACP and the Struggle for Colonial Liberation, 1941–1960* (New York: Cambridge University Press, 2014).

19. See, for example, Stokely Carmichael and Charles V. Hamilton, *Black Power: The Politics of Liberation in America* (New York: Random House, 1967); Martin Luther King Jr., *Where Do We Go from Here: Chaos or Community* (New York: Harper and Row, 1964); Robert F. Williams, *Negroes with Guns* (New York: Marzani and Munsell, 1962); Maegan Parker Brooks and Davis W. Houck, *The Speeches of Fannie Lou Hamer: To Tell It Like It is* (Jackson: University Press of Mississippi, 2013). For historical analysis of these intellectual trends see, for example, Barbara Ransby, *Eslanda: The Large and Unconventional Life of Mrs. Paul Robeson* (New Haven, Conn.: Yale University Press, 2013); Ashley Farmer, *Remaking Black Power: How Black Women Transformed an Era* (Chapel Hill: University of North Carolina Press, 2017); Timothy Tyson, *Radio Free Dixie: Robert F. Williams and the Roots of Black Power* (Chapel Hill: University of North Carolina Press, 2001); Peniel Joseph, *Stokely: A Life* (New York, Civitas Books, 2016).

20. Robin D. G. Kelley, "'But a Local Phase of a World Problem': Black History's Global Vision, 1883–1950," *Journal of American History* 86 (1999): 1045–77.

21. Frank Guridy, *Forging Diaspora: Afro-Cubans and African Americans in a World of Empire and Jim Crow* (Chapel Hill: University of North Carolina Press, 2010).

22. Rayford Logan, *The Negro in American Life and Thought* (New York: Dial Press, 1964).

Part I

✦

Black Internationalism

Introduction

Michael O. West

In his own lifetime Booker T. Washington earned the ire of many African American intellectuals, as much for his perceived anti-intellectualism as for his accommodationist politics in the face of US apartheid, or Jim Crow. After discursively casting down his bucket at the Atlanta Exposition of 1895, the event that brought him fame, Washington went on to cast a long shadow over the discourse on black liberation in the United States. Directly and indirectly, and to varying degrees, his legacy helps to frame the three essays in this section of the book, all of which are set in the decades immediately following his death in 1915.

Celeste Day Moore's essay on "pedagogies of black internationalism" begins with one of Washington's more famous reproaches to what he regarded as black misguided priorities, which necessarily doubled as a dig at liberal arts education. A convinced germophobe as well as a champion of industrial training and wealth accumulation, Washington laid into the apocryphal black young man, "sitting down in a one-room cabin, with grease on his clothing, filth all around him, and weeds in the yard and garden, engaged in studying a French grammar." How absurd indeed!

Moore's task, and it is a formidable one, is to transform Washingtonian absurdity into black internationalism. Hers is a deft undertaking, accomplished by focusing on French language instruction at historically African American institutions of higher learning, notably Howard and Atlanta universities, in the interwar years. Amid the political, intellectual, and spiritual incarceration that was Jim Crow, Moore shows how black teachers and students gained entry into a wider world by studying French, which they directly linked to the larger struggle for black liberation.

A key figure in Moore's narrative is Mercer Cook, who taught French at both Howard and Atlanta. Cook had previously pursued graduate studies in Paris, where his larger education included attending the salon of the Martinique-born sisters Jane Nardal and Paulette Nardal, seminal if largely unsung figures in the making of négritude, the key expression in Francophone black internationalism in the interwar years. Cook's informal studies under the auspices of the Nardal sisters put him in good stead for teaching in the United States, where the great majority of his students, including at the graduate level, were African American women. These women, and others who similarly populated French-language classes at black universities and colleges, offered a sharp contrast, and rebuke, to Washington's caricature of a male autodidact, oblivious to the mess around him as he consumed his French grammar book. Furthermore, Moore argues, the labor of the female students, including their unpublished master's theses, formed an indispensable scaffolding for the publications that cemented the reputations of Cook and other African American male French scholars.

Literature in French about Haiti, some of it written by Haitian writers, was standard fare for Mercer Cook and his African American fellow French-language instructors. Haiti, with its glorious revolution and storied place in the global antislavery struggles of the nineteenth century, dramatically returned to Pan-African consciousness in the early decades of the twentieth century. The reason was not far to seek: the United States invaded Haiti in 1915 and occupied the country for a generation, until 1934. In what one biographer calls "one of the frankest articles he ever wrote," Washington, in failing health and with only a few months left to live, offered a qualified endorsement of the invasion and—this is the frank part—admonished the US government against turning Haiti into a "white man's country."[1]

A good many black people in the United States, Brandon R. Byrd shows in his essay, labored to end the occupation and ensure that Haiti would not become a white man's country. Among those protesting the occupation was Washington's widow, Margaret Murray Washington. Indeed members of her race, gender, and class, meaning middle-class African American women, are the main subjects of Byrd's essay.

Much has been written on the Pan-African reaction to the occupation of Haiti, most of it privileging male voices and activities. In locating a specifically "female domain" of opposition, Byrd has earned himself a place in the van-guard of scholars who are "gendering the occupation."[2] His larger argument is that the interwar period was a transformative moment in the evolution of black internationalism—witnessing as it did a shift from an elite-led, sacred-based, racial uplift tradition to a more proletarian-driven, secular-grounded emphasis on opposition to imperialism and capitalism—and that the Haitian antioccu-pation movement was a crucial factor in that transformation. As with the inter-locution between the study of the French language and black internationalism charted by Moore, so too with the opposition to occupied Haiti discussed by Byrd: history, notably the history of the Haitian Revolution, was summoned to bear witness to the crime and to speak truth to the Yankee occupiers.

The women whose antioccupation activities he chronicles, Byrd informs us, inhabited a "liminal" space between the old and new forms of black inter-nationalism. Except they seem more committed to the former than to the latter, their Protestant missionizing zeal in respect of Vodou-Catholic Haiti distinctly reminiscent of such figures as James Theodore Holly, the staunchly anti-Catholic Episcopalian minister who promoted African American emi-gration to Haiti in the nineteenth century.[3] Echoes of Washington are also evident in the work of women like Nannie Helen Burroughs and Harriett

Gibbs Marshall, who combined opposition to the occupation with promoting industrial education for the Haitian masses (as Washington had done in his endorsement of the invasion) and in championing "Bible, bath, and broom" in occupied Haiti. Marshall would go on to cofound the antioccupation Save Haiti League, which Byrd has very usefully rescued from obscurity. The League's activities included a drive to petition the US president to end the occupation—an appeal that may well have been modeled on the successful campaign to pardon the imprisoned Marcus Garvey, whose movement was centrally involved in the struggles around occupied Haiti.[4]

There is (in the current state of research) not much to indicate that Bernardo Ruiz Suárez had any real interest in the Haiti question, even though he resided in Harlem, perhaps the center of the antioccupation movement in the United States. An Afro-Cuban, Ruiz Suárez was every bit the New Negro, just like the subjects of the essays by Moore and Byrd. Ruiz Suárez's unjustly obscure book, *The Color Question in the Two Americas*, translated from the Spanish and published in 1922, is the focus of Reena N. Goldthree's essay. Like Moore and Byrd, Goldthree is engaged in an exercise in translation—linguistic, cultural, political.

The "two Americas" in the title of Ruiz Suárez's book are Cuba and the United States, the main subject being the quest for black liberation in both societies. With the crucial exception of Haiti, where the revolution dispatched slavery, colonialism, and white supremacy (even if it did not settle the color question), black citizenship was a vexing issue in all postemancipation societies of the Americas. In the United States a brief experiment in nonracial democracy—launched by constitutional amendments granting color-blind birthright citizenship and universal male franchise—notoriously ended in the blood-soaked, white supremacist counterrevolution that gave birth to Jim Crow. By contrast, Cuba, like most of the Latin American nations, officially and formally rejected apartheid even as it actually and systematically excluded people of African descent from the upper reaches of state and society alike. Behind this façade of supposed racial democracy, with its occasional nod to the token black exception that proved the rule, lurked a racist Leviathan of a state, policing black consciousness and ready, ever ready, to drown black mobilization in a bloodbath, as evidenced by the massacres in Ruiz Suárez's Cuba in 1912.

A fundamental argument of Ruiz Suárez, Goldthree calls it his "provocative thesis," is that these ostensibly divergent racial regimes produced similar outcomes: actual segregation and putative assimilation, respectively, left African Americans and Afro-Cubans without a "racial personality." This argument is provocative because it goes against received wisdom, which holds that the totalitarian nature of US apartheid endowed African Americans with a collective consciousness, in effect a "racial personality," that was either nonexistent or comparatively undeveloped among black people in Latin America. Yet, as Goldthree notes, Ruiz Suárez's argument is far from consistent, and elsewhere his book, using muscular and masculinist language, bestows on

African Americans an apparently unique sense of group combination that seems to qualify as "racial personality."

The racial personality projected by the Garvey movement was, however, too much for Ruiz Suárez. Although a black internationalist, or more properly a black pan-Americanist, he was no Pan-Africanist, rejecting as he did the view that transnational black combination required a continental African homeland. This was, practically, a call for erasure—a motion to delete the diaspora concept from black struggles outside of Africa, specifically in the Americas. To the famous poetic query of fellow Harlemite and New Negro bard Countee Cullen—"What is Africa to me?"—Ruiz Suárez seemed content to answer nothing, or very little. It followed that he rejected the emigrationist or "Back to Africa" plank in Garveyism, which he derisively labeled the "Go to Africa" movement. That rousing cry of Garveyism—"Africa for the Africans, at home and abroad"—apparently rang hallow to Ruiz Suárez.

In 1922, the same year his book came out, Goldthree notes, Ruiz Suárez became a Spanish-language columnist for the *New York Age*, a Harlem-based, anti-Garvey newspaper. The *Age*, which carried his death-bed endorsement turned admonition of the invasion of Haiti, previously served as a mouthpiece for Washington in his ideological struggles against his African American detractors. A black internationalist in his own accommodationist way, Washington also took a keen interest in Cuba, recruiting numbers of Afro-Cubans to his Tuskegee Institute. In the post–World War I era, colonialists and other traducers of black folk worldwide picked up the mantle of the now deceased Washington, seeking to advance an industrial-training, apartheid-deferring counterpoint to more radical brands of black and other forms of internationalisms, most notably Garveyism and communism.[5] Yet even Garveyism, with which communists worldwide famously feuded, owed a debt to Washington (who, like Ruiz Suárez, was no friend of emigrationism), as seen in Garvey's reverence for the "Great Sage of Tuskegee."

The essays in this section focus on three key centers of black life and thought in the modern world—the United States, Haiti, and Cuba—and the ties that bound them at an especially crucial moment, the two decades between the two world wars of the twentieth century. The struggles and movements charted by Moore, Byrd, and Goldthree during the interwar years, an era of colonialism and neocolonialism, of apartheid and neo-apartheid, precariously stood athwart the past and the future. Individually and collectively these three essays contain vital lessons about the black intellectual tradition and its corollary, the struggle for black liberation everywhere, then and now.

Notes

1. Louis R. Harlan, *Booker T. Washington: The Wizard of Tuskegee, 1901–1915* (New York: Oxford University Press, 1983), 446.

2. Raphael Dalleo, *American Imperialism's Undead: The Occupation of Haiti and the Rise of Caribbean Anticolonialism* (Charlottesville: University of Virginia Press, 2016), 101–21.

3. James Theodore Holly, *A Vindication of the Capacity of the Negro Race for Self-Government and Civilized Progress* ((New Haven, Conn.: W. H. Stanley, 1857).

4. Dalleo argues that Garvey, unlike a number of prominent female Garveyites, was more interested in the Haitian Revolution than in occupied Haiti. See Dalleo, *American Imperialism's Undead.*

5. The literature on the Tuskegee model of black development worldwide is considerable. For an early example, see Louis R. Harlan, "Booker T. Washington and the White Man's Burden," *American Historical Review* 71, no. 2 (1966): 441–67. A recent addition is Andrew E. Barnes, *Global Christianity and the Black Atlantic: Tuskegee, Colonialism, and the Shaping of African Industrial Education* (Waco, Tex.: Baylor University Press, 2017).

"Every Wide-Awake Negro Teacher of French Should Know"

The Pedagogies of Black Internationalism in the Early Twentieth Century

Celeste Day Moore

In his 1901 autobiography, *Up from Slavery*, Booker T. Washington offered an iconic, if infamous, representation of intellectual ambition. In the course of his travels, he wrote, "one of the saddest things" he had seen was a young man, "sitting down in a one-room cabin, with grease on his clothing, filth all around him, and weeds in the yard and garden, engaged in studying a French grammar."[1] In Washington's eyes, the young man's devotion to French studies had rendered him incapable of addressing—or even seeing—the "poverty, the untidiness, the want of system and thrift" that surrounded him, and thus exemplified the necessity of Washington's own program of industrial education.[2] Two years later it was this same scene that fueled W. E. B. Du Bois's critique of Washington's educational vision. While Washington had rendered the "picture of a lone black boy poring over a French grammar amid the weeds and dirt of a neglected home" into "the acme of absurdities," Du Bois embraced the power of language—and the French language in particular—to elevate and ennoble black life. He sketched a very different scene: "I sit with Shakespeare and he winces not. Across the color line I move arm in arm with Balzac and Dumas, where smiling men and welcoming women glide in gilded halls." For Du Bois the sight of a young man consumed by the study of French did not evince failure but instead heralded progress. Lost in the intricacies of a new tongue, this young man might begin to "soar in the dim blue air above the smoke," where he could rediscover what is lost "on earth by being black."[3]

Returning to this foundational debate in African American intellectual history, I am struck by the curious place of the French language within it. Why was it the French grammar in particular that signified at once the apparent absurdity of black ambition and the dream of elevated intellectual intercourse? Moreover, why has the French language, and France itself, continued to exert such representational power in African American history? In recent years this question has been taken up by a range of scholars who have tracked the movement of African American writers, musicians, artists, students, and scholars to

France, where they sought new opportunities to create, write, and perform.[4] While these expatriates envisioned, and in some cases found, a life freed from the yoke of American racism, they nevertheless found themselves ensnared by racial (and racist) ideologies that simultaneously elevated African Americans and denigrated France's own colonial populations.[5] By investigating the lived experiences of these contradictions, scholars have illuminated key dimensions of African American and French colonial histories and mapped the history of twentieth-century black internationalism.[6] For even as they struggled to negotiate this racial terrain, African Americans nevertheless found within it new means of building diasporic connections, political movements, and camaraderie among African-descended people. Through their work the language of colonialism was transformed into a critical tool with which allegiances were built, for even linguistic failures and mistranslations offered a heuristic for understanding the possibilities and limitations in claiming racial identities.[7]

While the problem of language remains at the center of my inquiry, this essay turns from the foreign to the domestic sphere to locate the history of black internationalism in the instruction of French at historically black colleges and universities in the 1930s. Spatially and materially bounded by Jim Crow, educators at these institutions still found in French a powerful means to connect African American students to the changing world around them. After first outlining the pedagogical priorities for African American educators in this period, I focus on the departments of romance languages at Howard and Atlanta Universities, where French instruction depended on the gendered division of labor among African American men and women.[8] While the initial interest in French was fueled in part by a desire to lay claim to its civilizational associations, its instruction would institutionalize African American intellectual production and also the networks of black internationalism, which was now reshaped by black-authored textbooks, distinct pedagogical strategies, and new approaches to support graduate training. By changing the mode of language instruction, this cohort of teachers and students in turn changed the political, cultural, and linguistic terms with which African Americans negotiated their relationships to the world.

Though driven by distinct political and pedagogical priorities, the instruction of French at African American colleges and universities reflected broader transformations in language study in the early part of the twentieth century.[9] The classical curriculum, with its required study of Greek and Latin, was dominant throughout the nineteenth century, but by the 1880s modern languages had become increasingly important to higher education, thanks in no small part to the tremendous resources marshaled by the Alliance Française to promote French language and culture abroad.[10] For African Americans the importance of French was rooted in the historical connection to the French

Caribbean, and Haiti in particular, but also in the confidence in French color blindness, which had been reinforced by both soldiers and the black press following World War I.[11] By the 1920s a number of African American students had begun formal studies in romance languages at historically white colleges and universities, including Amherst, Chicago, Columbia, Cornell, Harvard, Radcliffe, Smith, and Williams.[12] While the study of French opened new doors, including the opportunity to study and live in Paris and in some cases offered a means to resist other forms of racial and gender exclusion, it was nevertheless defined by racism. As a student at Amherst College, Mercer Cook recalled later that he was initially interested in joining the US Foreign Service, but because this particular path was "closed to people of my complexion," he decided instead to teach French.[13] Having objected to the implementation of vocational training at Dunbar High School, where she taught French, Anna Julia Cooper studied at the Sorbonne in Paris, where she received a doctorate in 1925 for her dissertation on the relationship of the French Revolution to slavery in the Caribbean.[14] Georgiana Simpson had earned her doctorate in German philology in 1921 from the University of Chicago largely through summer and correspondence courses (to avoid the indignities imposed upon her by the administration), after which she edited a critical edition and translation of a French biography of Toussaint Louverture.[15]

While African American scholars were allowed provisional acceptance into graduate programs at white-dominated universities and colleges, they were most often excluded from teaching in these same institutions. Instead this cohort of teachers was hired to teach foreign languages at African American high schools, land grant colleges, and private liberal arts colleges, the latter of whose classical liberal curriculum was slowly gaining support from white philanthropists, missionaries, and benevolent societies.[16] In 1933 W. Napoleon Rivers Jr., then professor of romance languages at North Carolina Agricultural and Technical College, published a study of modern language instruction at African American colleges. After surveying thirty institutions, including Florida A&M College, Howard University, Morehouse College, Shaw University, Tuskegee Institute, and Virginia State College, Rivers outlined their curricular and extracurricular offerings, noting that most schools offered a wide range of courses at both the beginning and advanced levels and that enrollment in all courses was dominated by women, who were also most often "the ranking students in languages." He found that while there was much interest in modern languages in general, French accounted for nearly two-thirds of the thirty-five thousand students enrolled in language courses that year. As a specialist in French poetry, Rivers was undeniably enthusiastic, but he was frustrated by the continued lack of resources at these same institutions. Few could provide enough books or language laboratory equipment or offer advanced degrees for African American teachers, who in turn could not study abroad or join national societies and organizations, even those where "there is not known to exist any opposition to Negro membership."[17] Moreover no undergraduate students had been awarded a Franco-American scholarship or been accepted into the University of Delaware's junior year abroad program, the only one of its kind.[18] While Rivers's study was focused on colleges and universities, his concerns echoed those articulated by contemporary studies of African American secondary school language instruction, which noted the limited financial resources for textbooks and libraries, large class sizes, limited time for extracurricular clubs, and, as Catherine Grigsby noted in 1931, little if any access to graduate training for African American teachers.[19] In this, the inequities in language instruction reflected the broader structural inequality that defined formal education in the Jim Crow South, where local and state governments provided starkly different resources for schools based on race.[20]

In light of the many challenges facing African American educators in this period, Rivers's interest in extracurricular clubs and study abroad programs could appear as frivolous today as they likely did to cotemporary adherents of industrial education. However, Rivers, along with other educators in the field, explicitly linked language instruction to the struggle for social equality and intellectual freedom. One of their central concerns was the French language curriculum itself, which rarely if ever depicted black people. Indeed a later survey of African American high schools in West Virginia found that most teachers employed the standard French grammar textbooks, whose maps of France were strictly hexagonal and did not mention African-descended people aside from offering a translation of "Blacky" to "Noiraud" in the vocabulary list.[21] Despite these limitations, most of the teachers surveyed were willing to include "racial" questions in their curricula by introducing, for example, "the inspiring career of Toussaint Louverture in Haiti, of the Dumas family in France, etc."[22] Rivers contended that the study of modern foreign languages offered an "inexhaustible mine to the Negro," for whom "racial pride" ought to drive an academic inquiry into the lives of "those men of African descent to whom the foreign idioms were adopted mother tongues." Because their "achievements and distinctions" had been heretofore "passed over unnoticed, intentionally concealed, or grievously misinterpreted" by white scholars, there was much work to be done by "scholarly minds that are sympathetic, just, and unbiased."[23] Echoing Carter G. Woodson's *The Mis-education of the Negro* (1933), which critiqued the indoctrination of black dependence in American schools, Rivers focused on the ways in which curricular choices could severely curtail the potential intellectual authority of African American students and scholars.

It is fitting, then, that in November 1933 Rivers presented this pedagogical vision in Washington, D.C., at the annual meeting of the Association for the Study of Negro Life and History (ASNLH), which had the previous year called for a renewed commitment to modern languages.[24] At the meeting Rivers took part in a panel on modern languages and literatures, for which he was joined by V. B. Spratlin, who was then chair of Howard University's Department of Romance Languages, as well as Dean E. P. Davis at Howard and John F. Matheus at West Virginia State College.[25] In his paper Rivers defined the moral and political stakes of learning new languages. The history of no "race of people," he wrote, had been "falsified more, in writing, than that of the Negro." If African Americans learned French, they could examine the sources themselves and discover the facts that had been "obscured, falsified, or omitted," and ultimately "combat falsehood with truth." In this effort he was particularly critical of French colonial accounts, in which "pejorative adjectives" were used to describe the African rulers "who defended their homeland against civilized invaders." After reviewing the accepted interpretations of Samory, "King of the Niger," for example, it became clear to Rivers that when "the white scholar goes to the sources," he does not return with the "whole truth" but instead "brings back the matter which fits into the well-established grooves of the Nordic mind, relative to the Negro." By learning French and directly engaging with its literature, African American scholars could thus "dam the flow of lies in the form of English translations, lectures, interpretations, and appraisals on matters concerning foreign Negroes." In addition to correcting the historical record, Rivers suggested that foreign-language acquisition would enable African American students to expand their minds. If restricted to reading only work "written in the language of his oppressor," a student would accept, "unwittingly and without protest," those ideologies "designed to enslave his mind forever." By reading in another language, students would be introduced to a "larger world of ideas" and "new zones for mental and emotional adventure," thus ameliorating the "provincial-mindedness already induced to an acute degree by slave psychology and the knowledge of only one language."[26] Linking monolingualism to slavery, Rivers directly challenged the ideological basis for industrial education, transforming the French grammar into a tool of empowerment, self-determination, and, ultimately, manhood.

Equally committed to this task of rehabilitating French was Mercer Cook, who joined the Department of Romance Languages at Howard University in 1927.[27] While Howard had offered courses in French since the 1870s, it was not until the 1920s that it began to offer both introductory courses as well as more specialized courses in French literature.[28] These course offerings were supplemented by a lively extracurricular commitment to all things French and, in particular, the development of the Société Française (later Cercle Français), which was formed in 1919 by Professor Metz Lochard to promote French in lectures, poetry readings, and its annual soirée at Liberty Hall, "to which eminent French people are often invited."[29] Although the Cercle Français was coeducational, as Howard had been since its founding, the club was dominated by women, who composed roughly two-thirds of the membership and frequently held leadership positions.[30] In addition, while Howard students and faculty sponsored the Cercle Français, it also attracted a large number of women either enrolled in or teaching at local colleges and secondary schools, including faculty like Mary G. Brewer, who was then professor of French at Miner Teachers College, as well as faculty and students from Dunbar High School.[31]

A native of the District—and son of composer Will Marion Cook and singer Abbie Mitchell—Cook had himself graduated from Dunbar High School in 1920. After completing a degree in French literature at Amherst College in 1925, he received a fellowship to attend a preparatory school for French-language teachers (École de Préparation des Professeurs de Français à l'Etranger) at the University of Paris.[32] In addition to his formal studies, Cook joined a unique intellectual space in the Parisian suburb of Clamart. It was there that two Martiniquan sisters, Jane and Paulette Nardal, hosted a biweekly salon for black students, writers, artists, and intellectuals from throughout the African diaspora, including Aimé Césaire, Léopold Senghor, Claude McKay, Countee Cullen, Alain Locke, and Carter G. Woodson. The salons were formative in the creation of a vibrant print cultural world of black internationalism in the 1920s and 1930s, which was itself critical to the development of *négritude*, a movement of Francophone writers that advocated a celebration of black life, history, and culture.[33] It was in these salons that Cook first met Louis Achille, a cousin of the Nardal sisters who had moved to Paris from Martinique in 1926 to begin his studies at the prestigious Lycée Louis-le-Grand. Having befriended fellow colonial students Césaire and Senghor at the *lycée*, Achille then brought them to the salons, where they met African American students and writers.

These diasporic relationships remained critical for Cook, who returned to the United States in 1927 to begin doctoral studies in French at Brown University as well as a teaching post in the Department of Romance Languages at Howard.[34] In 1931, after arranging an interview with Alain Locke, Cook extended an invitation to Achille to join the department that fall.[35] Working with Achille, Cook took a leading role in reorganizing the Cercle Français and changing the departmental curriculum. In 1932 the Baltimore *Afro-American* reported that the Sunday afternoon meeting of the club had been hosted by Anna Julia Cooper at her home on T Street, where she welcomed Dantès Bellegarde, then minister of Haiti, to the United States, who "urged the study of French to cultivate international friendship with the Haitians," as well as Miss Fay Hershaw, an elementary teacher who had brought home souvenirs from the 1931 Colonial Exposition in Paris.[36] Perhaps mimicking the salons in Paris, the club thus became a space in which to define—and debate—black identity. Cook was also critical to rethinking the department's course offerings, which now included The Negro in French Literature, and in training graduate students, which the department began to accept in 1932.[37] In keeping with the gendered interest and commitment to French, almost all of his graduate students were women, whose theses focused on the role of black people in French literature: Mary Edna Burke's "Honoré de Balzac's Conception of the

Negro" (1933), Cecie Roberta Jenkins's "Voltaire and the Negro" (1936), Valerie Ethelyn Parks's "Napoleon and the Negro" (1935), Alice A. Foster's "Lafayette and the Negro" (1935), Marian C. Bowden's "Saint-Pierre and the Negro" (1938), and Martha B. Kendrick's "The Negro as Seen by Contemporary French Writers" (1941). Most had attended Dunbar High School before enrolling at Howard and, following their master's degrees, would teach French throughout the United States at both the secondary and college level.

Building on his work in the classroom and his graduate students' research, in 1934 Cook published an essay, "On Reading French," which he addressed to the "average Negro student of French" who takes the course "against the advice of parents or well-meaning friends."[38] Perhaps conscious of Booker T. Washington's own admonition, Cook underscored the importance of studying not only French but also those texts that examine black subjects. In this vein, Cook was quick to cite his own forthcoming volume, *Le Noir*, which compiled works by twenty-nine French authors who referenced black people.[39] The selections in this new book were wide-ranging, including Théophile Gautier's account of the Shakespearean actor Ira Aldridge, the racial theories of the Comte de Buffon, and André Gide's account of his voyage to the Congo. While some selections highlighted the accomplishments of black men and women, others were marked by the French colonial racism with which Cook was no doubt familiar. Cook wrote in the preface that the collection was a "modest attempt to answer a purpose, the importance of which has become increasingly apparent to the writer during his several years of experience as a teacher of French in colored schools." In short, he wanted his students to know that while the standard books might indicate otherwise, the "Negro has not been overlooked in French literature to the same extent that he has been neglected in the French courses of our Negro Schools and colleges." In offering these selections, he assured his readers that he was by no means "attempting to prescribe a literary racial line," likely forestalling potential criticism. This effort was instead, he argued, motivated by a belief that his students "have the right to know" what Maupassant, Hugo, and Lamartine "had to say about the Negro."[40]

Building on these selections, Cook's volume offered a distinct way of teaching French to African American students, who were invited to engage in and potentially debate these canonical texts. Accompanying each literary selection was a set of exercises and questions, which, in addition to ensuring basic comprehension of plot and vocabulary, sanctioned the students' desire to dispute the assumptions or characterizations in these texts. In this way Buffon's own account of the habits and customs of the Ethiopians became a site of contestation for the reader, prompted by Cook's question: "Do you believe that this history is true or false?" In response to Gautier's account of African people, Cook's discussion questions clarify his characterization but then push back, asking the students to consider: "Are all African women in fact ugly?" After reading a short story by Maupassant, Cook invited his readers to consider why the author had made his black characters speak in a form of pidgin rather than standard French. Cook's framing of the texts focused his students' attention on the possibilities and limits of translation. At the end of the book is a short glossary of relevant vocabulary, which invited students once again to query the categories of race, whether it was *noir* or *nègre* or *noirâtre* (blackish). Reflecting on Balzac's *Le Père Goriot*, Cook's discussion guide questioned the novelist's definition of *nègre* and asked the reader to assess whether this word could in fact "express the personal ideas" of Balzac with regards to slavery." Cook's decision to highlight how black people figured into French literature was above all a way of enabling his students to locate themselves in an alternative linguistic and cultural realm. The book's central aim was, he argued, to inform his students, to "let them know what has been written concerning them in this beautiful foreign tongue, the intricacies of which they are attempting to master."[41] Drawing together the "intricacies" of learning a language and the complexities of forging a black identity in the modern world, Cook's formulation underscored the epistemological dimensions of racial identity. In learning about themselves in a new language, students would read and discuss black lives in radically different terms. By virtue of the discussion guides that Cook offered, they were also invited to question those same terms, perhaps then locating themselves outside of the very structures that had first provided the terms of racialization. In this they would find new terms of racialization, but taken together this contrast might deepen their understanding of the structures of racism. As Cook noted, "If a tragic note is sometimes sounded in these pages, the reader must remember that the history of the Negro is not without an occasional minor."[42] Rather than presenting French as a means of escaping racism, Cook's text facilitated a deeper inquiry into its many permutations.

The collection soon captured the attention of reviewers in popular publications, including the *Amsterdam News* and *The Crisis*, as well as academic journals.[43] Writing in the *Journal of Negro Education,* Rivers gave a glowing review, praising this "composite picture, in miniature, of the Negro in French thought" as "teachable, informing, and interesting."[44] Spratlin's review in the *Journal of Negro History* recommended the text to the "teacher of French who desires to see an occasional black face among the Perrichons, Poiriers, and Colombas who invade his class-room."[45] Reviewers in mainstream French publications were less convinced. In the *Modern Language Journal*, Gilbert E. Mills first expressed doubt that he would be able to judge its reception among African Americans, since he was "unacquainted with Negro psychology." He nevertheless critiqued the book as one that would have an adverse effect on interracial relations. Given the broader interest in improving international relations, he argued that "any textbook which does not improve inter-racial relations is out of harmony with modern thought."[46] Although Mills interpreted this approach to be at odds with the cultivation of foreign relations, Cook's text was rooted in the political debates at Howard, where scholars questioned the racist foundations of the study of international relations and imperialism.[47] While some of his colleagues rejected colonialism in all its permutations, Cook and other French scholars sought to rehabilitate this colonial language, believing it capable of creating new links among African-descended people.

Building on growing interest in the book—which would soon be used in one rural West Virginia high school as a "supplementary reader" to standard readers and grammars—Cook translated and condensed Alexandre Dumas's novel *Georges* for serial publication in the *Baltimore Afro-American* from September 1935 through January 1936.[48] In promoting the work of "France's greatest colored author," the *Afro-American* reproduced caricatures of the author to help explain that Dumas was "often satirized by his enemies, who used many of the epithets that white Americans employ today against colored people."[49] The following year Dumas's novel was published in French by ASNLH's own Associated Publishers, edited by Rivers, John Matheus, and Messaoud Belateche and marketed as a "race novel" for the intermediate French reader.[50] As the editors noted in the preface, the novel presented "the triumph of a colored man over the bars of race prejudice, a triumph realized through self-respect, physical courage, and a purposeful intolerance for racial injustice." Like Cook, the editors included questions for each chapter, asking students to directly reckon with Dumas's treatment of race and racial characteristics in the novel. The questions also pointed to a distinct ideological framework for understanding black French life, whether it was the way one character finds pride once "he finds himself in the midst of Blacks" or in referring to the marooned slaves as the "unknown heroes of Liberty."[51]

After completing his dissertation, Cook left Howard in 1936 to join the Department of Romance Languages at Atlanta University.[52] Now a member of the only other romance languages department to offer graduate training to African American students, Cook continued to advise undergraduate and graduate students at Atlanta as well as at Morehouse and Spelman colleges. Similar to Howard, the majority of his students were African American women, including Sara Harris Cureton, Florrie Florence Jackson, Naomi Mills Garrett, Jeannette Frances Spurell, Marian Mae Speight, and Carolyn Lemon, all of whom wrote master's theses in the department. While the previous cohort at Howard had focused on the place of black people within the writings of well-known white French authors, several in this group turned to black French authors, including Dumas but also René Maran, whose novels were the focus of Speight's thesis. Drawing on her own interviews with the author, she focused on the ways in which Maran "portrays his African brothers."[53] Lemon, who completed her thesis, "Victor Hugo and the Negro," in 1936, was the first African American student to receive a Franco-American Student Exchange fellowship from the Institute of International Education to study at the University of Paris in 1937.[54] However, her participation in the exchange program was met with some trepidation by the Institute's Student

Bureau, which believed it to be impossible to place African American students in French schools.[55]

While supporting his own students in their training as French scholars and teachers, Cook also focused on the possibilities of extending this training to secondary school teachers, most of whom were unable to maintain graduate coursework and a full teaching load during the academic year. In 1936 Cook joined with faculty at Spelman and Morehouse to create a six-week French Institute in the Atlanta University Summer School. It was "the first of its kind to be set up in a Negro university" and provided graduate and undergraduate courses in French.[56] The supervising instructors included Louis Achille, who traveled from Washington to Atlanta each summer to join the Institute; Edward Allen Jones, then professor of French at Morehouse College; and Billie Geter Thomas, who had taught at Bethune-Cookman College before coming to Spelman in 1933.[57] While some of the enrolled students might have been able to complete graduate studies in French at other institutions, including Middlebury, McGill, and Columbia, the opportunity to do so in an African American school made what could have been an unpleasant and alienating educational experience one that fostered community among black educators. In addition to undergraduate courses in elementary French, the Institute offered graduate courses "in the Negro in French civilization," as well as opportunities to speak French over meals.[58] Moreover Cook and his wife, Vashti Cook—who held a diploma from the Alliance Française and a certificate from the University of Paris—created a French-language program at Atlanta University's Oglethorpe Elementary School, a private laboratory school for the children of faculty at Atlanta, Morehouse, and Spelman. By incorporating "simple conversations, songs, games, and other natural methods of acquiring a new language," the *Chicago Defender* reported, students were "making remarkable progress" in learning French.[59] It also served as an important training opportunity for future students. In 1936, inspired by the "increasing interest in French literature by and about Negroes," Cook had inaugurated a new series by Atlanta University Press, which published two novels focused on black lives that were to be used in French classes.[60]

In 1938 Cook published an essay on these experiences, speaking directly to those educators who believe that "the languages have little or no value in our schools." It was for precisely that reason, he argued, that they had created the Institute, which provided African American teachers with a respite from this pedagogical myopia and also from the many other problems they faced in teaching French, be it the excessive teaching loads, low salaries, or the limited opportunities to study abroad. By enrolling in the Institute, these teachers would learn how to teach this material to African American students. They might bring in stories "concerning Frenchmen of color" or tell their classes "the story of Haïti and that her inhabitants still speak French despite the fact that she won her independence more than one hundred years ago" or, when learning to sing "La Marseillaise," might also introduce Lamartine's *Marseillaise Noire*. They would be introduced to current library services and publications, like *Illustration*'s recent special issue devoted to the French Antilles, a topic that "every wide-awake Negro teacher of French should know." Indeed, Cook concluded, "the Negro needs not technical or industrial instruction alone, nor will the social sciences alone prove to be the long sought panacea." If "taught with breadth of vision, sincerity and proficiency," nothing could "more effectively combat narrow mindedness than an acquaintance with the civilization of another people."[61] Cook's essay reflected the deepening commitment to French as a means of expanding the worlds of African American students in the Jim Crow South. By learning an alternative language of civilization, they might begin to challenge the assumptions that were built into their own linguistic worlds, which encoded black life as inferior, uncivilized, and unworthy of ambition. When Cook spoke of "narrow mindedness," it was not a blithe or banal hope of openness to new experiences or possibilities; instead it underscored the critical need for black students to see beyond the confines of segregation.

However, in making sense of this worldview—and this pedagogical *and* political commitment to French language acquisition—it is not enough to simply look at Cook or the other men whose vision was propagated in journals and textbooks in this period. These intellectual syntheses and statements depended largely on the work of women, whose master's theses delved into the place of black people in French literature, who supervised classroom training, who organized French clubs and associations, and who taught introductory French courses while completing their degrees. It was these women—and the many others whose names and courses are unrecorded—who employed these new French grammars to teach their students. While their stories are yet to be told, the effect of their labor is visible in the interventions that Cook and Rivers made in this period.[62] It is through a situated examination of this work, then, that we discover a new kind of archive of black internationalism, one that would inspire children and college students alike to turn to their French grammars and to the world. By focusing on this "domestic" intellectual and pedagogical production, we can expand the boundaries of black internationalism and deepen our understanding of the intellectual labor that undergirded the black intellectual tradition.

Notes

1. Booker T. Washington, *Up from Slavery* (New York: Doubleday, 1901), 122.

2. Booker T. Washington, "The Awakening of the Negro," *Atlantic Monthly* 78 (September 1896): 322–28.

3. W. E. B. Du Bois, *The Souls of Black Folk* (Chicago: McClurg, 1903), 43, 109, 108.

4. On the history of African Americans in France, see Tracey Denean Sharpley-Whiting, *Bricktop's Paris: African American Women in Paris between the Two World Wars* (Albany: State University of New York Press, 2015); Tyler Stovall, *Paris Noir: African Americans in the City of Light* (Boston: Houghton Mifflin, 1996); William A. Shack, *Harlem in Montmartre: A Paris Jazz Story between the Great Wars* (Berkeley: University of California Press, 2001); Michel Fabre, *From Harlem to Paris: Black American Writers in France, 1840–1980* (Urbana: University of Illinois Press, 1991).

5. On this paradox, see Sue Peabody and Tyler Edward Stovall, eds., *The Color of Liberty: Histories of Race in France* (Durham, N.C.: Duke University Press, 2003); Petrine Archer-Straw, *Negrophilia: Avant-Garde Paris and Black Culture in the 1920s* (London: Thames & Hudson, 2000); Trica Danielle Keaton and T. Denean Sharpley-Whiting, eds., *Black France / France Noire: The History and Politics of Blackness* (Durham, N.C.: Duke University Press, 2012).

6. Some key texts in this rich historiographical tradition include Michael O. West and William G. Martin, eds., *From Toussaint to Tupac: The Black International since the Age of Revolution* (Chapel Hill: University of North Carolina Press, 2009); Robin D. G. Kelley, "But a Local Phase of a World Problem: Black History's Global Vision, 1883–1950," *Journal of American History* 86, no. 3 (1999): 1045–77; Minkah Makalani, *In the Cause of Freedom: Radical Black Internationalism from Harlem to London, 1917–1939* (Chapel Hill: University of North Carolina Press, 2011); Gerald Horne, *Black and Red: W. E. B. Du Bois and the Afro-American Response to the Cold War, 1944–1963* (Albany: State University of New York Press, 1986); Penny M. Von Eschen, *Race against Empire: Black Americans and Anticolonialism, 1937–1957* (Ithaca, N.Y.: Cornell University Press, 1997); Frank Andre Guridy, *Forging Diaspora: Afro-Cubans and African Americans in a World of Empire and Jim Crow* (Chapel Hill: University of North Carolina Press, 2010); Lara Putnam, *Radical Moves: Caribbean Migrants and the Politics of Race in the Jazz Age* (Chapel Hill: University of North Carolina Press, 2013).

7. On this, see Brent Hayes Edwards, *The Practice of Diaspora: Literature, Translation, and the Rise of Black Internationalism* (Cambridge, Mass.: Harvard University Press, 2003).

8. For recent work that has deepened the field's understanding of black women's internationalism, see Keisha N. Blain, *Set the World on Fire: Black Nationalist Women and the Global Struggle for Freedom* (Philadelphia: University of Pennsylvania Press, 2018); Keisha N. Blain, "'We Want to Set the World on Fire': Black Nationalist Women and Diasporic Politics in the New Negro World, 1940–1944," *Journal of Social History* 49, no. 1 (2015): 194–212; Barbara Ransby, *Eslanda: The Large and Unconventional Life of Mrs. Paul Robeson* (New Haven, Conn.: Yale University Press, 2013); Barbara Savage, "Professor Merze Tate: Diplomatic Historian, Cosmopolitan Woman," in *Toward an Intellectual History of Black Women,* edited by Mia Bay et al. (Chapel Hill: University of North Carolina Press, 2015), 252–72.

9. In narrating this history, I am indebted to two bibliographies on the subject. See Clarence Harvey Mills, "Selective Annotative Bibliography on the Negro and Foreign Languages," *Journal of Negro Education,* 8, no. 2 (1939): 170–76;

James J. Davis, "Foreign Language Study and Afro-Americans: An Annotated Bibliography, 1931–1988," *Journal of Negro Education* 58, no. 4 (1989): 558–67.

10. See Maurice Brueziere, *L'alliance française: Histoire d'une institution, 1883–1993* (Paris: Hachette, 1993). In 1883, for example, scholars formed the Modern Language Association to promote the use and study of modern languages. On language instruction in this period, see Algernon Coleman, *The Teaching of Modern Foreign Languages in the United States* (New York: Macmillan,1929). On French, see Richard H. Pells, *Not Like Us: How Europeans Have Loved, Hated, and Transformed American Culture since World War II* (New York: Basic Books, 1997), 31–32.

11. On this discourse during and after World War I, see especially Chad L. Williams, *Torchbearers of Democracy: African American Soldiers in the World War I Era* (Chapel Hill: University of North Carolina Press, 2010); Stovall, *Paris Noir*; Fabre, *From Harlem to Paris*.

12. This cohort included Rupert Lloyd, John Matheus, Edward A. Jones, Mercer Cook, W. Napoleon Rivers, as well as a number of women, including Etnah Rochon Boutte, Theodora R. Boyd, Catherine Grigsby, Georgiana Simpson, and Anna Julia Cooper.

13. Mercer Cook, interview by Ruth S. Njiri, June 24, 1981, Silver Spring, Md., transcript, Phelps-Stoke Fund's Oral History Project on former Black Chiefs of Mission, Writings by Mercer Cook, Mercer Cook Papers, Box 157-5, Folder 6, Manuscript Division, Moorland-Spingarn Research Center (MSRC), Howard University, Washington, D.C.

14. On Cooper, see Vivian M. May, *Anna Julia Cooper, Visionary Black Feminist: A Critical Introduction* (New York: Routledge, 2012).

15. Georgiana R. Simpson, ed., *Toussaint Louverture, surnommé le premier des noirs* (Washington, D.C.: Associated Publishers, 1924).

16. On African Americans and higher education, see James D. Anderson, *The Education of Blacks in the South, 1860–1935* (Chapel Hill: University of North Carolina Press, 2010), esp. chapter 7.

17. W. Napoleon Rivers, "A Study of the Modern Foreign Languages in Thirty Negro Colleges," *Journal of Negro Education* 2, no. 4 (1933): 487, 490, 489. It was not until 1937 that the College Language Association was formed to support teachers of English and foreign languages in historically African American colleges and universities.

18. Rivers, "A Study of the Modern," 490–91.

19. John F. Matheus, "A Negro State College Looks at Foreign Language," *Journal of Negro Education* 7, no. 2 (1938): 158–59; Catherine V. Grigsby, "The Status of the Teaching of French in Virginia High Schools," *Virginia Teachers Bulletin* 8, no. 2 (1931): 4–5.

20. See also Hilary J. Moss, *Schooling Citizens: The Struggle for African American Education in Antebellum America* (Chicago: University of Chicago Press, 2010); Anderson, *The Education of Blacks in the South, 1860–1935*.

21. W. H. Fraser and J. Squair, *Standard French Grammar* (Boston: D. C. Heath, 1931).

22. Fraser and Squair, *Standard French Grammar*, 158.

23. Rivers, "A Study of the Modern," 490.

24. "Notes," *Journal of Negro History* 18 (October 1933): 487–89.

25. "Proceedings of the Annual Meeting of the Association for the Study of Negro Life and History Held in Washington, D.C., from October 29 to November 1, 1933," *Journal of Negro History* 19, no. 1 (1934): 7–8.

26. Napoleon W. Rivers, "Why Negroes Should Study Romance Languages and Literature," *Journal of Negro History* 19, no 2 (1934): 119, 126, 123, 133, 131, 134.

27. On Cook, see Félix Germain's recent essay, in which he argues that Cook helped to "create conceptual frameworks and theoretical tools" that remain critical to black French studies. While focused on a different historical moment and disciplinary question, Germain underscores the unrecognized importance of Cook in the history of African American studies and black internationalism. Felix Germain, "Mercer Cook and the Origins of Black French Studies," *French Politics, Culture & Society* 34, no. 1 (2016): 66–85.

28. Walter Dyson, *Howard University: The Capstone of Negro Education, a History 1867–1940* (Washington, D.C.: Howard University Press, 1941), 157. See also James J. Davis's departmental history in the Howard University Archives, MSRC.

29. Howard University, "The Echo: 1920," *Howard University Yearbooks*, Book 101; "The Enopron: 1921," Book 186; "The Bison: 1925," Book 106, MSRC, http://dh.howard.edu/bison_yearbooks/.

30. The estimate was based on a survey of fifteen years of yearbooks. See note 29.

31. On the membership of the Cercle Français, see the Howard University yearbooks. See "Helen W. Burrell, 1902–1960," *Modern Language Journal* 44, no. 7 (1960): 295. Dunbar's teaching staff had included Carter G. Woodson, Jessie Fauset, Anna Julia Cooper, and Georgiana Simpson, all of whom taught classical and romance languages at the school.

32. Allison Stewart, *First Class: The Legacy of Dunbar, America's First Black Public High School* (Chicago: Lawrence Hill Books, 2013), 99.

33. On the role of the Nardal sisters in shaping the négritude movement, see Edwards, *The Practice of Diaspora*; T. Denean Sharpley-Whiting, *Negritude Women* (Minneapolis: University of Minnesota Press, 2002). On négritude more generally, see Lilyan Kesteloot, *Black Writers in French: A Literary History of Negritude*, translated by Ellen Conroy Kennedy (Philadelphia: Temple University Press, 1974); Gary Wilder, *The French Imperial Nation-State: Negritude and Colonial Humanism between the Two World Wars* (Chicago: University of Chicago Press, 2005).

34. "Howard Drops Prof. Mills, Appoints 4 Instructors," *Afro-American* (Baltimore), July 30, 1927. Cook arrived the same year as Valaurez B. Spratlin, who led Spanish-language instruction in the department.

35. Interview by Emmanuelle Payen, Radio Fourviere, Lyon, January 19, 1974, Private Collection of Dominique Achille, Caen. Cook had taken a leave of absence and returned along with Achille in 1931. "Sixty-three New Members on Howard University Faculty," *Chicago Defender*, national edition, October 11, 1930.

36. "Bellegarde Addresses D.C. French Club," *Afro-American* (Baltimore), February 13, 1932.

37. James J. Davis, "Master's Theses on Afro-French and Afro-Hispanic Literatures and Cultures and African American Images in French and Spanish Literatures Produced by Howard University's Department of Romance Languages

from 1933–1993" (2005), Educational Resources Information Center database, ED385164.

38. Mercer Cook, "On Reading French," *Quarterly Review of Higher Education among Negroes* 1 (1934): 42.

39. He first published on this in 1933. Mercer Cook, "Edouard de Laboulaye and the Negro," *Journal of Negro History* 18, no. 3 (1933): 246–55. See also Fernand Masse, "The Negro Race in French Literature," *Journal of Negro History* 18, no. 3 (1933): 225–45.

40. Mercer Cook, *Le Noir, Morceaux choisis de vingt-neuf Français célèbres* (New York: American Book, 1934), v, vi.

41. Cook, "On Reading French," 43–44, vi.

42. Cook, "On Reading French," vi.

43. "Howard Professor Edits French Book," *Amsterdam News*, February 7, 1934; Guichard Parris, "French Text-Books and the Negro," *Crisis*, November 1935, 344–45.

44. W. Napoleon Rivers, review, *Journal of Negro Education* 3, no. 4 (1934): 627–28.

45. V. B. Spratlin, review, *Journal of Negro History* 20, no. 1 (1935): 86–89.

46. Gilbert E. Mills, review, *Modern Language Journal* 20, no. 4 (1936): 248–9. See also Leslie S. Brady, review of *Le Noir, French Review* 8, no. 6 (1935): 500–501.

47. On the history of the Howard School, see Robert Vitalis, *White World Order, Black Power Politics: The Birth of American International Relations* (Ithaca, N.Y.: Cornell University Press, 2015). On the relationship of African American scholars to Africa, see Jerry Gershenhorn, "'Not an Academic Affair': African American Scholars and the Development of African Studies Programs in the United States, 1942–1960, *Journal of African American History* 94, no. 1 (2009): 44–68.

48. On its use in schools, see John F. Matheus, "A Negro State College Looks at Foreign Language," *Journal of Negro Education* 7, no 2 (1938): 158.

49. "France's Greatest Fiction Writer Deals with Race Problems of His Day," *Afro-American* (Baltimore), September 28, 1935; "Alexandre Dumas, World's Greatest Fiction Writer, Whose Novel, 'Georges,' Starts in the AFRO Next Week," *Afro-American* (Baltimore), September 21, 1935.

50. Alexandre Dumas, *Georges: An Intermediate French Reader*, edited by W. Napoleon Rivers, John F. Matheus, and Messaoud Belateche (Washington, D.C.: Associated Publisher, 1936), i. On Matheus, see Fabre, *From Harlem to Paris*, 132.

51. Dumas, *Georges*, ii, 103–15.

52. Will Mercer Cook, "French Travelers in the United States, 1840–1875," Ph.D. dissertation, Brown University, 1936. According to the *Afro-American*, he had been denied a year's leave of absence and was also promised a larger salary in Atlanta. "Mercer Cook to Quit Post at Howard U.," *Afro-American* (Baltimore), February 8, 1936.

53. Marian Mae Speight, "The Negro in the Novels of Rene Maran" (1940), ETD Collection for AUC Robert W. Woodruff Library, EP17454, http://digitalcommons.auctr.edu/dissertations/EP17454.

54. "Theses for the Year," *South Atlantic Bulletin* (South Atlantic Modern Language Association) 4, no. 2 (1938): 4–5; "Carolyn Lemon of Atlanta University Given Scholarship for Year's Study in France," press release, 1937, Florence M.

Read Presidential Records, Box 190, Folder 20, Atlanta University Archives, Archives Research Center, Robert W. Woodruff Library, Atlanta University.

55. It also unsettled the Office National des Universités et Ecoles Françaises, which sought a French student from Martinique, Guadeloupe, "or some other French colony" and finally settled on a "little colored lady from Martinique" named Mireille Césaire. Despite their enthusiasm for the student, the committee feared that she would face racist treatment in the United States and that she would suffer without contact with the white population. In response Acting President Florence M. Read proposed that Césaire be put in touch with Miss Billie Geter, a former student of Cook and a French instructor at Spelman who was currently in Paris. She also noted that Cook was well acquainted with the student's brother Aimé Césaire, who had first met Cook in Paris in 1926 and had by then begun work on his *Cahier d'un retour au pays natal* (1939). Jessie Douglass, secretary, Student Bureau, Institute of International Education, to Florence M. Read, Atlanta University, January 13, 1937, Box 190, Folder 20, Archives Research Center, Robert W. Woodruff Library, Atlanta University.

56. "Starts 11th Year Teaching French at Atlanta Univ.," *Chicago Defender*, June 8, 1940.

57. "School for French Profs. to Be Held," *Chicago Defender*, April 11, 1936.

58. Martin D. Jenkins, "Negro Higher Education," *Journal of Negro Education* 5, no. 4 (1936): 667.

59. "Atlanta Children Taking Up French Books Are Waived," *Chicago Defender*, February 13, 1937.

60. Mercer Cook and Guichard Parris, eds., *Alexander Privat d'Anglemont's Les singes de Dieu et les hommes du Diable and Madame de Duras's Ourika* (Atlanta, Ga.: Atlanta University Press, 1936). Several years later Cook would also publish *Five French Negro Authors* (Washington, D.C.: Associated Publishers, 1943).

61. Mercer Cook, "The Teaching of French in Negro Schools," *Journal of Negro Education* 7, no. 2 (1938): 147, 149–50, 153, 154.

62. In 1939, for example, Cook built on his graduate students' work on black French writers to define the "race problem" in Paris and the French West Indies, first in an address at Atlanta University in December 1938. Mercer Cook, "The Race Problem in Paris and the French West Indies," *Journal of Negro Education* 8, no. 4 (1939): 673–80.

Afro-Cuban Intellectuals and the New Negro Renaissance

Bernardo Ruiz Suárez's *The Color Question in the Two Americas*

Reena N. Goldthree

In the summer of 1922 Bernardo Ruiz Suárez published *The Color Question in the Two Americas*, a comparative study of "the conditions in which the colored race lives in Central and South America . . . and in the United States."[1] Written during Ruiz Suárez's residency in Harlem, the nonfiction work blurred the boundaries between historical narrative and political commentary, invoking the author's lived experience as a Cuban of African descent, theories of racial difference, and sociopolitical analysis. In the book's foreword, Ruiz Suárez characterized the monograph as a descriptive account of race relations, explicitly disavowing any prescriptive agenda. "In the following pages, I have essayed to set forth, not in the vein of a critic but rather as an apprentice and an observer," he insisted. "In presenting my impressions of the color question, I hardly need to state that I have no theory to offer, with the force of dogma, for the solution or attenuation of the problems arising from the relations of the white and colored races in the United States."[2]

Ruiz Suárez's trenchant critiques of white supremacy and antiblack violence belied his authorial guise as an unassuming observer. Indeed in *The Color Question in the Two Americas*, the Afro-Cuban intellectual sought to recast public debates about the future of the "colored race" by offering a hemispheric perspective on the path to black liberation. His internationalist vision of black freedom decentered three major themes of diasporic thought: Africa (as a site of origin and displacement), the history of chattel slavery, and the creative power of black cultural forms.[3] Instead he articulated strategies to confront antiblack policies in the Western Hemisphere, arguing that black self-determination could be realized by establishing autonomous institutions—including a separate "Black Nation within a White Nation"—in the Americas rather than through repatriation to Africa.

Originally written in Spanish, *The Color Question in the Two Americas* debuted in the United States in English translation, marking Ruiz Suárez's initial foray into the black intellectual scene in New York. Announcements and reviews heralding the book's release appeared in the *New York Age, New York Times Book Review and Magazine, Southern Workman*, and the Universal Negro Improvement Association (UNIA)'s *Negro World*.[4] Ruiz Suárez also dispatched autographed copies of the book to several Harlem luminaries, including Hubert Harrison, William Ferris, and Arturo Schomburg. In his handwritten note to Schomburg, Ruiz Suárez thanked the famed Afro–Puerto Rican bibliophile and journalist for being "the first friend that I met in New York," offering a tantalizing clue to how Ruiz Suárez might have gained access to publication and speaking opportunities in the United States.[5]

The cosmopolitan milieu in Harlem—forged by multilingual, literate black residents with ties across the African diaspora—provided an ideal springboard for the Cuban writer. In the aftermath of the book's release, he achieved heightened visibility as a public intellectual, producing work in both Spanish and English. In August 1922 he represented Cuba at the UNIA's Third International Convention of Negro Peoples of the World, held in New York City. His lecture at the convention subsequently appeared in the Spanish section of the *Negro World*.[6] Months later Ruiz Suárez launched his own Spanish-language section in the *New York Age*, Harlem's leading African American newspaper. The section—written "por y para la Colonia Hispano Americano de la Raza de Color que reside en los Estados Unidos de Norte América" (by and for the Hispanic American Colony of the Colored Race that resides in the United States of America)—featured news reports from Latin America and the United States, *crónicas*, and poetry.[7] To promote his work as a writer, Ruiz Suárez gave public lectures in Harlem on topics such as "the future of the colored race in Spanish America" and "Latin American conception of the colored American."[8] His intellectual activities in the United States extended beyond Harlem as well. In 1923 he toured two of the nation's preeminent institutions of higher learning for black students: Hampton Institute in Virginia and Howard University in Washington, D.C.[9] He also maintained close ties to the Cuban immigrant community in Florida, collaborating with the Sociedad La Unión Martí-Maceo in Ybor City to publish a lecture on the *mulato* general Antonio Maceo.[10] Thus Ruiz Suárez, like his better-known contemporary Schomburg, participated in a "multicultural black alliance" that encompassed African Americans, Afro-Latinos, and British West Indians.[11]

Ruiz Suárez has received only passing attention from scholars of black internationalism, black intellectual history, and the Harlem Renaissance, despite his extensive archive of published work.[12] This essay offers a critical analysis of *The Color Question in the Two Americas*, situating Ruiz Suárez's understudied monograph in the context of black activism in Harlem and Havana and placing it in dialogue with his other writings from the period. In doing so I seek to contribute to a growing body of literature that foregrounds New York City as a critical site of Afro-Cuban intellectual production, particularly in regard to race and nationalism.[13] To begin, I examine Ruiz Suárez's provocative thesis that Afro-Cubans and African Americans lacked a "racial personality." I argue that Ruiz Suárez's theory of racial personality is structured around a series of binary oppositions that stage African Americans as the counterpoint to Afro-Cubans. Then I shed light on Ruiz Suárez's conception of nationality by analyzing his critique of the UNIA's African repatriation proposals. Revisiting his argument that "nationality is based . . . on sentiments of association" and a "community of interests" rather than territorial claims, I suggest that Ruiz Suárez anticipated social constructivist approaches to nationalism.[14] To conclude, I trace how Ruiz Suárez reappropriated the rhetoric of democracy to critique US policy at home and abroad, highlighting the entwined evils of racism and imperialism.

Historians have detailed the resurgence of black internationalism during the 1920s, tracing how it functioned as a political ideology, a collective consciousness, and an organizing praxis.[15] The "revival" of black internationalism, as Michael O. West and William G. Martin note, was spurred by the dislocations of World War I, the mass migration of people of African descent in the Americas, increasing urbanization, and the global circulation of black periodicals.[16] Harlem, as the most visible hub of the Black International during this era, provided a vital organizing platform for race-conscious migrants from the Spanish Caribbean. Moving between Anglophone and Hispanophone black communities in Harlem, intellectuals like Ruiz Suárez evoked and enacted an internationalist conception of the New Negro. They also contributed firsthand knowledge about the global modalities of racism, bringing attention to anti-black violence and marginalization beyond the United States.

Black Transnationalism and the "Harlem-Havana Nexus"

Ruiz Suárez's hemispheric framing of the color question reflected his own itinerant journeys. Born in Santiago de Cuba, Ruiz Suárez spent his formative years in a locale known for its rich tradition of political activism and dense network of Afro-Cuban *sociedades de color*.[17] Black civic life in the city was buoyed by an unusually high literacy rate: 53 percent of Santiagueros of color could read and write at the turn of the century.[18] Ruiz Suárez completed his secondary education in his hometown and then enrolled at the University of Havana Law School, a remarkable feat given that Cuba, according to the 1899 census, had only three black lawyers on the entire island.[19] Sometime in the years following graduation, he began his sojourn abroad. He moved first to the Republic of Panama, where he likely encountered black migrant laborers from the British West Indies and French Caribbean. After practicing law in Panama, he moved to Colombia to study political science at Central University in Bogotá.[20] By the early 1920s he had resettled in the United States, joining the forty thousand black immigrants who arrived in New York City between 1900 and 1930.[21]

Photo of Bernardo Ruiz Suárez, from his
The Color Question in the Two Americas
(New York: Hunt, 1922).

Ruiz Suárez worked as an attorney before immigrating to the United States, but he established himself in Harlem as a writer, editor, and speaker. Through his varied intellectual endeavors, he chronicled the plight of black communities in the Americas, giving concerted attention to those in Cuba and the United States. Noting his preoccupation with African Americans, he explained, "Having devoted myself, as a young man, to secure, with the aid of other right-thinking elements, the improvement of the condition of the colored race in my native land, I early came in contact, through the periodical press as well as books devoted to the subject, with the development of thought and action in regard to the problem affecting the millions of black people of the United States."[22] Fueled by his initial exposure to African American life in newspapers and scholarly works, Ruiz Suárez desired to meet his "Anglo-American brother" in person. "I had always been seduced by the fantastic tales which reached my foreign ears and eyes from the pages of the book of life of the people of the United States," he wrote with characteristic flourish. "Ever more insinuating, ever more persuasive, that seductiveness caused me to abandon the soil of my beloved Cuba and come to this land of inconceivable potentialities, so as to get a closer view of its greatness and an intimate understanding of its defects."[23]

In *The Color Question in the Two Americas*, Ruiz Suárez claimed that his interest in black life in the United States was unusual, suggesting that the "colored people of Spanish America" knew "very little" about African Americans and viewed them with "contempt." In actuality black activists in Cuba and the United States had participated in transnational exchanges since the nineteenth century.[24] Following the US military intervention in Cuba in 1898, Afro-Cubans and African Americans frequently "reached across cultural and linguistic differences to develop cultural exchanges, forge economic relationships, and construct political solidarities." These interactions, as Frank Guridy relates, were "based on the idea that they belonged to a larger African diaspora, or the 'colored race,' rooted in the perception of a shared history of enslavement and concretized by the motive to develop crossnational relations as a means of negotiating the intertwined processes of U.S. imperialism and of racism in Cuba and the United States during the opening decades of the century."[25]

Ties between the two black communities flourished during the 1920s, adding a transnational dimension to the New Negro Renaissance.[26] The global resurgence of black activism during this watershed period, as Robin D. G. Kelley maintains, was "the product of a particular historical convergence—the expansion of U.S. and European empires, settler colonialism, an increasingly industrialized racial capitalism, and their attendant processes: expropriation, proletarianization, massive migration, urbanization, rapid technological development, and war."[27] For Afro-Cubans and African Americans, the transnational black press, inexpensive steamship travel, and shared experiences of oppression at the hands of the US government bolstered links between Harlem and Havana's Afro-descended avant-garde.[28]

For Ruiz Suárez and other Afro-Cuban commentators, Harlem was the mecca of black life in North America, and the neighborhood's urbane sophisticates represented the "synthetic, typical colored man of the United States." "To the stranger expecting to find the typical kennels of the underdog, such as the hovels of the poor which disgrace many a European city, the native quarters in South Africa, or the old Chinatown in Havana, the colored section of New York is an agreeable revelation," Ruiz Suárez apprised readers.[29] Black Cubans closely followed developments in Harlem in newspaper columns such as "Ideales de una Raza" in Havana's *Diario de la Marina*. During its three-year run, that column covered the work of US-based black organizations such as the National Association for the Advancement of Colored People (NAACP), condemned Jim Crow policies enacted by the US government, and debated the merits of black nationalist groups like the UNIA, in addition to addressing local racial concerns in Cuba. Harlem was also invoked frequently in Afro-Cuban literature and artwork. In the 1929 poem "El camino de Harlem" (The Road to Harlem), for example, Nicolás Guillén condemned racial prejudice in Cuba and warned that the island was dangerously close to taking the "road" of legalized racial segregation, exemplified by the United States.[30]

If Harlem "cast [a] most captivating spell" for many Afro-Cubans, black scholars and activists in the United States likewise sought to cultivate stra-

tegic partnerships with race-conscious islanders.[31] In the decades following
the War of 1898, Booker T. Washington recruited dozens of Afro-Cuban
students to study at Tuskegee Institute as part of his campaign to spread
industrial education to the island.[32] Members of the NAACP also followed
the work of Afro-Cuban activists, with Schomburg publishing biographical
sketches of prominent Afro-Cuban leaders in the association's journal, *The
Crisis*.[33] Schomburg also corresponded privately with prominent Cubans of
color, including Guillén, the journalist Gustavo Urrutia, and the painter Pastor
Argudin.[34] Members of Harlem's burgeoning British West Indian community similarly developed important connections with Afro-Cubans.[35] In 1921
Marcus Garvey, the Jamaican-born president-general of the UNIA, traveled
to Cuba in a visit that received front-page coverage in Havana's *El Heraldo
de Cuba*.[36] Speaking in Havana—as well as the Cuban cities of Morón, Santiago, Nuevitas, Banes, and Camagüey—Garvey sought subscriptions for his
Black Star Line and urged black Cubans to become members of the UNIA.[37]
By 1926 Cuba had fifty-two UNIA divisions, more than any nation outside
of the United States, and the association continued to attract followers until
it was outlawed by the Cuban government in 1929.[38] While Cuban UNIA
divisions included British Caribbean migrant workers as well as Afro-Cubans,
it is significant that Garvey appointed Eduardo V. Morales, a bilingual Cuban
writer and labor union activist, as the island's UNIA commissioner.[39]

Translation simultaneously enabled and enriched the cultures of black
internationalism that linked Harlem and Havana. The practice of translation
was particularly important for Afro-Cuban thinkers who engaged in dia-
logues with Harlem's predominantly Anglophone black intelligentsia. Translation comprised not only the "simple and direct identification of equivalent
words and concepts in two languages" but also the act of explaining new
racial terminologies, conceptions of blackness, and geographically specific
histories of racial exclusion.[40] Ruiz Suárez engaged in translation as a twofold
process: he embraced translation as a linguistic exercise, publishing in both
English and Spanish, while also using translation as a sociocultural tool to
foster understanding between black communities in Latin America and the
United States. His writings illuminate the "constitutive multilingualism of
black internationalism" and expose the attendant challenges black writers
faced when narrating race across linguistic and national divides.[41]

Black Activism and the Problem of "Racial Personality" in Cuba and the United States

Divided into seventeen short thematic chapters, *The Color Question in the
Two Americas* surveyed the sociopolitical condition of Afro-Cubans and
African Americans in the volatile decades following emancipation. In the
book Ruiz Suárez concerned himself with the fate of black people as a racial

collective—writing of the "black American," the "Hispanic black man," and the "black people of the American countries"—instead of highlighting the achievements of prominent individuals. Central to his analysis was the idea of racial personality, an amorphous concept that combined pseudo-scientific ideologies of racial difference and emergent theories of human personality. Articulated in the nineteenth-century writings of Edward Wilmot Blyden and J. W. E. Bowen, racial personality supposedly described the unique attributes, outlook, and contributions of the world's racial groups.[42] While Blyden and Bowen invoked racial personality as a means to illuminate the distinctive gifts of the Negro race, Ruiz Suárez made the provocative claim that Afro-Cubans and African Americans did not possess a racial personality at all.

The "lack of a definite, affirmative racial personality in the Afro-Cuban as well as the Afro-American," Ruiz Suárez announced to readers, was "traceable to opposite causes."[43] To explain the absence of racial personality, *The Color Question in the Two Americas* employed a series of binaries, mobilizing the United States and Cuba as archetypes of segregationist and assimilationist racial regimes. In the aftermath of emancipation in the United States (1865) and in Cuba (1886), the two nations embraced contrasting approaches to managing racial heterogeneity. In Cuba, despite multiple forms of racial bias, the official rhetoric of "raceless nationality" allowed blacks and *mulatos* to live in "an atmosphere of apparent cordiality with the white race."[44] Duped by their white countrymen's insincere "hand of fellowship," Ruiz Suárez alleged, Cubans of color had "no aspirations other than those of their *white brothers*."[45] Cuba's assimilationist rhetoric, then, was doubly insidious: it was rarely realized in practice, and it stymied the development of racial solidarity among Afro-Cubans. Ruiz Suárez bemoaned the fact that the "self-seeking tolerance" of Cuban whites had "nullified and destroyed" any "racial personality" among blacks and *mulatos*, who composed 27 percent of the island's total population.[46]

If race relations in Cuba were defined by assimilationist policies and the myth of racial equality, then the regime of legalized racial segregation in the United States presented a strikingly different terrain. Yet the codified exclusions of Jim Crow too precluded African Americans from cultivating their own racial personality. "The black American has no personality, and indeed no existence at all, in relation to the life of the white man," Ruiz Suárez maintained. Not only were African Americans prevented from exercising the rights afforded to them as US citizens, but they were also debased and dehumanized by white racists. Convinced of their racial superiority, whites in the United States regarded the black man with "haughty disdain," viewing him "simply as a negro, an indefinite and indefinable thing, a beast at most."[47]

Nonetheless, in Ruiz Suárez's estimation, the "general disrespect of the whites" was "not without its positive advantages for the colored people."[48] Whereas Afro-Cubans were fractured along lines of class and skin color, African Americans managed their own businesses, churches, and educational

institutions in segregated neighborhoods. Pointing to these ventures, Ruiz
Suárez reasoned that Jim Crow had promoted heightened solidarity and racial
consciousness among African Americans, a claim also articulated by the Mar-
tinican intellectual Jane Nardal.[49] The dual injustices of overt discrimination
and legalized exclusion compelled African Americans to mobilize along racial
lines to ensure self-preservation. Not only did the "black people of the United
States know just where they stand," they were "stimulated and compelled by
the outspoken prejudice of the whites to develop a distinctive racial consciousness and pride." While the "pusillanimous and simple-minded" might prefer
Cuba's false embrace of racial equality, scoffed Ruiz Suárez, the "methods of
the Anglo-Saxon" would ultimately appeal to "strong and noble spirits, to
sincere and loyal men" of the black race.[50]

Despite his celebrations of racial consciousness, Ruiz Suárez advocated for
a process of selective cultural assimilation, writing that black people could
achieve social mobility by "observing the ways of the white man so as to
adapt some of them to his needs." Yet he also framed assimilation—even
when embraced pragmatically by black communities—as a deeply fraught
process. In particular he alerted black residents on both sides of the Florida
Straits to the embodied perils of absorption and asphyxiation. In *The Color
Question in the Two Americas*, narratives about absorption and asphyxiation
signified the ways in which whites, either by marginalizing or incorporating
peoples of African descent, could destroy black communities. Ruiz Suárez
referenced the act of absorption—the process in which one entity is incorpo-
rated completely into a larger entity or group—to describe totalizing efforts to
acculturate members of the black race. In Spanish America, he explained, the
guise of "simulated equality" stifled racial unity and also "permits the whites
to absorb and represent every cultural principle" of black men and women.
Black communities in the United States and in colonized Africa similarly were
engaged in a pitched struggle "against absorption by the overwhelming influence of the white race."[51]

The peril of asphyxiation—a condition in which one has been deprived of
oxygen, often resulting in death—loomed even more ominously in the text.
Asphyxiation, in Ruiz Suárez's writing, signaled the hazards of both psychic
and physical strangulation. When describing the Afro-Cuban society Club
Atenas as a potential model of intraracial fraternity—a place where the "fair
mulatto" could find fellowship with the "pure black man"—he stressed that
the organization could exist as a site of autonomous racial activism only if
whites did not decimate its ranks through absorption and asphyxiation.[52] In
the case of the United States, asphyxiation posed a distinctly mortal threat.
After reflecting upon African Americans' lack of a "racial personality," Ruiz
Suárez abruptly turned his attention to the hazards of interracial encounters in
the United States, proclaiming, "Whenever the two [races] come in contact the
black man is submerged and asphyxiated."[53] Yet the author failed to reconcile
his recurring warnings about the risks of absorption and asphyxiation with

his calls for assimilation. As a result the tension between what was sought (assimilation) and what was feared (absorption and asphyxiation) remained unresolved in the book.

The tropes of activity and passivity—movement and inaction—furnished an additional binary to depict black life in the United States and Cuba. Using deeply masculinist language, Ruiz Suárez valorized activity, a word that appeared over a dozen times in *The Color Question in the Two Americas*, and correlated action with racial progress and virile manhood.[54] In a passage pervaded with aquatic imagery, he contrasted the sea and a "motionless" lake to dramatize the danger of inactivity. The waters of the sea, like an active race, are "wholesome" because they are in "constant flux and reflux." "The black people, not alone of the United States, but of the whole civilized world, must act like the waves of the sea. They must constantly be in motion," he advised. Racial groups that failed to embrace activity—those that did not "constantly renovate their ideals, their customs, [and] their modes of action"—would be like "stagnant waters" filled with "inferior organisms." Any race that was not "constantly in motion" would be "useless as a factor in civilization."[55]

African Americans exemplified racial progress and virility for Ruiz Suárez, providing a counterpoint to the supposed docility of Afro-Cubans. Racial segregation and extralegal racial violence, though "rough and brutal and contemptuous," had propelled African Americans to act collectively on behalf of the race. Heaping praise on the black Harlemite, Ruiz Suárez proclaimed, "Living in an atmosphere of activity, he cannot but be industrious. His ideas are accompanied by action; he does not leave for tomorrow what he can do today, for he knows and appreciates the value of time and of things." By contrast, the author demeaned his fellow Afro-Cubans as "impotent spectator[s]," insinuating that his countrymen lacked power politically (and sexually).[56]

There were strict limits to Ruiz Suárez's call for activity, however. If it was "criminal to remain stationary when it is possible to go ahead," it was even more imprudent for black activists to challenge white dominance through armed resistance. The "excessive stimulation . . . of the racial consciousness of the colored American," he wrote, "is accompanied with the ever present danger of a sudden and violent reaction."[57] Ruiz Suárez's rejection of armed resistance as a protest tactic was linked directly to the brutal suppression of black activists in republican Cuba. Writing ten years after the state-sponsored massacre of thousands of Afro-Cubans in 1912, he sympathetically recounted the history of the Partido Independiente de Color (Independent Party of Color, PIC) and its "shortlived and unhappy revolution."[58] In a chapter titled "The Lesson of Revolution," Ruiz Suárez conceded that African Americans' plight was worse than that of black Cubans in 1912, and he further confessed that it was unreasonable to expect black Americans to contain their frustrations through "songs of mirth." Yet, citing the traumatic legacy of the PIC's demonstration in 1912, Ruiz Suárez made it clear that he rejected any efforts to win racial equality through armed struggle. Asserting that "patience, plodding, and peace" should guide African Americans' fight for racial justice, he warned that "revolution would be suicidal for the black people of the United States." Learning from the Cuban government's campaign of terror against black activists in 1912, African Americans should exhibit their fortitude in a manner that Cuban protestors could not—"by surviving."[59]

In his cautionary tale about the 1912 massacre, Ruiz Suárez drew upon the poetry of Jamaican writer Claude McKay. The inclusion of McKay's "If We Must Die," an unflinching ode to black self-defense written in response to the US race riots of 1919, struck a discordant note in a passage urging African Americans not to take up arms. It is easy to read Ruiz Suárez's invocation of "If We Must Die" as an example of the "misapprehensions and misreadings" Brent Hayes Edwards suggests are constitutive of translated exchanges in the diaspora.[60] However, I want to suggest that Ruiz Suárez employed McKay's searing verse to simultaneously acknowledge and redirect African American militancy. The Cuban author argued that McKay's acclaimed sonnet demonstrated that black people were not "beasts" who could thoughtlessly shed their blood, but rather were people who "must not die and need not die." "The black American," he reasoned, "cannot afford to risk on a throw of the dice the success he has achieved and the conquests which the future will open to him through his assimilative capacity." While extolling McKay's most celebrated poem as "virile and resonant," he ultimately urged readers to eschew militancy in favor of "peaceful evolution" "under the inspiration of competent leaders."[61]

Wading deeper into the debate over black protest strategies, Ruiz Suárez devoted an entire chapter of *The Color Question in the Two Americas* to the UNIA's African repatriation initiative. He roundly attacked the UNIA's call for voluntary emigration, characterizing the proposal as "misdirected" and ill conceived. Any attempt to create a sovereign black nation in West Africa would be "totally ineffective," he forecast, because Africans and their descendants in the Americas "would lack the very bond of moral identity on which such a union is predicated." If "millions of civilized black people went and hoisted . . . the flag of a new nation" on the continent, "their mission" would be "one of conquest and dominion over the native population" rather than a mutually beneficial project of racial liberation.[62]

Despite their shared racial categorization, black people reared in the Americas could never be "genuinely African." Ruiz Suárez called into question essentialist notions of black identity that privileged Africa as the "geographic fatherland," writing, "It is reasonably certain that no black man born and bred on this side of the Atlantic knows what it is to feel genuinely African, and it is doubtful whether any black alien has even a superficial sense of a common nationality with the African." The "line of ancestry" between African Americans and Africans had "long since disappeared, without leaving traces sufficient to re-establish a nexus of positive co-relation." Moreover, from a geopolitical standpoint, creating a new independent polity in West Africa would do little to subvert global antiblack racism. Given European colonial dominance over the African continent and African Americans' limited access to capital, Ruiz Suárez argued that the UNIA's proposed African state would have a precarious existence: it would be "backward" and "backless."[63]

Confronting US Racial Violence and Imperialism in the Era of the New Negro

For the majority of *The Color Question in the Two Americas*, Ruiz Suárez probed the origins and impact of racial discord. However, at the very beginning of the book and then in two brief chapters near the conclusion, he dissected exceptionalist narratives that celebrated the United States as a "symbol of democracy."[64] In his meditation on American democracy, he foregrounded racism and imperialism as constitutive features of the US political order. He also pondered whether the United States, which oppressed black citizens domestically while simultaneously engaging in imperialist projects overseas, could be classified as a democratic polity.

In contrast to his initial posture as "an apprentice for Americanization," Ruiz Suárez registered a stinging condemnation of US democratic pretensions. Whereas whites in the United States claimed to be culturally superior to other groups, their lack of "tolerance, mutual respect, [and] reciprocal consideration" hindered them from accomplishing their "full purpose in civilization." He elaborated: "In those countries where religion, education and other influences have softened the hearts of men, the sentiment of brotherhood tends to level the inequalities and barriers of race and give reality to that form of society which in Political Science is called Democracy. But the race which colonized and still forms the majority of the people of the United States, with its historical antecedents and its degrading record of bloodshed, cannot be classified, in the opinion of an impartial observer, as a democratic race."[65] Ruiz Suárez thus cast light on white Americans' long-standing involvement in colonialist projects—before and after 1898—to subvert self-congratulatory narratives of the United States as a beacon of democracy.

For Ruiz Suárez the violent racial landscape in the United States during the 1920s exposed the façade of representative democracy. The ritualized violence of lynching and US military interventions in the Caribbean and Latin America wholly belied the nation's official commitment to democratic principles. Rehearsing popular narratives of former US president Abraham Lincoln as the Great Emancipator, Ruiz Suárez asserted, "The people and the public powers of the United States have fallen far short of the ideal of Lincoln, not only in the various groups of the population, but especially as regards the attitude of the white man towards the black man." Noting the complicity of the executive and legislative branches of the US government in perpetuating the "Lynch Law," he condemned whites for denying African Americans "the most elemental claims of justice." He went on to ask how the US government could be trusted to respect the sovereignty and rights of people in foreign lands if its leaders had shown no interest in protecting the lives of their own black citizens: "A nation that deprives its own citizens of their rights is not likely to have much genuine respect for the rights of other nations."[66]

In light of Cuba's repeated experience with US military interventions beginning in 1898, it is not surprising that Ruiz Suárez denounced the United States for exalting self-determination in principle while engaging in imperialist ventures in practice.[67] Highlighting the yawning disjuncture between the principles and practices of the United States, he concluded that the government had "by no means lived up to their professed abhorrence of autocracy and aggressive imperialism in their international affairs."[68] Given that the United States had intervened militarily in Cuba, Panama, Nicaragua, Mexico, Haiti, and the Dominican Republic between 1898 and 1922—in addition to taking possession of Puerto Rico and the Virgin Islands—*The Color Question in the Two Americas* provided an urgent and necessary warning about the expansion of US military power and its potential consequences for black people throughout the Western Hemisphere.

The Color Question in the Two Americas garnered notable attention in the United States during the early 1920s before fading into relative obscurity. While it remains unclear if the book ever circulated in Cuba (or elsewhere in Latin America), Ruiz Suárez's monograph provided an early example of comparative studies of race in the Americas. Recent critics of comparative historical studies have questioned comparison as a methodology, rightly noting that "overtly political comparisons" ultimately reify national ideologies and "produce the very notions, subjects, and experiences of national difference that in turn attract further comparative study."[69] This is a valuable insight as scholars increasingly seek to trace the flow of ideas, objects, and individuals across national boundaries in the wake of history's transnational turn. However, for Ruiz Suárez comparative analysis did not simply provide a means to accentuate the different racial systems in Cuba and the United States, scripting one country as a racial democracy and the other as a racist abyss. Rather he sought to delegitimize both countries' dominant narratives about race, belonging, and democracy, and he insisted fervently that the racial regimes in Cuba and the United States both marginalized black citizens (albeit with different results). Writing in a moment of global upheaval concerning the "color question," Ruiz Suárez sought to build solidarity among black people across the Americas by using translation and comparative analysis as tools for racial mobilization. Situating the histories of black activism on both sides of the Florida Straits in the same analytical framework was a tactic for advancing black internationalism and a shared project of racial liberation.

Notes

1. Advertisement, "The Color Question in the Two Americas," *New York Age*, February 3, 1923, 8. I would like to thank the editors of this anthology and John D. French and Barbara Savage for their comments on previous drafts of this essay. I would also like to acknowledge Fannie Theresa Rushing, Alexander Sotelo Eastman, Bennie Niles IV, Chloe J. Jones, and the librarians at the University of South Florida for their assistance.

2. Bernardo Ruiz Suárez, *The Color Question in the Two Americas*, translated by John Crosby Gordon (New York: Hunt, 1922).

3. David Scott, "That Event, This Memory: Notes on the Anthropology of African Diasporas in the New World," *Diaspora: A Journal of Transnational Studies* 1, no. 3 (1991): 261–84; Michelle Wright, *Becoming Black: Creating Identity in the African Diaspora* (Durham, N.C.: Duke University Press, 2004), 1–26.

4. "Latest Books," *New York Times Book Review and Magazine*, July 2, 1922, 29; "The Color Question in the Two Americas," *Negro World*, July 29, 1922, 2; "The Color Question in the Two Americas," *New York Age*, December 23, 1922, 5; "What Others Say," *Southern Workman* 52, no. 5 (1923): 252.

5. The full text of the notes reads, "En verdadero afecto para el primer amigo que conocí en Nueva York, Sr. Arturo Shomburg [Schomburg]." See handwritten note dated June 1922 from Ruiz Suárez to Schomburg in *The Color Question in the Two Americas*, copy 2, Jean Blackwell Hutson Research and Reference Division, Schomburg Center for Research in Black Culture, New York. For a comprehensive account of Schomburg's contributions to black life in New York City, see Vanessa K. Valdés, *Diasporic Blackness: The Life and Times of Arturo Alfonso Schomburg* (Albany: State University of New York Press, 2017).

6. "Dr. Suárez to Represent Cuba at Third International Convention," *Negro World*, July 29, 1922; Bernardo Ruiz Suárez, "El problema de razas en Cuba," *Negro World*, September 2, 1922.

7. "Sección en Español," *New York Age*, November 18, 1922. In the second week the column's masthead was revised to omit the crucial phrase "de la Raza de Color" (of the Colored Race). "Sección en Español," *New York Age*, November 25, 1922.

8. "Prof. Suárez Speaks at 135th St. 'Y,'" *Negro World*, November 11, 1922; "Dr. Suárez Lectures at Mother Zion Church," *New York Age*, December 23, 1922; "Dr. Suárez to Lecture," *New York Age*, December 30, 1922.

9. "Hampton Incidents," *Southern Workman* 52, no. 4 (1923): 198; "El Dr. Bernardo Ruiz Suárez ganó nuestro Segundo Premio," *La Nueva Democracia 5*, no. 3 (1924): 28.

10. Established by Afro-Cuban cigar workers in 1900, the Sociedad La Unión Martí-Maceo was a mutual aid society based in Tampa's Ybor City neighborhood. Susan D. Greenbaum, *More Than Black: Afro-Cubans in Tampa* (Gainesville: University Press of Florida, 2002), 148–77. For Ruiz Suárez's published lecture on Antonio Maceo, see *Maceo: The Liberator of Cuba* (Tampa: Tampa Bulletin Publishing, 1924). The published lecture is available in the La Unión Martí-Maceo Collection, Series 6, Subseries shelf 1, Special Collections, University of South Florida Library, Tampa.

11. Jesse Hoffnung-Garskof, "The Migrations of Arturo Schomburg: On Being *Antillano*, Negro, and Puerto Rican in New York, 1891–1938," *Journal of American Ethnic History* 21, no.1 (2001): 28. On the migratory circuits that brought Afro-Caribbeans to Harlem, see Lara Putnam, "Provincializing Harlem: The 'Negro Metropolis' as Northern Frontier of a Connected Caribbean," *Modernism/Modernity* 20, no. 3 (2013): 469–84.

12. See, for example, Rosalie Schwartz, "Cuba's Roaring Twenties: Race Consciousness and the Column 'Ideales de una Raza,'" in *Between Race and Empire: African-Americans and Cubans before the Cuban Revolution*, edited by Lisa Brock and Digna Castañeda Fuertes (Philadelphia: Temple University Press, 1998), 105; Nancy Raquel Mirabal, "Scripting Race, Finding Place: African Americans, Afro-Cubans, and the Diasporic Imaginary in the United States," in *Neither Enemies nor Friends: Latinos, Blacks, Afro-Latinos*, edited by Anani Dzidzienyo and Suzanne Oboler (New York: Palgrave Macmillan, 2005), 198–99; Gerald Horne, *Race to Revolution: The U.S. and Cuba During Slavery and Jim Crow* (New York: Monthly Review Press, 2014), 191, 200, 212, 221.

13. See Frank Andre Guridy, *Forging Diaspora: Afro-Cubans and African Americans in a World of Empire and Jim Crow* (Chapel Hill: University of North Carolina Press, 2010); Antonio López, *Unbecoming Blackness: The Diaspora Cultures of Afro-Cuban America* (New York: New York University Press, 2012); Nancy Raquel Mirabal, *Suspect Freedoms: The Racial and Sexual Politics of Cubanidad in New York, 1823–1957* (New York: New York University Press, 2016).

14. Ruiz Suárez, *The Color Question in the Two Americas*, 57.

15. For example, Brent Hayes Edwards, *The Practice of Diaspora: Literature, Translation, and the Rise of Black Internationalism* (Cambridge, Mass.: Harvard University Press, 2003); Michelle Ann Stephens, *Black Empire: The Masculine Global Imaginary of Caribbean Intellectuals in the United States, 1914–1962* (Durham, N.C.: Duke University Press, 2005); Minkah Makalani, *In the Cause of Freedom: Radical Black Internationalism from Harlem to London, 1917–1939* (Chapel Hill: University of North Carolina Press, 2011); Lara Putnam, *Radical Moves: Caribbean Migrants and the Politics of Race in the Jazz Age* (Chapel Hill: University of North Carolina Press, 2013).

16. Michael O. West and William G. Martin, introduction to *From Toussaint to Tupac: The Black International Since the Age of Revolution*, edited by Michael O. West, William G. Martin, and Fanon Che Wilkins (Chapel Hill: University of North Carolina Press, 2009), 8–9.

17. I have not been able to identify Ruiz Suárez's precise date of birth. However, photographic portraits and the dates of his earliest published works suggest that he was born in the 1880s or 1890s. Aline Helg, *Our Rightful Share: The Afro-Cuban Struggle for Equality, 1886–1912* (Chapel Hill: University of North Carolina Press, 1995), 49–50, 145; David Sartorius, *Ever Faithful: Race, Loyalty, and the Ends of Empire in Spanish Cuba* (Durham, N.C.: Duke University Press, 2013), 134–42; Alexander Sotelo Eastman, "Binding Freedom: Cuba's Black Public Sphere, 1868–1912," Ph.D. dissertation, Washington University, 2016.

18. US War Department, Office Director, Census of Cuba, *Report on the Census of Cuba, 1899* (Washington, D.C.: Government Printing Office, 1900), 384.

19. US War Department, Office Director, Census of Cuba, *Report on the Census of Cuba, 1899*, 462. On the widespread discrimination that Afro-Cubans faced in their efforts to secure employment, see Alejandro de la Fuente, *A Nation for All: Race, Inequality, and Politics in Twentieth-Century Cuba* (Chapel Hill: University of North Carolina Press, 2001), 99–137.

20. The biographical information provided here is drawn from a profile of Ruiz Suárez published after he won second prize in an essay competition. "El Dr. Bernardo Ruiz Suárez ganó nuestro Segundo Premio," *La Nueva Democracia 5*, no. 3 (1924): 28.

21. Hoffnung-Garskof, "The Migrations of Arturo Schomburg," 27.

22. Ruiz Suárez, *The Color Question in the Two Americas*, 16.

23. Ruiz Suárez, *The Color Question in the Two Americas*, foreword, n.p.

24. Brock and Castañeda Fuertes, *Between Race and Empire*; Guridy, *Forging Diaspora*.

25. Guridy, *Forging Diaspora*, 2.

26. On the ties between Harlem and Havana during the New Negro Renaissance, see Monika Kaup, "'Our America' That Is Not One: Transnational Black Atlantic Disclosures in Nicolás Guillén and Langston Hughes," *Discourse 22*, no. 3 (2000): 87–113; John Patrick Leary, "Havana Reads the Harlem Renaissance: Langston Hughes, Nicolás Guillén, and the Dialectics of Transnational American Literature," *Comparative Literature Studies 47*, no. 2 (2010): 133–58; Ricardo René Laremont and Lisa Yun, "The Havana Afrocubano Movement and the Harlem Renaissance: The Role of the Intellectual in the Formation of Racial and National Identity," *Souls 1*, no. 2 (1999): 18–30; David Luis-Brown, "Cuban Negrismo, Mexican Indigenismo: Contesting Neocolonialism in the New Negro Movement," in *Escape from New York: The New Negro Renaissance beyond Harlem*, edited by Davarian L. Baldwin and Minkah Makalani (Minneapolis: University of Minnesota Press, 2013), 53–76.

27. Robin D. G. Kelley, foreword to *Escape from New York*, ix.

28. On the role of black-run periodicals in fostering black internationalism in the 1920s, see Lara Putnam, "'Nothing Matters but Color': Transnational Circuits, the Interwar Caribbean, and the Black International," in West et al., *From Toussaint to Tupac*, 118–22; Lara Putnam, "Circum-Atlantic Print Circuits and Internationalism from the Peripheries in the Interwar Era," in *Print Culture Histories beyond the Metropolis*, edited be James J. Connolly, Patrick Collier, Frank Felsenstein, Kenneth R. Hall, and Robert Hall (Toronto: University of Toronto Press, 2016), 215–39.

29. Ruiz Suárez, *The Color Question in the Two Americas*, foreword, n.p., 69.

30. Nicolás Guillén, "El camino de Harlem," *Diario de la Marina*, April 21, 1929.

31. Schwartz, "Cuba's Roaring Twenties," 109.

32. Guridy, *Forging Diaspora*, 17–60.

33. For example, Arthur A. Schomburg, "General Evaristo Estenoz," *The Crisis*, July 1912, 143–44.

34. Hoffnung-Garskof, "The Migrations of Arturo Schomburg," 38–39; Kevin Meehan, *People Get Ready: African American and Caribbean Cultural Exchange* (Jackson: University Press of Mississippi, 2009), 52–75.

35. On Afro-Caribbean immigrants in Harlem during the World War I era, see Irma Watkins-Owens, *Blood Relations: Caribbean Immigrants and the Harlem*

Community, 1900–1930 (Bloomington: Indiana University Press, 1996); Winston James, *Holding Aloft the Banner of Ethiopia: Caribbean Radicalism in Early Twentieth Century America* (New York: Verso, 1998).

36. On the UNIA in Cuba, see Tomás Fernandez Robaina, "Marcus Garvey in Cuba: Urrutia, Cubans, and Black Nationalism," in Brock and Castañeda Fuertes, *Between Race and Empire*, 120; Marc C. McLeod, "'Sin dejar de ser cubanos': Cuban Blacks and the Challenges of Garveyism in Cuba," *Caribbean Studies* 31, no. 1 (2003): 75–105; Guridy, "Making New Negroes in Cuba: Garveyism as a Transcultural Movement," in *Escape from New York*, 183–204; Frances Peace Sullivan, "'Forging Ahead' in Banes, Cuba: Garveyism in a United Fruit Company Town," *New West Indian Guide* 88 (2014): 231–61.

37. The Spanish-language section of the *Negro World* was first published on October 8, 1921. The newspaper launched a section in French on February 2, 1924. Robert A. Hill, ed. *The Marcus Garvey and Universal Negro Improvement Association Papers* (Berkeley: University of California Press, 2006), 10:176.

38. Rupert Lewis, *Marcus Garvey: Anti-Colonial Champion* (Trenton, N.J.: Africa World Press, 1988), 112; James, *Holding Aloft the Banner of Ethiopia*, 366.

39. Guridy, *Forging Diaspora*. On Morales's labor activism, see Carla Burnett, "'Unity Is Strength': Labor, Race, Garveyism, and the 1920 Panama Canal Strike," *Global South* 6, no. 2 (2012): 39–64.

40. Valdés, *Diasporic Blackness*, 23.

41. Vera M. Kutzinksi, *The Worlds of Langston Hughes: Modernism and Translation in the Americas* (Ithaca, N.Y.: Cornell University Press, 2012), 237.

42. Edward W. Blyden, *Black Spokesman: Selected Published Writings of Edward Wilmot Blyden* (New York: Humanities Press, 1971), 201; J. W. E. Bowen, "An Appeal to the King" (1895), in *The New Negro: Readings on Race, Representation, and African American Culture, 1892–1938*, edited by Henry Louis Gates Jr. and Gene Andrew Jarrett (Princeton, N.J.: Princeton University Press, 2007), 32.

43. Ruiz Suárez, *The Color Question in the Two Americas*, 24.

44. Ruiz Suárez, *The Color Question in the Two Americas*, 22. On the origins and impact of the discourse of raceless nationalism in Cuba, see Ada Ferrer, *Insurgent Cuba: Race, Nation, and Revolution, 1868–1898* (Chapel Hill: University of North Carolina Press, 1999), 7–10; de la Fuente, *A Nation for All*, 26–39; Devyn Spence Benson, *Antiracism in Cuba: The Unfinished Revolution* (Chapel Hill: University of North Carolina Press, 2016), 10–13. On theories of race and racial difference in republican Cuba, see Alejandra Bronfman, *Measures of Equality: Social Science, Citizenship, and Race in Cuba, 1902–1940* (Chapel Hill: University of North Carolina Press, 2004).

45. Ruiz Suárez, *The Color Question in the Two Americas*, 22 (emphasis in original).

46. Ruiz Suárez, *The Color Question in the Two Americas*, 22–23; Dirección General del Censo, *Census of the Republic of Cuba*, 1919 (Havana: Maza, Arroyo y Caso, 1922), 303.

47. Ruiz Suárez, *The Color Question in the Two Americas*, 26, 24.

48. Ruiz Suárez, *The Color Question in the Two Americas*, 20.

49. Jane Nardal, "Internationalisme noir," *La Dépêche africaine*, February 15, 1928.

50. Ruiz Suárez, *The Color Question in the Two Americas*, 20, 35, 24.

51. Ruiz Suárez, *The Color Question in the Two Americas*, 63, 26, 17.

52. Ruiz Suárez, *The Color Question in the Two Americas*, 88–89. On the role of Club Atenas in Afro-Cuban politics, see Guridy, *Forging Diaspora*, 57–59, 85–88, 135–36; Melina Pappademos, *Black Political Activism and the Cuban Republic* (Chapel Hill: University of North Carolina Press, 2011), 165–67, 190, 197–98.

53. Ruiz Suárez, *The Color Question in the Two Americas*, 26.

54. For examples of the ways in which Ruiz Suárez discusses "activity," see *The Color Question in the Two Americas*, 24, 32, 53, 70, and 71. There is one passage in the text in which he associates activity with women in the United States (104).

55. Ruiz Suárez, *The Color Question in the Two Americas*, 52–53.

56. Ruiz Suárez, *The Color Question in the Two Americas*, 32, 34.

57. Ruiz Suárez, *The Color Question in the Two Americas*, 52, 35.

58. Ruiz Suárez, *The Color Question in the Two Americas*, 43. On the massacre of 1912 in Cuba, see Helg, *Our Rightful Share*, 161–226; Aviva Chomsky, "The Aftermath of Repression: Race and Nation in Cuba after 1912," *Journal of Iberian and Latin American Research* 4, no. 2 (1998): 1–40. For a comparative perspective on the 1912 massacre, see Aline Helg, "Black Men, Racial Stereotyping, and Violence in the U.S. South and Cuba at the Turn of the Century," *Comparative Studies in Society and History* 42, no. 3 (2000): 576–604.

59. Ruiz Suárez, *The Color Question in the Two Americas*, 48, 36, 48.

60. Edwards, *The Practice of Diaspora*, 5.

61. Ruiz Suárez, *The Color Question in the Two Americas*, 36, 48, 32.

62. Ruiz Suárez, *The Color Question in the Two Americas*, 56, 57–58.

63. Ruiz Suárez, *The Color Question in the Two Americas*, 56–58.

64. Ruiz Suárez, *The Color Question in the Two Americas*, 59.

65. Ruiz Suárez, *The Color Question in the Two Americas*, 92, 19.

66. Ruiz Suárez, *The Color Question in the Two Americas*, 18–19, 93, 94–95.

67. On the impact of US military interventions on race relations in Cuba after 1898, see Helg, *Our Rightful Share*, esp. chapter 3.

68. Ruiz Suárez, *The Color Question in the Two Americas*, 95.

69. Micol Seigel, "Beyond Compare: Comparative Method after the Transnational Turn," *Radical History Review* 91, no. 1 (2005): 63.

"To Start Something to Help These People"

African American Women and the Occupation of Haiti, 1915–1934

Brandon R. Byrd

On July 28, 1915, US marines landed on the shores outside of Port-au-Prince. US policymakers justified the invasion by pointing to the death of Haitian president Vilbrun Guillaume Sam at the hands of a mob incensed by the recent executions of political prisoners. But this unrest was more a convenience than a concern for the invaders. With the outbreak of World War I portending a German encroachment in the Caribbean, Woodrow Wilson now identified the insurrection in Port-au-Prince as a perfect excuse to realize long-standing US military and economic aspirations. He promoted the invasion as a humanitarian intervention, as a reluctant and impermanent means of bringing order out of chaos in Haiti.[1]

Numerous works show that African Americans saw through yet another threadbare lie told in defense of white supremacy. In particular they demonstrate the extent to which organizations established or led by black men opposed the US occupation of Haiti.[2] Although welcome, this scholarship has obscured the complicated ways in which black women confronted the US occupation of Haiti. To be sure, black women throughout the United States became vocal antioccupation activists. The more prominent among them created a female domain in the antioccupation movement by promoting greater awareness of Haitian history, reporting on the excesses of the US marines stationed in Haiti, and making the restoration of Haitian independence the central goal of their organizations. At the same time, though, some of these same middle-class and elite black women spoke of the need to civilize Haiti. The schools and philanthropic groups they created in Haiti emerged from imperialist discourses and sometimes relied upon the ideological structures of the US occupation to fulfill their mission: the uplift of the Haitian masses from material and moral poverty to Victorian respectability.

In the end these competing impulses—to demand Haitian independence while attempting to correct Haiti's perceived deficiencies—reveal a remarkable moment in black intellectual history. The period between the two world wars was a time in which blacks throughout the African diaspora amplified their attacks on white supremacy. Haitian and African American intellectuals moved beyond the bourgeois black nationalism of the nineteenth century toward a black internationalism that featured critiques of capitalism, opposition to imperialism, and vindications of black working-class culture. This process was, however, complex and uneven. Older ideas about racial progress lingered even as new understandings of gender, race, and nationality emerged. Nothing better illustrates this truth or better exposes the liminal state of black thought in the interwar period than the antioccupation efforts sustained by black women in the United States. Even as a cohort of African Americans articulated the roots of black internationalist feminism, they struggled to transcend the faith in respectability, bourgeois culture, and Western imperialism that had pervaded the intellectual traditions and communities in which they were raised.

A Female Domain in the Antioccupation Movement

Ordinary black women were incensed by what they read in the exposés on US imperialism produced by African Americans who lived in or traveled to Haiti. Some sent letters to black newspapers decrying the unwelcome intervention in Haitian affairs. Others voiced their discontent to leaders of the NAACP, members of the US State Department, or other high-ranking US officials. These protestors included Ana La Condre.[3] In an April 1920 edition of the *New York Age*, the leading black paper, La Condre "noticed an account of some of the outrages that are being committed in Haiti by the American army of occupation especially against the children."[4] These outrages, chronicled by an AME missionary working in Port-au-Prince, included an instance wherein "nine little [Haitian] girls, 8 to 12 years old, died as a result of being raped by American sailors."[5] These reported abuses moved La Condre to immediate action. A day after encountering them, she wrote the African American writer James Weldon Johnson to ask, "What can we do to put a stop to these heinous crimes?" Could the NAACP, she continued, "do something to have these men removed, and put colored soldiers in their place?" If La Condre failed to reflect on the futility of exchanging one occupying force for another, she did identify the behavior of US marines in Haiti as a pressing concern for blacks throughout the African diaspora. Her letter concluded with a succinct directive: if the accusations in the *Age* could be verified—and accounts of sexual violence against Haitians by US marines often were—then "surely we must do something."[6]

Defiant stances against the US occupation of Haiti also emerged from black women who held leadership roles in national organizations. Besides serving as one of New York's finest secondary school teachers, Layle Lane was a key organizer of the Empire State Federation of Colored Women's Clubs. In 1927 she wrote a letter on behalf of her organization to Frank B. Kellogg, the US secretary of state. Like his predecessor Charles Evans Hughes, Kellogg was a member of the Republican Party, which had received substantial support from African Americans since the 1850s. He might have expected this support to continue, but Lane advised Kellogg that the allegiance of black Republicans was not to be taken for granted. In her letter Lane coolly noted, "The Negroes of the United States are keenly interested in the actions of the American government in Haiti, and hope those actions will be such that we can support them with our approval and votes."[7] Lane insinuated that newly enfranchised women in the Empire State Federation and African Americans in general wanted an end to the occupation and a greater role in future policymaking decisions pertaining to Haiti. Any political party seeking the black vote needed to act in accordance with those wishes.

Addie Hunton was one of several elite black women who rallied support for the antioccupation cause among prospective black voters. By the early 1930s Hunton was an imposing figure in black America. Her leadership positions included service as president of the International Council of Women of the Darker Races (ICWDR), the Empire State Federation of Colored Women's Clubs, and the Circle for Peace and Foreign Relations. She was also a principal organizer of the Fourth Pan-African Congress in 1927 and held offices in the National Association of Colored Women (NACW) and the NAACP. She articulated the transnational nature of her commitment to racial equality and black progress in her position as the vice president and national field organizer in the latter organization. Speaking before the NAACP annual conference in May 1932, she lamented, "In India, Africa, Haiti and other parts of the world we are constantly agasp at the flagrant violation of the rights of darker peoples." The troubles of colonized and occupied colored people were not, however, insurmountable. Hunton praised members of the NAACP for ensuring that their organization "stretched its hands abroad to help in Africa, India and the Islands of the Sea." With their continued vigilance, she implied, black people the world over would transcend white supremacy. Haiti would once again be free.[8]

By making this hope for Haitian liberation clear, Hunton and her peers contributed to an emergent black internationalism. During the years between the two world wars, black intellectuals across the world voiced a common vision of freedom from and opposition to the residual effects of slavery and the immediate consequences of white colonialism and imperialism. They forged collaborations and solidarities across national and linguistic boundaries, in the process creating a transnational black or colored identity.[9] Black people in the United States played a crucial role in crafting this Black International through their protests of the US occupation of Haiti. They drew parallels between the experiences of Haitians and African Americans while critiquing the capitalist culture that seemed to serve white supremacy everywhere from Haiti to Harlem. Some even argued that Haitian schools needed to privilege Kreyòl rather than French. In insisting that a Haitian people educated in their vernacular were "splendid material for the building of a nation," Johnson and

Margaret Murray Washington, ca.
1910–15 (Bain Collection, Library
of Congress Prints and Photographs
Division).

his ilk rejected the traditional assumption that black folk needed to rise to
the standards of civilization set by bourgeois whites before they could assume
any semblance of self-government.[10] For them, black political and cultural
autonomy required no proof. Their validity was self-evident.

In fact middle-class and elite black women were not satisfied with blending
into a crowd of black internationals. They wanted to stand out. By 1922 black
clubwomen's experiences in international organizations led by white women
or black men resolved them to the founding of a new organization. That
year Margaret Murray Washington encouraged the formation of the ICWDR.
According to one member from Charlotte, North Carolina, the objective
of Booker T. Washington's widow was to establish "some kind of definite
cooperation among the women of all the darker races for the purpose of
studying the conditions under which each subgroup lived and progressed, of
disseminating knowledge of their handicaps and of their achievements, and
of stimulating by closer fellowship and understanding to higher endeavor."[11]
In other words, as white women asked black women to advocate for their sex
and as black men implored black women to support their race, the members
of the ICWDR insisted that they would do both in tandem. "We," Washington
informed her peers, "have a mission for *our* women the world over."[12]

The attempt to create a coalition of nonwhite women bound by a shared
opposition to white supremacy would grow into a robust black internation-

alist feminism linking Third World liberation struggles to women's rights.[13] More immediately, though, the ICWDR played a key role in the antioccupation movement. Its inaugural meeting brought together representatives from North America, Africa, Asia, and the Caribbean. Members included Haitian women who joined their African American counterparts in ensuring that the ICWDR concerned itself with Haiti. Participants in ICWDR study groups held during the 1920s and 1930s read works by Jean Price-Mars, the famed Haitian ethnologist who worked tirelessly for the removal of US troops from her country. Select ICWDR members gave public lectures on Haiti throughout the United States, while others worked to introduce Haitian history into the curriculum of US schools. The ICWDR made the assessment of the "conditions of the women and children of Haiti" its priority during its inaugural year and launched several investigations into those conditions. Through these actions, the members of the ICWDR crafted a counternarrative to the anti-Haitian propaganda promoted by the US government and the white press, built a greater understanding between Haitian and African American women, and constructed a stronger foundation for future relations between Haiti and the United States.[14]

Liberating Haiti, Uplifting Haitians

New modes of black thought and political protest were ascendant. Yet they were not quite triumphant. Limitations arose from the fact that the most prominent black women involved in antioccupation organizing had been born and educated in the nineteenth century. These women assigned great importance to churches, missions, mutual aid societies, charities, colleges, and patriarchal households. They emphasized Protestantism, race pride, self-help, thrift, temperance, and chastity. In the parlance of their day, adhering to the bourgeois values shared by Anglo-Americans and participating in the institutions that cultivated them defined individuals and communities as respectable or not. And African Americans had to be respectable. As US race relations deteriorated in the late nineteenth and early twentieth centuries, Hunton and her peers surmised that African Americans could improve their political and social status by augmenting protest with programs of racial uplift. Consequently they assumed responsibility for reforming the morals and manners of black sharecroppers, domestics, and laborers throughout the United States.[15]

Even as black women critiqued the US occupation of Haiti, some demonstrated a lingering commitment to these traditions of racial uplift and civilizationist Pan-Africanism.[16] Nannie Helen Burroughs was one of them. On October 19, 1909, the future ICWDR executive board member became the first principal of the National Training School for Women and Girls (NTS) in Washington, D.C. The curriculum established by the Virginia native and her colleagues in the Woman's Convention of the National Baptist Convention had two principal components. First, the working-class women who attended the NTS gained employable skills by training in domestic science. Second, they practiced public speaking, read about current events, and took academic courses that stressed self-help, race consciousness, and Christian charity. Altogether the NTS experience was meant to uplift the very least among black women.[17]

Haitian women were conspicuous among those upon whom Burroughs sought to impart the lessons of the "Bible, bath, and broom." Between 1909 and 1920 two cousins, Alice Pierre Alexis and Christina François, attended the NTS. The two women received high marks in scholarship, deportment, laundering skills, and other categories upon which NTS teachers evaluated their charges.[18] Alexis, in particular, did much to distinguish herself. The granddaughter of the former Haitian president Pierre Nord Alexis earned certificates in subjects ranging from hairdressing and manicuring to millinery and domestic training during her time in Washington. At the 1916 NTS commencement ceremonies, Alexis was even awarded a cash prize for outstanding performance in the domestic science curriculum and tasked with explaining "why we teach practical housekeeping and home making."[19] This recognition was not unusual. Year after year Burroughs and her peers lauded Alexis for meeting their lofty expectations. The Haitian woman garnered acclaim for being "skilled with the needle and industrious in her general habits" and earned commendations for speaking French "fluently" while eschewing Kreyòl. Alexis was, in the estimation of Burroughs, "a very cultured little lady."[20]

A unique set of expectations came with this honorific. Burroughs wanted most African Americans at the NTS to focus on becoming respectable representatives of black people in the United States, but she anticipated that a Haitian lady such as Alexis would uplift her benighted compatriots. Completion of the certificate program in missionary training became the means of accomplishing this task. In reports given to annual meetings of the Woman's Convention, Burroughs praised Alexis as "desirable material out of which to make a cultured, consecrated, faithful missionary." She noted that Alexis did "beautiful needlework" and insisted that the participation of her Haitian pupil in a "literary and missionary training course" along with a class in millinery would "be great help to her in the Mission School." In fact Burroughs believed that Alexis might become one of the greatest promoters of the gospel of respectability abroad. Just a few years before the US occupation, she assured her fellow black Baptist women that Alexis would "imbibe the American spirit of energy and aggressiveness that will make her a power on the Haytian mission field."[21] The danger of US "aggressiveness" overseas was becoming quite clear at the outset of the twentieth century. Yet it was just as apparent that the idea of American exceptionalism that emboldened US military interventions in the Caribbean would continue to resonate with the NTS principal and her peers.

Indeed black Baptist leaders promoted the US occupation of Haiti as a unique opportunity even after it became clear that Haitians suffered under it. Haitian missions were a main topic of discussion at the 1917 meeting of the National Baptist Convention. The report provided to the main body of black Baptists by the Lott Carey Convention revealed that it hoped "to begin work in Haiti on a very large scale" because "that island at our very door needs the Gospel, and needs it now." The dissolution of Haitian sovereignty was presented as an incentive for rather than a deterrent to missionary work. "Because our own Government is exercising a kind of protectorate over Haiti," the Convention reported, "we believe they may be induced to co-operate with a united effort on our part to aid in a great industrial and religious awakening among the people of that island."[22] This report came in the same year that US officials in Haiti sentenced Charlemagne Péralte to the system of slave labor known as the corvée. As the future nationalist rebel planned his escape and an imminent attempt to drive the marines out of his country, some black Baptists still tried to accommodate the unwanted intervention in Haiti. Outspoken leaders even attempted to use it to their—and what they assumed to be Haitians'—best advantage. In their estimation a foreign occupation could be benevolent. It could impart civilization upon ordinary Haitians in dire need of it.

Similar ideas emerged among black clubwomen who bore witness to the occupation. In 1926 the Women's International League for Peace and Freedom (WILPF) organized a committee to travel to Haiti for a three-week investigation of the occupation. The eclectic group emerged from the various subsets of the interwar liberal reform movement. It consisted of a Quaker professor of economics from the University of Chicago, two representatives of the US branch of the WILPF, and one member of the Fellowship of Reconciliation, a leading peace organization. The committee also included two "representative colored women," Hunton and Charlotte Atwood. By the time of the investigation, Hunton was the ICWDR president and the NACW vice president. Atwood had become an English teacher at Dunbar High School (formerly the M Street High School) after graduating from Wellesley, the prestigious private women's liberal arts college in eastern Massachusetts. Both black elites made significant contributions to a report that presented the committee's findings about the military occupation and offered their final recommendation for the restoration of Haitian independence. But in doing so they revealed a lingering ambivalence about the role of foreigners in the "Black Republic."[23]

Atwood's contribution to *Occupied Haiti*, the report published a year after the committee returned to the United States, was a chapter on health and sanitation. In it Atwood detailed the myriad diseases that afflicted ordinary Haitians. Malaria, syphilis, yaws, tuberculosis, hookworm, ringworm, and dysentery, she reported, remained far too prevalent due to a number of factors, including malnourishment, lack of medical care, and the contamination of water, soil, and food with human excrement. The English teacher noted the efforts made by US physicians to combat these diseases. In particular she focused on the work of the Service d'Hygiène in Haiti. Initially established as a way of ensuring that the US marines did not suffer the same fate as past foreign armies who were ravaged by disease in their attempts to conquer Haiti, the Service d'Hygiène had begun to shift its attention toward the Haitian population. Atwood acknowledged that, by the time her committee made its investigations, US officials had established ten public health districts, eleven hospitals, sixteen rural dispensaries, and more than one hundred rural clinics.[24]

These efforts were perhaps more shrewd than magnanimous. US marines killed as many as eleven thousand Haitians while stationed in Haiti. Several testified that it was common for their drunken comrades to rape Haitian women. Many southerners in the occupying forces even boasted that they thought nothing of shooting "niggers" who would have been subject to the same treatment back home. In fact they ensured that the mistreatment of the Haitian masses continued even after the restoration of Haitian sovereignty. In the ensuing decades countless more Haitians would die from violence inflicted by the gendarmerie, the Haitian military force reorganized and reinforced during the occupation. Making preventative and curative health care more accessible to ordinary Haitians thus became an effective way for the US government to hide these realities of occupation from casual observers. In effect the outreach of the Service d'Hygiène was a thin veneer of altruism and so-called civilization placed over the brutal subjugation of a sovereign nation.[25]

Atwood was not entirely taken by this propaganda. But she was not unimpressed by it, either. In her chapter she remarked that the financial priorities of US occupation officials led to an "inability" on the part of the Service d'Hygiène to "provide a living wage" for the Haitian physicians it hoped to assimilate into its medical program. Moreover she decried the lack of funds devoted to public health in occupied Haiti. She pointed out that the paltry $8,000 afforded to the National Medical School each year was "inadequate to provide any equipment worthy [of] the name, or to pay full-time professors." Worse still was the dearth of medical supplies in the countryside. Atwood reminded her readers that "it would seem to be in the interest of economy and of sound building for the future" to "look first to the health of the people on whom the future of Haiti must of necessity depend." This was a key issue for Atwood. Despite her misgivings about the Service d'Hygiène, she remained optimistic that it was a benefit to Haitians. She applauded that organization for "overcoming the serious health conditions as rapidly as the nature of things and their budgetary allowance will permit." She even cited agreement from Haitians: "From what I could see and hear, there is more good feeling, and less hard feeling among Haitians toward the Service d'Hygiène, than toward any other branch of the American Occupation."[26] Put simply, some Haitians were appreciative beneficiaries of the gifts of US imperialism.

The sources that informed Atwood's opinion matter a great deal in hindsight even if she downplayed their influence at the time. The WILPF investigative committee claimed to have made "every effort to meet informants of different shades of opinion." It did not, however, attempt to speak with confidants from different walks of life. The "many types" of people encountered by the US investigators included "French priests, Protestant missionaries, technical employees of the Occupation, and Haitian teachers, professors and doctors."[27] Atwood thus had little ability to claim that there was "more good feeling, and less hard feeling among Haitians toward the Service d'Hygiène," at least not without modifying "Haitians" with "elite." Yet she did make that sweeping claim. For Atwood and her peers, educated foreigners and the Haitian professionals in whom they confided were more than qualified to speak on behalf of the black masses. This myopia shaped their attitudes toward the occupation. The Dunbar faculty member finished her report on health and sanitation by insisting, "Whatever of money or time or energy is spent in getting a common viewpoint for Americans and Haitians, and in working shoulder to shoulder to a common end, is not only not a useless expenditure, but the only way to safeguard what America has put into Haiti in the last ten years, and plans to continue putting in so long as the Occupation lasts. When Americans learn to work *with* and not merely *for* Haitians, and not until then will their efforts be truly fruitful."[28] This statement suggests that the occupation had worthwhile elements. It implies that Americans needed to retain a leading role in shaping Haitian public policy. Overall it reveals the tenuous relationship between Atwood's genuine support for Haitian independence and her competing commitment to a program of uplift that relied on cooperation among US imperialists, black reformers, and Haitian elites.

Similar ideological tensions appear within ICWDR president Addie Hunton's contribution to the WILPF investigative report. The chapter of *Occupied Haiti* she co-authored with the white peace activist Emily Greene Balch focused on race relations in Haiti. It began by noting that Haitians were "like the colored people of the United States in having an African inheritance with an intermixture . . . of white blood and Western civilization," while stressing that they were unlike their African American counterparts in one crucial regard: Haitians had been a free and independent people for more than a century. Consequently "there was almost nothing before the Occupation to make Haitians racially self-conscious or to create an 'inferiority complex' with its inconsistent but equally natural resultants—a morbid lack of self-confidence and self-assertiveness."[29] This changed with the occupation. According to the two authors, "friendly" relations between Haitian elites and US officials soured once the wives of those officials arrived in Haiti. At that point Haitians concluded that the white Americans, spooked by the specter of interracial sex, drew "the color line . . . much as it is in the southern part of the United States."[30] The investigative committee observed the same.

And yet, even as Hunton and Balch protested these realities and called for the restoration of Haitian independence, they held out hope that a US presence in Haiti need not be detrimental to Haitians. To their credit, both women

challenged US officials who claimed widespread support among Haitian peasants as well as the few Haitian elites who profited from their complicity
with the occupiers. They pointed out that it was "hard to believe that given
the deep-seated traditional belief that the return of the white men spelled a
return of slavery . . . the peasants do not feel uneasy under their new white
masters. They certainly do not appear . . . pleased as one passes them on the
road."[31] The latter sentence, however, again revealed the shortcomings of the
WILPF investigation despite its more useful insights. Like Atwood, Hunton
and Balch passed by but did not speak with ordinary Haitians during their
three weeks in Haiti. Instead the two reformers found it more appropriate to
speak for them.

Thus Hunton and her peers remained adamant that a transnational program of racial uplift was an excellent way to guarantee the vitality of an
independent Haiti. In particular an ICWDR officer, Harriett Gibbs Marshall,
graduate of Oberlin College and founder of the Washington Conservatory of
Music, took it upon herself to guarantee that Haitian elites and their African
American collaborators realized their "responsibility toward the great peasant
mass of the island." Arriving in Haiti in 1922, after her husband became the
clerk at the Port-au-Prince legation and the sole black member of the occupation regime, Marshall wasted little time in advertising the perceived social
underdevelopment of her new city. She wrote letters back home claiming that
only 5 percent of Haitians were "highly cultured," while the rest toiled in a
state "sad to behold." Popular misrepresentations of Haitian history encouraged this opinion. Marshall insisted that the devastation of the Haitian Revolution and the "inhuman treatment" that inspired the slave insurrection had
left Haitians "ill prepared for establishing and maintaining a republican government where head, heart, and hand would be joined to develop the country,
educate and protect its citizens." They had left the Haitian masses neglected.
Marshall characterized Haitian peasants as primitive, as a people "longing
for the gifts of this era, for breadth of vision, for modern methods, for opportunity . . . for justice and assistance." In her rendition Haitian peasants who
had maintained a vibrant counter-plantation system for generations became
an amorphous entity subordinate to Haitian elites who lacked "the technique
and resources for development of social work for the masses."[32]

For Marshall the dearth of social service organizations and the prevalence
of US marines were comparable obstacles to Haitian progress. She found
that the "majority [of Haitians] . . . cannot read or write." These high rates
of illiteracy, she surmised, indicated poor domestic training rather than systemic problems in the Haitian educational system that US officials ignored.
She alleged that Haitian "homes and family life are in a primitive condition,"
clear evidence that Haitians were in "need [of] all kinds of home and occu-
pational training." In turn the deficiencies of domestic life in Haiti suggested
to Marshall the failings of ordinary Haitian women. Instead of imbuing their
husbands and children with sound morals, they were "seen dressed in burlap

and flour bags or tattered rags hardly covering their bodies." That Marshall provided an explanation—the low wages received by Haitian laborers—for the inappropriate dress she claimed to have observed does little to alter the substance of her message. The black clubwoman speculated that the interrelated absences of education, domestic training, and Victorian womanhood placed strict limitations on Haitian prosperity. How, she seemed to ask the recipients of her letters, could Haiti maintain a prosperous independence even if it cast off the yoke of US oppression? The obvious response was that it could not. And so Marshall attempted, "with God's help, to start something to help these people" save their country and, in the process, vindicate black self-government.[33]

More specifically Marshall tried to establish "some form of social work organization . . . which would show the educated, cultured few [Haitians] how they can help the impoverished many." She visited the most prominent families and the most elite clubs in Port-au-Prince, selling them on the idea of building new social welfare projects in the Haitian capital. Not content with the promises of patronage that she received from former Haitian presidents, leading diplomats, and wealthy businessmen and their families, Marshall also appealed to black organizations, including the Empire State Federation of Colored Women's Clubs. It was her expectation that her peers would understand what was at stake in helping Haiti, a country that one of her correspondents, the director of the first school of social work for African Americans, called "an example of the Negro's inability to develop any sort of civilization" to some observers and "a concrete example of the possibilities of the Negro in self-government" to others.[34]

Marshall's efforts bore fruit in March 1926. That year the Oberlin graduate and her Haitian collaborators, a group of elite women that included a Haitian member of the ICWDR, formed L'Oeuvre des Femmes Haitiennes pour l'Organisation du Travail (Charity of Haitian Women for the Organizing of Labor). Branches throughout Haiti promoted "native industry" and assisted Haitians "without means," especially youth who could not afford a "practical education." In addition Marshall, who became the vice president of the social service organization, advanced a US auxiliary that she hoped would not only provide financial support for the Haitian branches but also establish a model for improved relations between US citizens and Haitians.[35] Despite the assertions of some historians, such efforts were far from "strictly charitable." As US politicians attempted to disrupt solidarities among African Americans and Haitians, Marshall insisted that the plight of occupied Haiti was a matter "in which every colored American is interested."[36] Her reform initiatives were a reflection of this Pan-African spirit. They confirmed the attitudes of Haitian journalists who insisted that "the Black Party in the United States is still the only organization which naturally, sincerely and automatically sympathize with the republic of Haiti" and "understand[s] the true needs of the Haitian Negroes."[37]

There is little doubt that Marshall thought herself well aware of the needs of the "Haitian Negroes." Months after its founding, L'Ouevre opened the Jean Joseph Industrial School in Port-au-Prince. It was a national institution with a broad mission to "develop Native Industries and afford a practical education for the [Haitian] Masses." To that end it featured programs of business, physical culture, English-language learning, hygiene, and social service while emphasizing a department of native arts that instructed "unlettered" pupils of both sexes in the "production and sale of active products and the fabrication of native materials into paper." At the same time, though, the Jean Joseph was a female-centered organization. Marshall assigned great importance to the education of Haitian girls by female instructors at the industrial school because she thought there was no historical record of "outstanding achievements" by Haitian women.[38] This was, of course, a hindrance to the progress of Haiti. One of her Haitian colleagues explained why, stressing, "It is important to initiate young girls to the basic principles of housekeeping that are the foundation of the good and healthy family life. They will learn to properly do the work that is becoming of women, suggesting to them the noble ambition of becoming a 'mama' one day. They would learn how to wash, iron, and cook without thinking. To this last point, we will never know enough how much influence one 'good broth' can have on husbands."[39] The Jean Joseph was, in other words, the manifestation of the belief that working-class black women had a special role in their communities. By achieving respectability—as housewives and homemakers, educators and mothers—they would deflect racist accusations of immorality and ensure that their compatriots would have bourgeois moral values along with technical skills.[40]

From the perspective of Marshall and the officers of L'Ouevre, the effort to create an export-oriented, self-sufficient Haiti was futile unless accompanied by an attempt to mold respectable Haitian women. Accordingly they assumed that their initiatives deserved the full support of all those who sympathized with Haiti. Pamphlets for the Jean Joseph produced under the watch of Marshall, the head of its executive committee, insisted that Haitians had responded to "the call of the oppressed [and] to the call of liberty" by helping the Continental Army lay siege to British forces in Savannah during the American Revolution. This aid had gone unrecognized, but US citizens now had the chance to rectify that wrong. Annual donations ranging from $1 to $100 would repay Haiti for her contributions to US independence, augment its "meager national resources," and aid Haitian peasants hoping to earn an "honest livelihood."[41] This last expectation was of special importance. As other black activists chastised Calvin Coolidge for maintaining the occupation, Marshall implored the Republican US president to recognize the good that his black compatriots could still accomplish in Haiti. She insisted that African Americans had found "the Haitian of thought and vision ready to cooperate enthusiastically in any work for the development of their country."[42] So they could not abandon the work of uplift now.

Just as Burroughs, Emily Williams, Atwood, and Hunton articulated a vision of reform in occupied Haiti, Marshall too had a clear interest in empowering Haitian women and uplifting the Haitian masses. But, like her peers, Marshall also assumed a tenuous position between complete opposition to the occupation and unintended complicity with US imperialism. In the summer of 1924 she wrote to US officials, hoping to gain permission to ship second-hand clothing from the United States to Haiti without its being subject to existing duties. She received mixed responses to her initial inquiry. In May 1924 Marshall heard from the office of the US secretary of state that the US Navy could provide free transport for "barrels of clothing, to be made over for poor children in Haiti."[43] Two months later, though, John H. Russell delivered less welcome news to Marshall. The US high commissioner in Haiti lamented that he was "in entire sympathy with the charitable object of your work" but had been told by US customs officials that there was no way to "provide for the free entry of clothing for charitable purposes."[44] There is little reason to question Russell's genuineness. Offering US largesse and extending a broader civilizing mission to Haitians cohered with the entrenched worldview of the white marine officer who believed that the average Haitian was "more or less an animal," possessing "the mentality of a child" and bordering "on a state of savagery."[45]

To Save Bleeding Haiti

In 1929, after returning to the United States, Marshall and her husband established the Save Haiti League. Its goal was simple: to restore Haitian independence. Advertisements for the antioccupation organization implored US citizens to live up to their "ideals of justice and liberty," to "protest," and to avoid assuming the "role of imperialistic overlord" in the Caribbean. League petitions appearing in the black press helped would-be activists take this preferred stance. They asked individuals to place their signature and address below the following statement: "I hereby petition President Hoover to withdraw the military occupation from Haiti." Many did. The Harlem offices of the Save Haiti League received petitions from small towns and cities in Virginia, Missouri, and everywhere in between. Indeed the Marshalls rallied their most prominent peers to their cause. The membership of the Save Haiti League included Mary McLeod Bethune, the *Baltimore Afro-American* editor Carl Murphy, the *Pittsburgh Courier* editor Robert L. Vann, the *New York Amsterdam News* editor William M. Kelley, the historian Rayford Logan, and the businesswoman Maggie Lena Walker. The organization was, in effect, a who's who of interwar black America.[46]

Countless African Americans of the era were taken by such impassioned pleas for racial justice. Many scholars of the US occupation of Haiti have been too. Brenda Gayle Plummer has insisted that the public declarations of the Save Haiti League prove that "increasing numbers of blacks abandoned the notion of participation in the [occupation] regime as they came to see it as undemocratic, racist, and unproductive." From her point of view, the heightened opposition of African Americans to the occupation was a reflection of their shifting attitudes about political protest in the United States. African Americans, Plummer continues, "foreswore the belief that Haitians could profit from accommodationism, as they likewise rejected this formula for themselves." Put simply, "militancy among blacks in the 1920s underlined the Afro-American response to the Haitian question."[47]

Upon closer inspection, the actions and words of middle-class and elite black women belie Plummer's assertions and similar arguments offered by other scholars. The "evaluations" of Haitians by leading African Americans did not change entirely with the "decline of the accommodationist outlook, the greater prominence of civil rights organizations, and resurgent black nationalism" after World War I.[48] Some African Americans still regarded Haitian peasants as a people in dire need of the type of racial uplift programs that emerged in the late nineteenth century. Some continued to insist that religious ideologies and social welfare organizations imported and initiated by foreigners would ensure that a liberated Haiti was a "better" Haiti. In general, then, a cohort of leading black women in the United States did not complete the transition from "racial uplift ideology" to an internationalism that recognized fully the "shared history of oppression against European and American imperialism."[49] They persisted in the assumption that they had transcended their own oppression to an extent that allowed them or even required them to redeem black women of different nationalities and social status.

There is no doubt that college-educated and middle-aged black women did oppose the US occupation of Haiti. But it is a mistake to assign our hopes to the women of an earlier era, to contend that their reaction to the occupation reflected an unambiguous "political maturation."[50] It was not always clear from whom or what the officers of the ICWDR or the Women's Convention of the National Baptist Convention or the Jean Joseph Industrial School thought Haiti needed saving. Was it the imperialism and capitalism that reinforced white supremacy? Was it the failings of black leaders who had not provided appropriate solutions to the problems facing their communities? Or was it both? For black women raised in a period when white supremacists used innumerable legal and extralegal means to reconfigure the racial domination weakened by the abolition of US slavery, the answers were not so simple. Still invested in an older strategy of contesting Jim Crow—emphasizing respectability and prioritizing Western theories of civilization, promoting elitist visions of Pan-African organizing, and spreading the gospel of racial uplift— hey could not fully form a black feminist internationalism that would address the plight of colonized and oppressed black women in a more egalitarian way. That is not an indictment of those women who sought solutions to a transnational "race problem," who hoped to deliver blacks in the United States and

Haiti from racism and occupation. Instead it is an acknowledgment of their key role in a moment of transition in black intellectual history. In considering ways to not only improve but also free Haiti, Marshall, Hunton, Burroughs, Williams, and their colleagues laid the groundwork for a subsequent generation of middle-class and elite black women who would construct an activist program more inclusive of working-class Haitians and less shackled to the social conservatism that privileged the hegemonic values and national chauvinism of bourgeois US Americans.

Notes

1. The authoritative English-language treatment of the occupation remains Hans Schmidt, *The United States Occupation of Haiti, 1915–1934* (New Brunswick, N.J.: Rutgers University Press, 1971).

2. James Weldon Johnson, "The Truth about Haiti: An N.A.A.C.P. Investigation," *Crisis* 20, no. 5 (1920): 224. On African American protest of the US occupation of Haiti, see Brenda Gayle Plummer, "The Afro-American Response to the Occupation of Haiti," *Phylon* 43, no. 2 (2nd qtr., 1982): 125–43; Leon D. Pamphile, "The NAACP and the American Occupation of Haiti," *Phylon* 47, no. 1 (1st qtr., 1986): 91–100.

3. It is difficult to verify the race and ethnicity of La Condre, but several factors suggest that she was of African descent. She was a member of the NAACP and subscribed to *New York Age*. Moreover contemporaries from the West Indies sharing her last name appear in naturalization petitions and other city records. I have searched the census for an Ana La Condre (or Anne LeCondre, as she is addressed in a return letter from the NAACP) but have not found her. A boarder in Manhattan named George Lacondre does appear in the 1940 New York census. It registers his birthplace as the Dutch West Indies and lists his race as black.

4. Ana L. La Condre to the secretary of the NAACP, April 18, 1920, Records of the National Association for the Advancement of Colored People, Administrative Files, Manuscript Division, Library of Congress (hereafter cited as NAACP Papers).

5. "Charge Americans Commit Grave Offenses in Haiti," *New York Age,* April 17, 1920.

6. La Condre to the secretary of the NAACP.

7. Layle Lane to the secretary of state, December 17, 1927, Decimal File 838.00/2424.

8. Addie Hunton, speech at annual conference of the NAACP, May 1932, the NAACP Papers.

9. Key works on black internationalism include Penny von Eschen, *Race against Empire: Black Americans and Anticolonialism, 1937–1957* (Ithaca, N.Y.: Cornell University Press, 1997); Brent Hayes Edwards, *The Practice of Diaspora: Literature, Translation, and the Rise of Black Internationalism* (Cambridge, Mass.: Harvard University Press, 2003); Michael O. West, William G. Martin, and Fanon Che Wilkins, eds., *From Toussaint to Tupac: The Black International since the Age*

of Revolution (Chapel Hill: University of North Carolina Press, 2009); Minkah Makalani, *In the Cause of Freedom: Radical Black Internationalism from Harlem to London, 1917–1939* (Chapel Hill: University of North Carolina Press, 2011).

10. James Weldon Johnson, "Self-Determining Haiti," *The Nation*, September 25, 1920, 345–57.

11. Mary Jackson McCrorey to Margaret Murray Washington, May 16, 1924, Mary Church Terrell Papers, Moorland-Spingarn Research Center, Howard University.

12. Margaret Murray Washington to Mary Church Terrell, April 28, 1924, Mary Church Terrell Papers, Library of Congress (emphasis added).

13. Notable works on female black internationals include Cheryl Higashida, *Black Internationalist Feminism: Women Writers of the Black Left, 1945–1995* (Urbana: University of Illinois Press, 2012); Grace Louise Sanders, "La Voix des Femmes: Haitian Women's Rights, National Politics, and Black Activism in Port-au-Prince and Montreal, 1934–1986," Ph.D. dissertation, University of Michigan, 2013; Keisha N. Blain, *Set the World on Fire: Black Nationalist Women and the Global Struggle for Freedom* (Philadelphia: University of Pennsylvania Press, 2018).

14. On the collaboration between elite black women in Haiti and in the United States in the ICWDR, see Sanders, "La Voix des Femmes," 80–94.

15. The best treatments of the politics of respectability and racial uplift remain Evelyn Brooks Higginbotham, *Righteous Discontent: The Women's Movement in the Black Baptist Church, 1880–1920* (Cambridge, Mass.: Harvard University Press, 1993); Kevin K. Gaines, *Uplifting the Race: Black Leadership, Politics, and Culture in the Twentieth Century* (Chapel Hill: University of North Carolina Press, 1996).

16. This longer preoccupation with reforming Haiti is the subject of my article "The Transnational Work of Moral Elevation: African American Women and the Reformation of Haiti, 1874–1934," *Palimpsest: A Journal on Women, Gender, and the Black International 5*, no. 2 (2016): 128–50.

17. The extensive scholarship on Burroughs and the NTS includes Evelyn Brooks Higginbotham, "Religion, Politics, and Gender: The Leadership of Nannie Helen Burroughs," in *This Far by Faith: Readings in African-American Women's Religious Biography*, edited by Judith Weisenfeld and Richard Newman (New York: Routledge, 1996), 140–57.

18. Student Records, Boxes 147 and 165, Nannie Helen Burroughs Papers, Manuscript Division, Library of Congress (hereafter cited as Burroughs Papers).

19. "National Training School Closing a Brilliant Affair," *Washington Bee*, June 10, 1916; "The Closing Week," *Washington Bee,* June 15, 1912; Graduate Certificates, Burroughs Papers.

20. Journal of the 10th Annual Session of the Woman's Convention, September 14–19, 1910, Microfilm Reel 14, Annuals/Journals of Black Baptist (National) National Conventions in America, Southern Baptist Historical Library and Archives, Nashville, Tenn. (hereafter cited as SBHLA).

21. Nannie Helen Burroughs, "Our Foreign Students," Journal of the 11th Annual Session of the Woman's Convention, September 1911, SBHLA.

22. Journal of the 36th Session of the National Baptist Convention, September 1917, SBHLA.

23. Emily Greene Balch, ed., *Occupied Haiti* (New York: Writers Publishing Company, 1927).

24. Charlotte Atwood, "Chapter VII: Health and Sanitation," in Balch, *Occupied Haiti*, 86–92; Matthew Davidson, "Public Health under United States Occupation," *Haiti: An Island Luminous,* accessed March 17, 2015, http://islandluminous.fiu.edu/part08-slide08.html.

25. The best treatment of the paternalistic and racist violence inflicted on Haitians during the occupation appears in Mary A. Renda, *Taking Haiti: Military Occupation and the Culture of U.S. Imperialism, 1915–1940* (Chapel Hill: University of North Carolina Press, 2001).

26. Atwood, "Health and Sanitation," 89, 90–91.

27. Balch, *Occupied Haiti*, v.

28. Atwood, "Health and Sanitation," 92.

29. Addie Hunton and Emily G. Balch, "Race Relations," in Balch, *Occupied Haiti*, 113–14.

30. Hunton and Balch, "Race Relations," 115.

31. Hunton and Balch, "Race Relations," 118.

32. Letter from Harriett Gibbs Marshall to Mrs. John M. Glenn, August 4, 1924, Washington Conservatory of Music Records, Box 112–2, Moorland-Spingarn Research Center, Manuscript Division, Howard University (hereafter cited as Washington Conservatory of Music Records).

33. Letter from Harriett Gibbs Marshall to Mrs. John M. Glenn, August 4, 1924, Washington Conservatory of Music Records.

34. Letter from Forrester B. Washington to Harriett Gibbs Marshall, January 30, 1928, Washington Conservatory of Music Records.

35. *L'Oeuvre de Femmes Haitien pour L'Organisation du Travail*, pamphlet, Washington Conservatory of Music Records.

36. Plummer, "The Afro-American Response to the Occupation of Haiti," 137; letter from Harriett Gibbs Marshall to Calvin Coolidge, September 12, 1924, Washington Conservatory of Music Records.

37. "Another Error Accredited to the United States by Design," *Nouvelliste*, July 7, 1924, Washington Conservatory of Music Records.

38. Harriett Gibbs Marshall Marshall, "Women of Haiti," unpublished and undated, Washington Conservatory of Music Records.

39. Letter from Rosina Jean Joseph to Mrs. John M. Glenn, quoted in Sanders, "La Voix des Femmes," 93.

40. On the discourses surrounding black home life during that time, see Michele Mitchell, *Righteous Propagation: African Americans and the Politics of Racial Destiny after Reconstruction* (Chapel Hill: University of North Carolina Press, 2004), 141–73.

41. Jean Joseph Industrial School, pamphlet, Washington Conservatory of Music Records. The pamphlet's statement that "eight hundred brave Haitians gave their lives for American independence at Savannah" is imprecise. Approximately 750 free men of color from Saint Domingue did volunteer to fight alongside Patriot forces at Savannah. At that point, however, they fought as French colonial subjects, not as citizens of an independent Haiti.

42. Letter from Marshall to Coolidge.

43. Edwin Clockson, on behalf of the secretary of state, to Harriet Gibbs Marshall, May 19, 1924, Washington Conservatory of Music Records.

44. Letter from John H. Russell to Harriett Gibbs Marshall, July 15, 1924, Washington Conservatory of Music Records.

45. Schmidt, *The United States Occupation of Haiti*, 125.

46. Petitions, Save Haiti League Business Records—Publicity and National Committee List, and Save Haiti League Business Records—Membership, Washington Conservatory of Music Records.

47. Plummer, "The Afro-American Response to the Occupation of Haiti," 142.

48. Plummer, "The Afro-American Response to the Occupation of Haiti," 125.

49. Lisa G. Materson, "African American Women's Global Journeys and the Construction of Cross-Ethnic Racial Identity," *Women's Studies International Forum* 32 (2009): 39.

50. Plummer, "The Afro-American Response to the Occupation of Haiti," 143.

Part II

✦

Religion and Spirituality

Introduction

Judith Weisenfeld

It is a truism that the black church has been a vital force in African American history, with individual churches and denominations serving as arenas for collective political action, fostering leadership, and supporting education and economic development. Commonplace accounts of African American history underscore the role that black religious collectives, primarily but not exclusively Protestant, have played in making space in slavery and freedom to affirm black humanity, cultivate creativity, nurture families, and enable spiritual expression. Yet religious thought often becomes marginalized in scholarly accounts of black intellectual history, receiving attention primarily in the narrowed context of discussion of black religious leaders as political actors. Nevertheless scholars of African American religious history have produced a body of work that attends to the intersections of religious and political discourses in civil rights activism and the forging of black collective identity through the production of sacred narratives of peoplehood.[1]

A long-standing critique by some African American intellectuals that religion was a diversion from what they saw as the more important work of political engagement supported arguments that religion and reason stand in opposition to one another. The fact that black congregations have been largely female undoubtedly contributes to the failure to engage religious thought and culture as of consequence in black intellectual history.[2] Frequently barred from ordination and formal leadership, black women made contributions to black religious life often in arenas and in cultural forms, such as music, prayer, healing, and service, not legible in conventional ways as intellectual work. In short, the sorts of things that take place in religious spaces—embodied religious expressions, cultural creativity in music and spoken word, and striving to connect to the divine—often do not appear useful for narratives of progress, modernity, political enfranchisement, and intellectual flourishing. In such a view the stuff of religious life may be, at best, spiritually sustaining but not intellectually productive and, at worst, anti-intellectual and limiting.

These three essays explore the intersection of black religions and intellectual history and challenge the relegation of religion to the margins of black intellectual life; they do so by extending into arenas beyond black church institutions. Taken together they raise questions about how we understand the nature of religious knowledge, challenge definitions of the religious and the secular, trouble the distinctions between these categories, and highlight new sources for pursing questions about religion and black intellectual history. While each essay extends in temporal and analytic directions specific to their topics, they cross paths in the early twentieth-century New Negro and Harlem Renaissance moment as a critical juncture in black thought, culture, and religion.

David Weinfeld's essay on Alain Locke explores the influence of engagement with the Baha'i faith on the development of the philosopher's perspective on race and his eventual embrace of secularism. Locke helped to frame the aesthetic and political contours of the New Negro movement through his editorial work on the 1925 "Harlem: Mecca of the New Negro" issue of *Survey Graphic* and the related anthology, *The New Negro*, both of which contained contributions attending to religion in black life. Weinfeld's important reminder that secularism should not be characterized solely as the absence of religion directs him to examine the moral and philosophical concerns that animated Locke's evolving position on religion and the New Negro. The Baha'i principle of "unity in diversity" contributed to Locke's deep commitment to highlighting African Americans' unique and profound cultural contributions, while it also supported his insistence on the universal principles these cultural productions offered. In Baha'i he found a religion more open to religious and racial diversity than he believed Christianity to be, and he rejected the latter as otherworldly and limited in its supernaturalism. While Locke converted to Baha'i, participated in the movement in the United States, and explored the tradition's history in travel and in writing, he eventually distanced himself from it, seeking what he felt would be more materially productive ideas and actions than a faith in unity could provide. Weinfeld's portrait of Locke reveals a secularism committed to cultural pluralism that is not evacuated of religious influence but that grew out of rigorous intellectual engagement with a variety of sources, including Baha'i. Weinfeld demonstrates, then, that it is impossible to understand the contours of Locke's secularism without attending to his history with the Baha'i tradition and, in doing so, directs us to examine in greater complexity the relationship between the religious and the secular among black intellectuals in the period.[3]

In his essay on African American secularism in the New Negro Renaissance of the 1920s, Christopher Cameron turns our attention to the black writers who, he argues, opened up space for the emergence of black freethought, an umbrella term he uses for atheists, agnostics, and secular humanists. Whereas, in Weinfeld's account, Locke's participation in the Baha'i faith assisted him in arriving at his own brand of secular cultural pluralism, Cameron sees a much more contentious engagement of religion, in the form of Christianity, in the work of the poet and playwright Langston Hughes and the novelist Nella Larsen.[4] Cameron highlights the conflict between Hughes's desire to believe in God and his skepticism of supernaturalism, a struggle made manifest in a number of poems Hughes wrote in the 1920s. Compounding this skepticism were Hughes's profound questions about how religion could account for or address racial violence and his abhorrence of manipulative preachers who prey financially on congregants. Ultimately Cameron's work shows that Hughes's embrace of freethinking secularism—putting his faith in black people rather than Jesus—was critical of Christianity but not entirely disentangled from it, as Hughes's use of religious themes and language in his poetry demonstrates.

In examining Larsen's 1928 novel, *Quicksand*, Cameron highlights her critique of black churches for emphasizing respectability and constraining black women's sexuality and independence. Larsen uses her main character, Helga, to explore the tension between fervent desire for faith and community and the disappointment of finding no satisfying answers within Christianity, much as Hughes wrote of his own struggles. Cameron argues that Larsen's rejection of black church religion as appealing to the weak and powerless characterized black freethinking more broadly. In Cameron's account, Larsen's freethought is less entangled with religion than Hughes's or Locke's, and he suggests that her rejection of Christian respectability and gendered oppression marks a critical starting point for the emergence of black freethinking radical politics.

Through an exploration of testimony, prophetic witness, and "grandmother wits," LeRhonda Manigault-Bryant provides a rich theoretical framework for interpreting black women as producers of religious knowledge. In directing our attention to black women's varied ways of knowing that derive from keen apprehension of perspective, lived experience, faith in things greater than oneself, and ancestral traditions, Manigault-Bryant challenges conventional understandings of the sources and substance of black intellectual history. Highlighting grand-maternal knowledge put forth by her own grandmothers as well as black cultural and intellectual grandmothers like Zora Neale Hurston, she underscores black women's work as moral agents and the intellectual fruits of practical wisdom derived from the complex wrestling with joy, pain, grief, human brokenness, and spiritual healing. By privileging black women's intergenerational moral wisdom, Manigault-Bryant's work reveals a different sort of critical engagement of the intellectual possibilities of religion than we see among the historical actors in Cameron's and Weinfeld's work. The grandmothers, daughters, and granddaughters we meet in this essay embrace and model a range of attitudes toward formal religious institutions and recognize and draw on a broad range of diasporic ancestral experiences. Manigault-Bryant's work explores the privileging of the solitary intellectual or the singular genius and emphasizes the significance of collective production of knowledge transmitted across generations. Her essay not only interrogates themes in the intellectual history of black women's prophetic witness; it models how black intellectuals can join in the collective project on knowledge production with their own work.

These rich essays open new directions for the study of religion and black intellectual history by attending carefully to religious influences and spiritual dimensions of cultural productions and dispositions we might easily take to be evacuated of religion. These scholars reveal the complexity of both black intellectual critiques of religion and the entanglements of religion and the secular in early twentieth-century black intellectual life. The sources and figures they examine point scholars to the variety of archives we must engage in order to expand our vision of the contributions of religion to black intellectual history, a charge relevant not only during the New Negro era but to other periods of African American history.

Notes

1. See, for example, Laurie Maffly-Kipp, *Setting Down the Sacred Past: African American Race Histories* (Cambridge, Mass.: Harvard University Press, 2010); Eddie S. Glaude, *Exodus! Religion, Race, and Nation in Early Nineteenth-Century Black America* (Chicago: University of Chicago Press, 2000).

2. Mia E. Bay, Farah J. Griffin, Martha S. Jones, and Barbara D. Savage, eds., *Toward an Intellectual History of Black Women* (Chapel Hill: University of North Carolina Press, 2015) is a notable exception in highlighting black women's contributions as producers of knowledge and recognizing religious thought as significant.

3. Josef Sorett engages similar concerns in *Spirit in the Dark: A Religious History of Racial Aesthetics* (New York: Oxford University Press, 2016).

4. For additional works that address the relationship of religion to early twentieth-century African American culture, see Wallace Best, *Langston's Salvation: American Religion and the Bard of Harlem* (New York: New York University Press, 2017); Craig Prentiss, *Staging Faith: Religion and African American Theater from the Harlem Renaissance to World War II* (New York: New York University Press, 2014); Judith Weisenfeld, *Hollywood Be Thy Name: African American Religion in American Film: 1929–1949* (Berkeley: University of California Press, 2007).

Isolated Believer

Alain Locke, Baha'i Secularist

David Weinfeld

In 1935, at age fifty, the Harlem Renaissance writer Alain LeRoy Locke, a phi-losophy professor at Howard University, contributed a chapter to his friend Horace Kallen's volume *American Philosophy Today and Tomorrow*. In a biographical preamble, Locke described himself as "more of a pagan than a Puritan" and "more of a humanist than a pragmatist." He then declared him-self a "universalist in religion" and a "cultural cosmopolitan" and labeled his philosophical outlook "cultural pluralism and value relativism."[1]

When Locke used the term "universalist in religion," he was subtly refer-ring to his adherence to the Baha'i faith, to which he had converted in 1918. In 1941, only six years after he wrote the chapter for Kallen's volume, Locke ended his official ties with religion due to lack of time and energy for the commitment and disillusionment with their ability to affect positive change on the race question. He wrote to a Baha'i friend, "I naturally am reluctant to sever a spiritual bond with the Bahai community, for I still hold to a firm belief in the truth of the Bahai principles." Though he "respectfully and regretfully" declined to renew his membership in the Washington, D.C. Baha'i organiza-tion, he declared himself an "'isolated believer.'"[2]

This designation, "isolated believer," reflected Locke's lifelong view of reli-gion, even before he became Baha'i. Locke wrote extensively on philosophy, politics, art, music, and many other topics. He rarely wrote about religion and was never known as a pious person. His private correspondence was devoid of religious language. Yet neither was he an outspoken nonbeliever like the Clar-ence Darrows of his day. As a result scholars have missed Locke's significance as an African American secularist. In the 2016 volume *Race and Secularism in America*, Locke is relegated to a single mention in a footnote.[3] The Locke biographer and literary scholar Charles Molesworth, meanwhile, has noted the fundamentally "modern and secular" character of the New Negro move-ment, equally "embodied" in all of Locke's writing, without analyzing that secularism further.[4] Locke is absent from scholarship on American secularism precisely because of his affiliation with the Baha'i, a religious group.

Ironically the key to understanding Locke's secularism is examining it alongside his Baha'i faith. He undergirded his universalist secular humanism with a spiritual foundation. His conversion to Baha'i was not a break but a continuation. It provided a religious framework for his overarching belief in the unity of humankind while explicitly sanctioning his pluralistic commitment to diversity in the realm of secular culture, a commitment he best expressed through the Harlem Renaissance.[5] While historians of the black experience privilege the roles of Judaism, Christianity, and Islam, particularly the black Protestant churches, this analysis of Locke's Baha'i faith enriches our understanding of twentieth-century black intellectual history by showing how an oft-ignored religion from nineteenth-century Persia provides a window into black secularism in the United States.

Locke should be acknowledged as a major secularist among African Americans. The New Negro movement of the 1920s that Locke helped lead was a movement of secular cultural nationalism. The writers and artists he championed—Langston Hughes, Zora Neale Hurston, and others—were not religiously oriented. Locke used the Baha'i faith, which preaches religious unity and cultural diversity, as a vehicle to bring about greater "race amity" in America. That nationalism sat on a foundation of cultural pluralism, the secular philosophy he developed in conversation with Kallen in 1906–8 at Harvard and Oxford.

Cultural pluralism responded to racism and nativism, as well as the assimilationist ideal of the melting pot. It posited that different ethnic groups could and should coexist in the same political entity. In celebrating diversity it shaped modern multiculturalism. Today multiculturalism usually includes religious diversity. Yet for Locke and Kallen, cultural pluralism was a secular ideal, referring to different immigrant groups, like Germans, Irish, and Italians, and defining Jews and blacks as national or cultural communities.

Secularism for Locke was not simply the absence of religiosity but an important philosophical orientation. Borrowing from the anthropologist Franz Boas, Locke ascribed a cultural definition to race and separated religion from race and culture. His views on religion emerged from his Philadelphia upbringing and his experiences at Harvard. His religious position, here called "Baha'i secularism," would be critical for the New Negro movement.

Locke edited and compiled the movement's bible, *The New Negro*, in 1925. This volume of essays, stories, poetry, and art did not mention Baha'i. Locke's cultural pluralism was political, not religious. He sought to create a sophisticated African American culture on par with elite European civilization to add to the larger tapestry of cultures in the United States. This was an artistic effort to advance civil rights. Though it failed as a civil rights initiative, the New Negro movement left a foundational legacy for modern black studies and aesthetics.

As intellectual godfather of the Harlem Renaissance in the 1920s, the first black Rhodes scholar at Oxford University in 1907, and a distinguished pragmatist philosopher for several decades, Locke was one of the most important African American thinkers of the twentieth century. In a 1927 letter W. E. B.

Du Bois wrote, "Locke is by long odds the best trained man among the younger American Negroes."[6] Locke scholars focus on the New Negro movement, his Rhodes Scholarship, his pragmatism, and his cultural pluralism. His religious and secularist commitments, largely unexamined, informed each of these facets of his life and merged in his dedication to Baha'i.

The Baha'i faith is a monotheistic religion that emerged in nineteenth-century Persia. Its leaders advocated the unity of God, of all religions, and of all humanity. They stood against race prejudice, making the religion attractive to ethnic minorities, including African Americans. The Baha'i principle Locke came to embrace was "unity in diversity." The Baha'i respected cultural differences in the name of upholding the religious unity of humankind. Religious unity implied that all religions shared the same foundation in monotheism and the same overarching moral framework.

When Locke converted to the Baha'i faith in 1918 the religion was less than a hundred years old.[7] In 1844 in Shiraz, Persia, a Muslim merchant named Siyyid Ali Muhammad prophesied a new religious leader who would unite mankind. He came to be known at the Báb, Arabic for "the gate." Though the Báb was executed for heresy in 1850, his follower, Mirza Husayn-Ali, a Tehran nobleman, claimed to be the prophet the Báb foretold, on par with Moses, Jesus, and Muhammad. He took a new name, Bahá'u'lláh, "Glory of God," and assumed leadership of the new faith. In 1852, accused of plotting to assassinate the shah, imprisoned, and exiled with his family to Baghdad, Bahá'u'lláh continued to spread his message of universal religion, undergirded by a common ethics and monotheism, accepting the legitimacy of the Abrahamic faiths, Judaism, Christianity, and Islam.

By 1863 Bahá'u'lláh had reinterpreted the Báb's religion, christening it Baha'i. He moved about the Middle East, often due to banishment, finally settling in Acre, Palestine, all the while preaching and composing major Baha'i texts. Bahá'u'lláh's son, born Abbas in 1844 but renamed 'Abdu'l-Bahá, or "Servant of Bahá," succeeded him. In 1907 'Abdu'l-Bahá moved the center of the Baha'i faith from Acre to Haifa. He increased his missionary activity, in 1911–13 touring Europe and North America. Either in England or the United States he may have encountered Locke, though Locke's recorded Baha'i activity only began in the 1920s.

Washington, D.C. in the early twentieth century had a small but energetic Baha'i community that included several African Americans. On March 22, 1911, the "colored believers" threw a "surprise farewell reception" for Louis George Gregory, a prominent black Baha'i. Gregory was about to make a pilgrimage to the religion's headquarters in Haifa, the first African American to do so. *Star of the West*, the Baha'i newspaper, counted "more than fifty of these believers and invited guests" at the house of Mr. and Mrs. Andrew Dyer, black Baha'is whose Washington home was "always open for meetings." Other African American attendees included Wilson Bruce Evans, the principal of the Armstrong Manual Training School for black youth (dedicated by

Booker T. Washington); the judge and former US consul to Madagascar Mifflin Wistar Gibbs; William Henry Harrison Hart, a lawyer and law professor at Howard; and Margaret Murrell, an English teacher at the Armstrong School.[8]

The following year 'Abdu'l-Bahá visited Washington.[9] He spoke (through a translator) at churches and other function halls, but also made a point of engaging the black community. On Tuesday, April 23, 1912, at noon, the Baha'i prophet lectured before over a thousand students and faculty of Howard University. That evening he addressed a packed house at the Metropolitan AME Church for a gathering sponsored by the Bethel Literary and Historical Society, an important African American intellectual organization. The *Washington Bee* covered the events, noting, "Quite a colony of colored Bahaists has been developed in Washington," referring to the black supporters of 'Abdu'l-Bahá as "earnest disciples."[10] The next night Mrs. Dyer hosted 'Abdu'l-Bahá's talk. The Baha'i prophet marveled at the racial harmony in the room, with over a hundred mostly white Baha'is in attendance at a black woman's home: "May the colored people be like sapphires and rubies, and the white be as diamonds and pearls; and their mixture, their unity will lend a charm to the composite. How delightful a spectacle it would be if there would be a real unity among them! . . . And now the American nation, be it colored or white, if they unite and be in accord, the Lights of the Oneness of Humanity will shine."[11]

Locke was not in attendance, though he likely interacted with members of the Washington Baha'i community after he began teaching at Howard in the fall of 1912. He kept his religious affiliation fairly private, even after his conversion in 1918. He occasionally participated in Baha'i ceremonies and functions, particularly events intended to encourage "race amity," the term that Baha'i in the United States used for racial harmony.[12] Locke helped organize two race amity conferences in 1921, in Washington and Springfield, Massachusetts, and another two in 1924, in New York and Philadelphia, speaking at all but the Springfield event. He occasionally wrote for Baha'i publications, though his pieces did not circulate widely.

Through this participation Locke came to know Louis Gregory, the leading black Baha'i, and furthered his active engagement with the faith. At the Philadelphia conference, in October 1924, Locke spoke on "art and culture" at the Convention for Amity between the Colored and White Races in America.[13] Gregory also participated in the event, and two years later, in February and March 1926, he invited Locke (then briefly fired from Howard for supporting more equitable pay for faculty) to go on a Baha'i lecture tour in Ohio and Florida. Locke also went on two pilgrimages to the Baha'i world headquarters in Haifa in 1923 and 1934. Still, he seldom publicly identified as Baha'i to people outside the religion. The Baha'i faith corresponded so well to Locke's philosophy of cosmopolitan cultural pluralism that making the connection explicit likely felt superfluous outside of Baha'i settings. To most of his American peers, this foreign faith would have seemed deeply unfamiliar.

Locke's secularism had deep roots. Born in Philadelphia in 1885, he lost his father six years later. Though his mother, Mary (Hawkins) Locke, raised her son Episcopalian, she was also inspired by ethical culture, the philosophy of Felix Adler, an interest she passed on to her son. Adler, the son of a New York Reform rabbi, left Judaism in 1876, thinking it too narrow and too focused on theology. He started his own movement, a secular religion that abandoned all Judaic particularism and opened itself up to gentile membership. Even more crucially, it eliminated all faith and theology from its ideology, arguing that morals mattered more than theism.

Locke embraced Adler's emphasis on education above any need for church attendance. After graduating from Philadelphia's Central High School, he attended the School of Pedagogy for a year, thinking he might enter the educational profession. In an essay he wrote in 1904, "Moral Training in Elementary Schools," for the school's journal, *The Teacher*, Locke quoted Adler, who stressed that schools not only develop the intellect but also "build up character." Adler had made education into a universal religion. Locke felt similarly, holding school above church and even family as an institution to inculcate morality in the young. "Is not the school custodian of the richest and most liable inheritance of man, the combined and formulated achievements of his thought and action?"[14]

That same year Locke wrote a school paper titled "The True Nature of a Church." His teacher, a Dr. Thompson, had asked, "What is a Church?," rejecting the commonplace definition of "a body of people united in a common divinity and a common creed." Instead, Thompson explained, "the essential idea of a church was that it should be so universal in doctrine and in intended scope as to include all humanity in its proper form of combination—the brotherhood of man."

Locke reasoned that "only a very few" of the world's religions could be counted as churches with a "self-imposed duty of universal realization." He found Thompson's argument "absorbingly interesting" due to the variety of "creeds, doctrines, and sects" known to humankind. He concluded, "The fallacy is not in adopting creeds, formulas and rituals, but in looking upon them as the essential elements without which true religion means nothing. How many realize that, in insisting upon these as necessary and always present elements, they are taking away the remote probability of a universalization of their religions and denying to themselves the right to the name of church?"[15] Locke valued religion as universal rather than particular. He believed that true religion functioned as universal philosophy that transcended the more particular religions of mankind.

Locke continued along this path at Harvard. He joined the Ethical Society, an organization loosely affiliated with Adler's movement. Whatever vestiges remained of his youthful Episcopalianism vanished completely. In his sophomore year he wrote his mother that he had become "quite a Unitarian by now." Compared to his Lutheran friend David Pfromm, Locke considered himself an "atheist," though he noted that to Pfromm's "childlike mind" atheism encompassed "Catholicism, Unitarianism and other such kindred religions." Locke recounted that when a friend wanted to have him baptized, he joked, "A bath is as much of a compromise with religion as I will make."[16] He occasionally attended Pfromm's services only "to please him."[17]

Locke spent the years 1907–10 in Oxford as a Rhodes scholar, and then the following year in Berlin. As an African American standing just over five feet tall and weighing about 100 pounds, Locke stood out in Europe. Germany, however, proved more tolerant of his skin color and his homosexuality, and he continued his education largely removed from issues of race and religion. The exception came in July 1911, when he attended the First Universal Races Congress in London, along with Felix Adler, Israel Zangwill, and W. E. B. Du Bois.

Another speaker, Wellesley Tudor Pole, an English representative of the Baha'i faith, read a letter from the Persian Baha'i leader 'Abdu'l-Bahá, son of the religion's founder, Bahá'u'lláh. Tudor Pole called for the "world-wide recognition of the underlying unity of religions and peoples." He stressed, however, that "the unification of Races is not intended to mean their suppression of their different characteristics in order that they may be blended into one, but would imply that these very differences are needed to constitute a harmonious whole, and that the duty of this age is to recognize the possibilities of development within each race in order that, in a spirit of love, mankind the world over may cooperate in working for Universal Peace."[18] 'Abdu'l-Bahá's letter reinforced this view with a floral analogy: "Consider the varieties of flowers in a garden. They seem but to enhance the loveliness of each other. When differences of colour, ideas, and character are found in the human Kingdom, and come under the control of the power of Unity, they too show their essential beauty and perfection."[19]

Locke may have attended this session and encountered Baha'i ideas there. Years later he recalled the First Universal Races Congress sparking his interest in "a comparative study of races" from a "scientific approach."[20] To Locke, science helped account for and categorize human variety, whereas religion facilitated spiritual unity. If he had any religious sentiments, they echoed those of the pragmatist philosopher William James, whose ideas Locke had encountered at Harvard and Oxford. James described religion as "the feelings, acts, and experiences of individual men in their solitude, so far as they apprehend themselves to stand in relation to whatever they may consider the divine."[21]

Locke's religion was personal rather than communal. Though he participated in some Baha'i activities, faith never served as his primary affiliation or identifier. He was a human being, a philosopher, an American, an African American. His religion was an acceptance of common humanity in a world of diversity. Baha'i provided a spiritual outlet for a secular philosophy he already believed.

Locke's cosmopolitan vision of cultural pluralism dovetailed with Baha'i rhetoric. In October 1911, a few months after the Universal Races Congress

Locke attended, 'Abdu'l-Bahá lectured in Paris on "beauty and harmony in diversity." He again used the metaphor of flowers in a garden, varied in "form and color" but sharing the same "origin." He described humanity the same way, "made up of many races, and its peoples are of different color, white, black, yellow, brown and red—but they all come from the same God, and all are servants to Him."[22]

These differences long caused hatred and bloodshed. Yet 'Abdu'l-Bahá insisted that differences were a blessing:

> Let us look rather at the beauty in diversity, the beauty of harmony, and learn a lesson from the vegetable creation. If you beheld a garden in which all the plants were the same as to form, color and perfume, it would not seem beautiful to you at all, but, rather, monotonous and dull. The garden which is pleasing to the eye and which makes the heart glad, is the garden in which are growing side by side flowers of every hue, form and perfume, and the joyous contrast of color is what makes for charm and beauty. . . . It is just the diversity and variety that constitutes its charm; each flower, each tree, each fruit, beside being beautiful in itself, brings out by contrast the qualities of the others, and shows to advantage the special loveliness of each and all.[23]

Then 'Abdu'l-Bahá offered a musical metaphor: "The diversity in the human family should be the cause of love and harmony, as it is in music where many different notes blend together in the making of a perfect chord. If you meet those of different race and color from yourself, do not mistrust them and withdraw yourself into your shell of conventionality, but rather be glad and show them kindness. Think of them as different colored roses growing in the beautiful garden of humanity, and rejoice to be among them."[24]

In using musical and garden metaphors, 'Abdu'l-Bahá established a dichotomy between the essential origins all humans shared, and their outward appearances and practices, which are different to ensure the world was interesting and exciting. This is precisely the dichotomy Alain Locke advanced through various endeavors, including the New Negro movement. Appreciating cultural difference led to an embrace of common humanity. The particular led to the universal.

By 1918 Locke had imbibed 'Abdu'l-Bahá's universalism enough to formally convert to the Baha'i faith.[25] His interactions with Baha'i leadership, however, came with Shoghi Effendi, who succeeded 'Abdu'l-Bahá in 1921. Effendi, a distant relative of 'Abdu'l-Bahá, had been born in Acre in 1897. Less a prophet and more a capable administrator, he spoke English, married a Christian woman from Montreal, Mary Maxwell, and proved a charismatic and accessible leader. Locke may have appreciated Effendi's temporal and physical nearness. Just as he had encountered Adler, the founder of the ethical culture movement, Locke met Effendi, leader of the Baha'i faith. Locke's experience of the ethical culture movement and the Baha'i faith was not distant, as it had been with Episcopalian Protestantism, but personal, immediate, and direct.

In 1923 Locke made a pilgrimage to Palestine to visit the Baha'i center in Haifa. He wrote about his experience the following year in an article titled "Impressions of Haifa," printed in the Baha'i journal *Star of the West*. His very first sentences evoked the universalism of his adopted faith: "Whether Bahai or non-Bahai, Haifa makes pilgrims of all who visit her. The place itself makes mystics of us all, for it shuts out the world of materiality with its own characteristic atmosphere." He compared the experience to the calm of a monastery, but without the feeling of being shut in, instead prompting the "opening of new vistas." It was not ascetic at all but combined the "joy and naturalness of a nature-cult with the ethical seriousness and purpose of a spiritual religion."[26]

Spirituality for Locke did not necessitate unreason. He found the shrines of the Báb and 'Abdu'l-Bahá "impressive" but also "modern." They gave the impression, "without mysticism and supernaturalness," of a religion very much alive. Christianity had "in such large measure forgotten" that lesson celebrated at Easter, "He is not here, He is risen." For Locke, the power of Christianity was in Jesus's message as "one of the greatest teachers in the world," his "spirit," not his divinity.[27]

Locke appreciated his guide in Haifa, the living and breathing Shoghi Effendi, the spiritual leader of the Baha'i community at that time. Locke was especially reassured by the "communion of ideas and ideals without the mediation of symbols," a feature of the Baha'i religion he deemed "novel." To Locke, "the only enlightened symbol of a religious or moral principle" was a human being who embodied that principle. In the Baha'i faith Locke found "the cure for the ills of western materialism" and a "destined mission of uniting in a common mood western and oriental minds."[28] He had found his universal religion, a source of spirituality individual in its manifestation yet available to all. It offered a shared ethics in a religious realm where, in Locke's mind, group variety led to strife. But that shared ethic enabled and undergirded cultural diversity, giving the world color and character.

In the 1920s, though continuing to teach philosophy, Locke put aside most of his philosophical pursuits to focus on the aesthetic and cultural realms. This shift culminated in his leadership of the New Negro movement, centered in Harlem. In the volume he compiled and edited in 1925, *The New Negro*, Locke contributed the introduction and several articles, including one titled "The Negro Spirituals." He opened this essay with a bold declarative statement: "The Spirituals are really the most characteristic product of the race genius as yet in America." He examined their contribution in an admiring but objective tone, skillfully navigating the universal and the particular. What made the spirituals "uniquely expressive of the Negro" also made them "deeply representative of the soil that produced them." Echoing W. E. B. Du

Bois's *Souls of Black Folk*, Locke labeled the spirituals both black and American, "nationally as well as racially characteristic."[29]

However, Locke took this expansive interpretation a step further, noting the spirituals' "immediate and compelling universality of appeal" that guaranteed "the immortality of those great folk expressions that survive not so much through being typical of a group or representative of a period but by virtue of being fundamentally and everlasting human." The Negro spirituals embodied a particularistic expression of a universal sentiment, of an emotion and an ethic that transcended ethnic and cultural boundaries. "This universality of the Spirituals" only increased over time. It outlasted the "contempt of the slave owners, the conventionalizations of formal religion, the repressions of Puritanism, the corruptions of sentimental balladry, and the neglect and disdain of second-generation respectability."[30]

Locke's implicit criticism of "formal religion" and the "repressions of Puritanism" are important here. For Locke, true religion could never be so narrow, so particular. The "formal" mainline Protestant denominations, of which the Puritan legacy was strongest, sought to stifle the spirituals from extending beyond their African American roots, deeming them inappropriate for their more enlightened Christianity. Locke believed the spirituals were "among the most genuine and outstanding expressions of Christian mood and feeling." He acknowledged that "there is no such thing as intrinsically religious music," that purportedly religious music contained the observable "interplay of the secular and religious." The spirituals displayed "sensuous and almost pagan elements." Nonetheless "something so intensely religious and so essentially Christian dominates the blend." He did not shy away from declaring, "The Spirituals are spiritual." To deny this would be "to rob them of their heritage" and would be "untrue to their tradition and to the folk genius" that birthed them.[31]

Though Locke valued their secular preservation, he observed that performances of the spirituals in concert halls and college campuses distorted their religious character. "They are essentially congregational, not theatrical." They were not, strictly speaking, art, though they could be source material for art. Yet to Locke they embodied the spirit of a particular people, African Americans, more effectively than jazz music. They more ably contributed to a universal American and global civilization. Their path to universality was through a musical Christianity that could appeal to religious and secular alike, to Christians and non-Christians, as folk art and folk culture. You did not have to adhere to the Judeo-Christian tradition to appreciate their spirituality.

In his discussion of the Negro spirituals, and in his essay on Haifa, Locke did not mention God. A divine being did not play a large role in his written output, in his appreciation of black music, or in his connection to the Baha'i religion. He admired the Baha'i ethic and philosophy, not its monotheism. In an unpublished and undated essay, "The Gospel for the Twentieth Century," he mentioned God, but in pragmatist rather than religious terms. "The pragmatic test and proof of the fatherhood of God is after all whether belief in it can realize the unity of mankind."[32] Implicitly employing James's principle of the "cash value" of an idea and his defense of faith in "The Will to Believe," Locke saw Baha'i monotheism as a means to an end, namely worldwide peace and spiritual unity.[33]

Locke lamented Christian otherworldly messianism, which rendered the notion of the "Brotherhood of Man" merely a "negligible corollary of the fatherhood of God." Without a peaceful payoff in *this* world, monotheistic belief was not worth much. The Baha'i faith, he gleaned, had more potential than Christianity did in that regard. He concluded his essay by quoting Bahá'u'lláh: "That all nations shall become one in faith, and all men as brothers; that the bonds of affection and unity between the sons of men should be strengthened; that diversity of religion should cease, and differences of race be annulled . . . These strifes and this bloodshed and discord must cease, and men be as one kindred and family."[34]

His longest essay for a Baha'i publication, "Unity in Diversity: A Baha'i Principle," written in the early 1930s, reads more like a philosophical treatise than a religious sermon. It evokes the same balance between universalism and particularism that his response to the Negro spirituals did ten years earlier. The subtitle of the essay reflects the quasi-secular affiliation Locke felt toward his adopted faith. What he admired about the Baha'i, what he made his own, were their principles much more than their beliefs. Locke understood that a "pure principle" served only to "motivate or sanction," noting that "mankind is not saved by declarations and professions of faith, but by works and ideas." His focus was the material world, which included the realm of rational thought. In celebrating a particular religion, he emphasized that religion's pragmatic value to broader civilization. Before referring to the Baha'i in the main text, he asserted, "The demand for universality is beyond doubt the most characteristic modern thing in the realm of spiritual values, and in the world of the mind that reflects this realm."[35]

The Baha'i faith offered a solution to the "present dilemma" felt by Locke and many others: "We feel and hope in the direction of universality, but still think and act particularistically." The Baha'i religion could help a variety of peoples "discover unity and spiritual equivalences under the differences." The principle of "unity in diversity" was a recipe for peace and reciprocity. A celebration of the spiritual and ethical similarities between all peoples, and an acknowledgment that these spiritual similarities outweighed cultural differences, paradoxically helped preserve cultural diversity. This principle allowed the cultural differences to flourish as sources of mutual appreciation, of reciprocity rather than conflict.[36]

Though Locke described the Baha'i as early adopters of this principle, his concern was not for their originality but for the pragmatism and persuasiveness of this message of peace. He thought it cruel to deny "oppressed classes and races" national expression in the face of racism and nationalism that consistently denigrated them. He cited "the partisanships of Indian Nationalism, or Chinese integrity, and independence, or Negro and proletarian self-assertion after generations of persecution and restriction." His solution, his *via media*, was not to demand "universalism" from these peoples, but instead to advocate "reciprocity," which entailed the preservation but also the "restriction of these movements to their own natural boundaries, areas and interests." He allowed for nationalism, but not imperialism and colonialism.[37]

Here, rather than attribute this idea to the Baha'i, he credited his old Harvard professor Josiah Royce, "one of the greatest of the American philosophers." Royce's "admirable principle of loyalty" was equivalent to the Baha'i principle of "unity in diversity." Royce advocated not only group loyalty, but "loyalty to loyalty," as in loyalty and respect for those who maintained a measure of group pride, even and especially if they were not of one's own group. This mutual respect allowed for "spiritual reciprocity."[38]

Locke envisioned translating the principles of universalism and reciprocity to the secular realm, into the "social and cultural fields," to enlist the support of the "most vigorous and intellectual elements in society." He challenged every "Baha'i believer," not to proselytize, but to "carry the universal dimension of tolerance and spiritual reciprocity into every particular cause and sectarianism he can reach. His function there is to share the loyalties of the group, but upon a different plane and with a higher perspective. He must partake of partisanship in order to work towards its transformation, and help keep it within his bounds of constructive and controlled self-assertion."[39] Locke struck a balanced tone. He never advocated cultural erasure or assimilation; instead he argued for "constructive and controlled self-assertion." Groups should distinguish themselves in an effort to improve the whole, never to overwhelm cultural units. The "loyalties of the group" should be shared, and appreciated, but on a higher, more spiritual plane. Writing in the 1930s, Locke designated the task for this decade as "transposing the traditional Baha'i reciprocity between religions into the social and cultural denominationalisms of nation, race, and class and vindicating anew upon this plane the precious legacy of the inspired teachings of 'Abdu'l-Bahá and Bahá'u'lláh."[40]

In a short 1936 essay, "The Orientation of Hope," Locke grouped himself among the "true Baha'i believers." He saw great value in "Baha'i principles" of universal "brotherhood, peace, and social justice," hoping they could be brought "to the attention of statesmen and men of practical affairs." In communicating these principles, he advised that while his fellow believers should remember the religious language in which they learned them, they should also "speak a language which the practical-minded man of affairs, and the realistic common man can and will understand." They must translate their message into "terms and ideas and practical issues of the present-day world." Locke remained loyal to the Baha'i but pragmatically applied their principles in a secular fashion.[41]

Locke singled out the Baha'i faith as particularly adept at navigating religious and racial diversity. In 1942 he coedited a volume with the anthropologist Bernhard Stern titled *When Peoples Meet: A Study in Race and Culture*. Locke and Stern described a "Christian cosmopolitanism" of the medieval period that led to a relatively "liberal racial attitude," yet maintained a stark separation with the most common religious other, the Jew. Christianity proved too narrow.[42]

Locke again criticized Christianity on a 1942 episode of the radio show *America's Town Meeting of the Air*, recorded at Howard University. The topic was "Is There a Spiritual Basis for World Unity?" Locke sat on a panel with three other Howard faculty; the university's president, Mordecai Johnson; the dean of the law school, Leon Ransom; and a professor of education, Doxey Wilkerson. Johnson spoke first, championing Christianity as a force for racial justice. Locke disagreed, observing, "One of the troubles of today's world tragedy is the fact that this same religion, of which Dr. Johnson has spoken with such grand idealisms, has, when institutionalized, been linked with politics, the flag and empire, the official church and sectarianism." He linked race and religion, finding little hope for world unity among the "superciliously self-appointed superior races aspiring to impose their preferred culture, self-righteous creeds and religions expounding monopolies on ways of life and salvation."[43]

Locke declared Christianity an enemy of racial progress and of cultural pluralism. When an audience member asked him for an alternative force for world unity, "a substitute for the spiritual ideas that you claim do not exist," Locke had a ready reply. "One of the tragic things which show our present limited horizons is that there are very few institutions where, let us say, the great philosophies of the East are studied; and when they are and as they are, we will be a little nearer to that spiritual unity, I think, that you think I don't believe in."[44] He likely meant the Baha'i faith but referred to "philosophies," not religions. To Locke, being Baha'i was a spiritual commitment that did not require supernatural beliefs.

In 1944 Locke reiterated this critique in an address at Mills College in Oakland, California, titled "Moral Imperatives for World Order." While people traditionally directed their loyalties toward nation, race, or religion, Locke hoped national loyalties would weaken with the dissolving and opening of borders. Race, meanwhile, needed to be transformed from the "fascist, blood-clan sense, which also is tribal and fetishist," into the Boasian definition of "race as a common culture and brotherhood." Locke opposed racial hierarchy, instead calling for a "confraternity of culture" and "an ideal of the parity of races and cultures."[45]

When it came to religion, Locke insisted, in accordance with Baha'i doctrine, that there were many spiritual paths to "salvation." He lamented the opposing view, "a tragic limitation of Christianity," which preached universalism but practiced monism. "If the Confucian expression of a Commandment means the same as the Christian expression, then it is the truth also and should so be recognized." Locke's denunciation of Christianity, his elevation of an Eastern religion, and his reference to a Commandment rather than a theological principle all reflected his commitment to secularism. Religions, for Locke, existed to provide spiritual expression and moral frameworks, not irrational or supernatural beliefs. They served a pragmatic function in this world, not the next. Locke concluded by linking nation, race, and religion again, not giving any precedence over the other but insisting they become "non-monopolistic and culturally tolerant" concepts "freed of sectarian bigotry."[46]

Locke wrote his final Baha'i essay, "Lessons in World Crisis," in 1945. The violence of the twentieth century provided an opportunity for a "terrestrial revelation of the essential and basic oneness of mankind." He praised "leading religious liberals" for their interfaith cooperation, helping to bridge the divides between Protestants and Catholics and Christians and Jews. He lamented, however, the lack of engagement with "Muslim and Oriental religious fronts," whose philosophies he believed better suited to universal justice. Again he distanced himself from Christianity, instead emphasizing "the essential parity of cultures," an idea that would provide a "spiritual foundation for any true world order of peoples and nations."[47]

When Locke died in 1954, Dr. Channing Tobias, an African American civil rights leader trained at Christian seminaries, presided over the funeral. None of the obituaries mentioned the Baha'i faith. Locke's cremated remains passed from one person to another until 2014, when they were finally buried in Congressional Cemetery on Capitol Hill in Washington. Katharine Bigelow, a prominent Baha'i, spoke at the ceremony, as did representatives of Howard University, the Alain Locke Society, and several Rhodes scholars. Members of the Kuumba Singers, Harvard's undergraduate African American choir, performed traditional spirituals, honoring Locke's musical taste. At graveside Robert James, another Baha'i representative, offered a prayer.

The Baha'i faith was one part of Locke's multifaceted existence, complementing his secularism, scholarly pursuits, aesthetic activism, and cultural pluralism. His 2014 gravestone reflects this cohesive compartmentalization. On the front, his epitaph reads: "PHILOSOPHER—EDUCATOR—COSMOPOLITAN— HERALD OF THE HARLEM RENAISSANCE—EXPONENT OF CULTURAL PLURALISM— PHILOSOPHY CHAIR, HOWARD UNIVERSITY—FIRST AFRICAN-AMERICAN RHODES SCHOLAR." Baha'i is not mentioned.

On the back of the stone are five images. In the center is a "dramatic art deco depiction" of an African woman's face with the sun as backdrop, drawn by the black painter Aaron Douglas during the Harlem Renaissance.[48] This image, first used as a book cover for Locke's copy of *The New Negro*, is adorned with the Latin words *Teneo Te, Africa*, "I hold you, my Africa," and *Ave, Aviis!*, "Hail, Grandmothers!," a tribute to his ancestral heritage. Each corner of the stone has a different symbol: the Greek letters *phi*, *beta*, and *sigma*, representing the black fraternity Locke joined at Howard; the *lambda*, a symbol for gay and lesbian rights; a Zimbabwe bird that was adopted by the American Association of Rhodes Scholars; and a nine-pointed star, emblem of the Baha'i faith. Those symbols are not labeled. Casual observers will not know of Locke's Baha'i affiliation and perhaps see only the universalism of the stars in heaven. Locke, Baha'i secularist and isolated believer, would likely have approved.

Notes

1. Alain LeRoy Locke, "Psychograph," for the article "Values and Imperatives," in *American Philosophy Today and Tomorrow*, edited by Horace Meyer Kallen and Sidney Hook (1935; Freeport, N.Y.: Books for Libraries Press, 1968), 312.

2. Alain Locke to Mariam Haney, March 30, 1941, Box 164-33, Folder 49, Alain Locke Papers, Moorland-Spingarn Research Center, Howard University, Washington, D.C. (hereafter cited as ALP), cited in Christopher Buck, *Alain Locke: Faith and Philosophy*, Studies in the Bábi and Bahá'í Religions, vol. 18 (Los Angeles: Kalimat Press, 2005), 177.

3. M. Cooper Harriss, "Two Ways of Looking at an Invisible Man: Race, the Secular, and Ralph Ellison's Invisible Theology," in *Race and Secularism in America*, edited by Jonathan Kahn and Vincent Lloyd (New York: Columbia University Press, 2016), 173n16.

4. Charles Molesworth, introduction to *The Works of Alain Locke* (New York: Oxford University Press, 2012), xii.

5. In a 1935 form for Baha'i records, Locke listed the year of his conversion as 1918 and the place as Washington, D.C.

6. W. E. B. Du Bois to Jesse Moorland, May 5, 1927, W. E. B. Du Bois Papers (MS 312), Special Collections and University Archives, University of Massachusetts–Amherst Libraries.

7. The following details are taken from the official website of the Baha'i faith, www.bahai.org, and from Buck, *Alain Locke*, 35–36.

8. Joseph H. Hannen, reporting Washington, D.C., news in *Star of the West* 2, no. 3 (1911): 9. See also Buck, *Alain Locke*, chapter 3, "The Early Washington D.C. Baha'i Community."

9. For more on this trip, see Guy Emerson Mount, "A Troubled Modernity: W. E. B. Du Bois, 'The Black Church,' and the Problem of Causality," in *'Abdu'l-Bahá's Journey West: The Course of Human Solidarity*, edited by Negar Mottahedeh (New York: Palgrave Macmillan, 2014), 85–110.

10. "Abdul Baha on Religious Unity," *Washington Bee*, April 27, 1912.

11. 'Abdu'l-Bahá, address in Washington, D.C. at home of Mrs. Dyer, April 24, 1912, translated by Dr. Ammen U. Fareed and recorded by Joseph H. Hannen, *Star of the West* 3, no. 3 (1912): 21–22.

12. Buck, *Alain Locke*, 69. The fifth chapter of Buck's book is titled "Race Amity."

13. "Convention for Amity Meets at Big Local Hall," *Pittsburgh Courier*, November 1, 1924.

14. Alain Locke, "Moral Training in Elementary Schools," *The Teacher* 8, no. 4 (1904): 96–97.

15. Alain Locke, "The True Nature of a Church," March 1, 1904, ALP.

16. Alain Locke to Mary Locke, November 3, 1906, Box 52, Folder 15, ALP.

17. Alain Locke to Mary Locke, November 18, 1906 Box 52, Folder 21, ALP.

18. Wellesley Tudor Pole, "The Baha'i Movement," in *A Recording of the Proceedings of the First Universal Races Congress Held at the University of London, July 26–29, 1911* (London: P. S. King and Son, 1911), 155.

19. 'Abdu'l-Bahá, "Letter from 'Abdu'l-Bahá to the First Universal Races Congress," translated by Wellesley Tudor Pole, in *A Recording of the Proceedings of First Universal Races Congress,* 156.

20. Alain LeRoy Locke, *Race Contacts and Interracial Relations,* ed. Jeffrey Stewart (Washington, D.C.: Howard University Press, 1992), 1. The lecture was first delivered in 1915. Also cited in Christopher Buck, "Race Leader, Social Philosopher, Baha'i Pluralist," *World Order* 36, no. 3 (2005): 12.

21. William James, *The Varieties of Religious Experience: A Study in Human Nature* (New York: Modern Library, 1902), 31.

22. 'Abdu'l-Bahá, "Beauty and Harmony in Diversity," *Paris Talks,* chapter 15, October 28, 1911, http://www.bahai.org/library/authoritative-texts/abdul-baha /paris-talks.

23. 'Abdu'l-Bahá, "Beauty and Harmony in Diversity."

24. 'Abdu'l-Bahá, "Beauty and Harmony in Diversity."

25. In 1935 Locke filled out a "Baha'i Historical Record," wherein he dated his own conversion to 1918, in Washington, D.C.

26. Alain Locke, "Impressions of Haifa," *Star of the West* 15, no. 1 (1924): 13.

27. Locke, "Impressions of Haifa," 13.

28. Locke, "Impressions of Haifa," 13–14.

29. Alain LeRoy Locke, "The Negro Spirituals," in *The New Negro,* edited by Alain LeRoy Locke (New York: Boni and Liveright, 1925), reprinted in Molesworth, *The Works of Alain Locke,* 105.

30. Locke, "The Negro Spirituals."

31. Locke, "The Negro Spirituals," 106.

32. Alain Locke, "The Gospel for the Twentieth Century," Box 164-143, Folder 3, ALP, cited in Buck, *Alain Locke,* 234.

33. William James, *Pragmatism* (New York: Longman's, 1907), uses the term "cash-value" several times. William James, *The Will to Believe* (New York: Longman's, 1897) .

34. Locke, "Gospel for the Twentieth Century," cited in Buck, *Alain Locke,* 234, 236.

35. Alain LeRoy Locke, "Unity in Diversity: A Baha'i Principle," in *The Baha'i World: A Biennial International Record,* vol. 5: *1932–1934* (New York: Baha'i Publishing Committee, 1936), reprinted in *The Philosophy of Alain Locke: Harlem Renaissance and Beyond,* edited by Leonard Harris (Philadelphia: Temple University Press, 1989), 134.

36. Locke, "Unity in Diversity," 135.

37. Locke, "Unity in Diversity," 136–37.

38. Locke, "Unity in Diversity," 137.

39. Locke, "Unity in Diversity," 137.

40. Locke, "Unity in Diversity," 138.

41. Alain Locke, "The Orientation of Hope," in *The Baha'i World,* vol. 5 (1936), reprinted in Harris, *The Philosophy of Alain Locke,* 130.

42. Alain Locke and Bernhard Stern, *When Peoples Meet: A Study in Race and Culture*, reprinted in Molesworth, *The Works of Alain Locke*, 375.

43. Alain Locke, "Is There a Spiritual Basis for World Unity," episode of *America's Town Meeting of the Air*, May 28, 1942, cited in Buck, *Alain Locke*, 179.

44. Locke, "Is There a Spiritual Basis for World Unity," 180.

45. Alain Locke, "Moral Imperatives for World Order," address delivered on June 20, 1944, at Mills College, Oakland, Calif., reprinted in Harris, *The Philosophy of Alain Locke*, 151–52.

46. Locke, "Moral Imperatives for World Order," 152.

47. Alain Locke, "Lessons in World Crisis, *Baha'i World* 9 (1945), 746. Also cited in Buck, *Alain Locke*, 230.

48. Francis Stead Sellers, "The 60-Year Journey of the Ashes of Alain Locke, Father of the Harlem Renaissance," *Washington Post Magazine*, September 12, 2014.

The New Negro Renaissance and African American Secularism

Christopher Cameron

From March 21 to 26, 1953, Langston Hughes testified before Senator Joseph McCarthy's Permanent Subcommittee on Investigations regarding the atheist and communist themes in his 1932 poem "Goodbye, Christ." At one point during the testimony, Senator Everett Dirksen of Illinois wanted to know whether Hughes thought the "Book is dead" (meaning the Bible) and whether or not "Goodbye, Christ" could be considered an accurate reflection of African American religious values. Dirksen noted that he was very familiar with African Americans and knew them to be "innately a very devout and religious people." Likely fearing jail or blacklisting, Hughes quickly disavowed the more radical religious and political sentiments of the poem. Yet the poem's very existence, as well as Dirksen's view that black people are naturally religious, speaks to a critical problem in the scholarship on African American religion, namely an inattention to expressions of atheism, agnosticism, and secular humanism in black thought. This chapter examines the rise and growth of African American secularism during the New Negro Renaissance of the 1920s and 1930s. Focusing on two secular thinkers, Langston Hughes and Nella Larsen, I argue that freethought was a key outgrowth of the New Negro Renaissance and constitutes a central innovation in black religious and intellectual life.[1]

Countless historians have demonstrated the key impact that the New Negro Renaissance and the Great Migration had on black religious life. The migration of 1.5 million black southerners to northern cities brought about a new sacred order that was dominated by women, who constituted more than 70 percent of members in many churches. With a lack of funds to build elaborate church structures, storefront churches became the most common ones created during the Migration. Many churches initiated social service programs, generally staffed by women, and cooperated in the promotion of black businesses, especially funeral homes. Worship patterns also changed significantly. Ministers tried to appeal to both the reason and emotions of their listeners, while gospel music came to replace classical music and Negro spirituals. Last, this period witnessed the massive growth of Pentecostalism, led by the evangelist William Seymour. It also saw the rise of dynamic ministers such as Father Divine and Aimee Semple McPherson, as well as the emergence of syncretistic forms of Islam such as the Moorish Science Temple, founded by Noble Drew Ali.[2]

While the Great Migration fostered this incredibly vibrant religious life among many blacks in the North, the literary and intellectual movement that has come to be known as the Harlem or New Negro Renaissance also paved the way for a more widespread freethought movement. Once the movement began, Harlem in particular and New York City more broadly became an attractive place for intellectuals and writers of all stripes. This situation, as well as the urbanization and industrialization prevalent throughout nineteenth- and early twentieth-century America, had significant implications for religious belief. For one, built structures now towered over nature and God's creation, diminishing their importance in the eyes of many. Also, as James Turner points out, once the nation became more urban, "Bible stories, built from the metaphors and folkways of a pastoral and agrarian people, lost their immediate emotional resonance." This is not to say that urbanization necessarily causes secularization. While some may come to religious skepticism as a result of living in a city, others might try to find community and kinship through participation in religious life. But for many people, including the writers and thinkers of the Harlem Renaissance, urban life helped foster religious skepticism.[3]

This religious skepticism constitutes a critical part of the black intellectual tradition during the twentieth century. Just as women came to dominate northern church life in the 1920s, so too would women such as Zora Neale Hurston and Nella Larsen became prominent theorists of secularism. Larsen strongly opposed the prevalent ties between religion and respectability among blacks and used her fictional works to articulate a vision of gender relations unbound by the mores of Christianity. Along with its influence on early black feminist thought, understanding black secularism helps shed light on the foundations of black radical political thought. Langston Hughes's career, and that of his contemporaries Hubert Harrison, Harry Haywood, and Louise Thompson Patterson, suggests that religious skepticism and freethought were motivating factors in becoming socialists and communists. Most scholars cite Caribbean immigration, the Black Belt thesis, and racism as the key reasons for growing political radicalism during this era. While these factors cannot be ignored, historians must also take seriously the ways that religious skepticism influenced political beliefs, especially since socialists and communists in the North strongly disavowed Christianity. Taking religious skepticism and nonbelief just as seriously as the influence of Christianity or Islam on political thought provides us with a richer picture of black radicalism in particular and black intellectual history more broadly.[4]

One of the principal figures of the New Negro Renaissance to embrace freethought was Langston Hughes. Hughes was born in Joplin, Missouri, in 1902 but spent most of his childhood in Lawrence, Kansas. With his father and mother separated and the latter traveling often to find work, Hughes went to live with his grandmother early on, in addition to spending stretches of time at the house of his relatives James and Mary Reed. It was while living with Auntie and Uncle Reed, as Hughes called them, that he first developed a fascination with black religion, but also distaste for church and eventual rejection of belief in Jesus. Auntie Reed ran the Sunday school at St. Luke's Methodist Episcopal Church in Lawrence, and while Langston was living with her she demanded he attend the school every week. He was not a fan of this requirement and noted that he came to loathe church after Auntie Reed made him stay inside on a beautiful spring day and memorize Bible verses while other kids played.[5]

It was after a revival service Hughes attended at the age of thirteen that he came to disbelieve in God. After spending the entire day in church, there was a special meeting for children in the evening, at which Hughes was placed on the mourner's bench with other kids who had not yet accepted Jesus. Before his experience on the bench, Hughes was a Trinitarian who believed that God used the Holy Spirit and Jesus to reconcile sinners to Himself. "My aunt told me that when you were saved you saw a light," he writes. "And something happened to you inside. And Jesus came into your life! And God was with you from then on! She said you could see and hear and feel Jesus in your soul. I believed her. I had heard a great many old people say the same thing and it seemed to me they ought to know. So I sat there calmly in the hot, crowded church, waiting for Jesus to come to me." The preacher called the children to come to Jesus, while the men and women of the church prayed over all of them. Some went; some just sat there on the mourner's bench. Through it all Hughes "kept waiting to *see* Jesus." Finally, there were just two children left on the bench who had yet to be saved, Hughes and a friend named Wesley. The temperature in the church being extremely high, Wesley could no longer take it and whispered to Hughes, "God damn! I'm tired o' sitting here. Let's get up and be saved." Wesley did just that and was saved, after which Hughes "was left all alone on the mourner's bench. My aunt came and knelt at my knees and cried, while prayers and songs swirled all around me in the little church. The whole congregation prayed for me alone, in a mighty wail of moans and voices. And I kept waiting serenely for Jesus, waiting, waiting—but he didn't come. I wanted to see him, but nothing happened to me. Nothing!"[6]

Hughes eventually started to feel bad that he was holding things up. It was getting late and the entire congregation had been there for hours praying over him and the other children. "I began to wonder what God thought about Wesley, who certainly hadn't seen Jesus either," he recalled. "God had not struck Wesley dead for taking his name in vain or for lying in the temple. So I decided that maybe to save further trouble, I'd better lie, too, and say that Jesus had come, and get up and be saved." Just as Wesley did, Hughes stood up and lied to the congregation, declaring that Jesus had come to him

Langston Hughes, 1943.
Photographer: Gordon Parks.
Library of Congress Prints and
Photographs Division.

and he had been saved. Everyone was proud of him, especially Auntie Reed, but he was not proud of himself and cried that night for one of the last times in his life. His aunt woke up and thought he was crying out of joy at having seen the Holy Ghost and accepted Jesus into his life, but Hughes admits, "I was really crying because I couldn't bear to tell her that I had lied, that I had deceived everybody in the church, that I hadn't seen Jesus, and that now I didn't believe there was a Jesus any more, since he didn't come to help me."[7]

There are a number of key ideas and moments in Hughes's recollection of how he came to disbelieve in God. First among these is the way that he describes his friend Wesley's eventual "conversion." While the congregation rejoices that Wesley finally decided to accept Jesus as his lord and savior, and Wesley likely also rejoiced that he no longer had to sit on the mourner's bench, Hughes knows the sordid truth behind this conversion, namely that it was one of expedience and that it actually began with an expression of blasphemy. By recalling Wesley's attempt to propitiate the church members through a feigned conversion, Hughes implicitly raises two questions: How widespread is this practice? How many individuals do we believe are Christian that converted only because of community pressure? Hughes does not take a direct jab at African American religiosity. He does, however, suggest that atheism, agnosticism, or other forms of freethought might be more widespread than most have imagined.

The primary reason Hughes gives for his own inability to believe is also telling. He indicates a sincere desire to believe in Jesus, yet simply cannot bring himself to take the Kierkegaardian leap of faith. By saying he could not see Jesus, and thus could not believe in him, Hughes wants the reader to know that his idea of reality is bounded by sensory perception and the analytic-technical bent of mind that Turner suggests became increasingly common in American society during the Industrial Revolution. If the pastor and others in the church could not physically demonstrate that Jesus existed, then Hughes had no reason to believe in him, despite the fact that he wanted very much to believe in a savior. Also, Hughes's time on the mourner's bench was a period fraught with anxiety, despite its relatively short duration. The fact that he seemingly received no assistance from Jesus in this time of trouble simply further confirmed for him the futility of religious belief.[8]

Hughes moved to Harlem in 1921 to attend Columbia University, an experience that likely served to deepen his religious skepticism. Harlem had recently undergone a period of intense transition. From 1910 to 1920 the number of African Americans in New York City doubled, and Harlem began its twenty-year transition into a primarily black neighborhood. In 1920 Harlem was bounded by Lexington Avenue on the east to St. Nicholas Avenue on the west, a distance of six blocks, and stretched from 125th to 145th streets, a distance of roughly one mile. A decade later the area had expanded fifteen blocks south and ten blocks north. In addition to its fast-paced growth, during the 1920s Harlem was home to some of the foremost intellectuals and activists in black America, including W. E. B. Du Bois, Charles Johnson, Elizabeth Hendrickson, and Amy Ashwood Garvey. In addition Harlem contained the offices of labor and civil rights leader A. Phillip Randolph and Chandler Owens's *Messenger* magazine, *The Crisis*, and *Opportunity*, three periodicals that would play a vital role in fostering the New Negro Renaissance. Marcus Garvey's United Negro Improvement Association had just begun to take off when Hughes arrived. The organization captivated thousands with its philosophy of black economic self-determination, race pride, and anti-imperialism; however, Garvey would begin to encounter opposition to his plans for American blacks to return to Africa in the early 1920s, especially after he attended a Ku Klux Klan meeting in Atlanta in June 1922.[9]

Hughes had begun writing poems even before his move to the mecca of black America, but after arriving there he began to explore in more depth religious themes such as the problem of evil and the nature and existence of God. Perhaps the first such work was his poem "Song for a Dark Girl," which appeared in his 1927 book *Fine Clothes to the Jew* but was first published in *The Crisis* five years earlier:

Way Down South in Dixie
(Break the heart of me)
They hung my young black lover
To a cross roads tree.

Way Down South in Dixie
(Break the heart of me)
I asked the white Lord Jesus
What was the use of prayer

Way Down South in Dixie
(Break the heart of me)
Love is a naked shadow
On a gnarled and naked tree

The subject of this poem is racial lynching, a practice that was becoming increasingly common during the 1920s. While the victims of lynching were often men, here Hughes highlights the plight of black women who fall victim to racial violence. He does so by mimicking the call-and-response pattern of African American religious music with the repetition of the refrain "Break the heart of me." Much of his poetry, and that of other New Negro writers, drew heavily from both Negro spirituals and the blues, but here Hughes uses black musical traditions to critique belief in "the white Lord Jesus" that is seemingly incapable of preventing the wanton destruction and mutilation of black bodies in the American South. Just as he himself had futilely tried to pray to Jesus a decade earlier, he notes that millions of African Americans engage in the same practice with the same results. His critique of African American religion in this poem also displays his political consciousness and growing belief in secular humanism. If Jesus cannot protect black people, then black people must take action to protect themselves.[10]

Hughes addressed the theme of divine powerlessness in a number of other works, including his poems "Litany" and "Who but the Lord." In the first of these he advises his reader to "gather up / In the arms of your pity . . . Gather up / In the arms of your love" the sick, the tired, and those who are viewed as the scum of Harlem because these are people "who expect / No love from above." Shifting the scenery away from the South and to the plight of the urban North, where hundreds of thousands of black southerners found themselves in the 1920s, Hughes draws attention to the lack of economic opportunities, poor housing, inadequate health care, and other social problems and posits that his readers must take pity on and show love to these people because God is not going to do so.[11]

Hughes highlights another persistent problem facing African Americans throughout the country in "Who but the Lord?," namely the problem of police brutality.

I looked and I saw
That man they call the Law.
He was coming
Down the street at me!
I had visions in my head
Of being laid out cold and dead,
Or else murdered
By the third degree.

I said, *o, Lord, if you can,*
Save me from that man!
Don't let him make a pulp out of me!
But the Lord he was not quick.
The Law raised up his stick
And beat the living hell
Out of me!

Now, I do not understand
Why God don't protect a man
From police brutality.
Being poor and black,
I've no weapon to strike back
So who but the Lord
Can protect me?

Hughes makes the connection between many blacks' class and racial identities, noting that victims of police violence often have no recourse because they are both "poor and black." With no one to stop police violence against blacks here on Earth, they naturally look to heaven for divine assistance but are once again let down. This is because God doesn't exist or because God is white and does not care about black people. Hughes and many other Renaissance writers are often unclear on just which claim they believe. Qiana Whitted argues that much of their literary production was concerned not so much with positing a definitive answer to the question of God's existence, but rather with "illustrating an angst-ridden process that is both critical and creative." Either way, the result is often the same for black writers such as Hughes, who posit that African Americans should stop looking to the church and to God to solve their problems and instead find their own creative solutions to the persistence of white racism.[12]

One of Hughes's most well-known and irreverent poems was "Goodbye, Christ" (1932), a poem that reiterates the main themes of his earlier work but in much stronger and more forceful language. Hughes wrote the poem while he and twenty-one other blacks were on a trip to Russia working on a film exploring American race relations. Otto Huiswoud, one of the foremost black communists in the United States, published the poem in the European magazine *Negro Worker*, which led to Hughes being bitterly attacked by black clergymen throughout the United States. Like some of his earlier pieces, in this poem Hughes is ambivalent about the existence of Jesus Christ but is clear that even if he does exist, human beings do not need him.

Listen, Christ,
You did alright in your day, I reckon—
But that day's gone now.
They ghosted you up a swell story, too,
Called it Bible—
But it's dead now,
The popes and the preachers've
Made too much money from it.
They've sold you to too many

Kings, generals, robbers, and killers—
Even to the Tzar and the Cossacks,
Even to Rockefeller's Church,
Even to THE SATURDAY EVENING POST.
You ain't no good no more.
They've pawned you
Till you've done wore out.

Goodbye,
Christ Jesus Lord God Jehova,
Beat it on away from here now.
Make way for a new guy with no religion at all—
A real guy named
Marx Communist Lenin Peasant Stalin Worker ME—

I said, ME!

Go ahead on now,
You're getting in the way of things, Lord.
And please take Saint Gandhi with you when you go,
And Saint Pope Pius,
And Saint Aimee McPherson,
And big black Saint Becton
Of the Consecrated Dime.
And step on the gas, Christ!
Move!

Don't be slow about movin'!
The world is mine from now on—

And nobody's gonna sell ME
To a king, or a general,
Or a millionaire. [13]

Hughes's central reason for rejecting human beings' need for a god in "Goodbye Christ" is the monetary value that people have placed on religious belief and the prosperity that it has brought to religious and political leaders throughout human history, especially at the expense of the working classes. Instead of black people benefiting from religion, Hughes argues, a secular ideology such as communism is much better suited to addressing the needs of individuals here on Earth. This is largely because communism has been articulated and spread by "a real guy," namely Karl Marx, Vladimir Lenin, Joseph Stalin, and others whose existence is not in doubt.

Hughes's views in the poem are influenced in part by his association with the "big black Saint Becton / Of the Consecrated Dime." He notes that in the early 1930s, George Becton facilitated some of the most amazing revivals Harlem had ever witnessed. Becton was born in April 1890 to Matthew and Lucy Becton and grew up in Clarksville, Texas, where he came to be known as the "boy clergyman." As a teenager he moved to Wilberforce, Ohio, to attend Payne Theological Seminary, where he earned a Bachelor of Divinity degree in 1910. He preached at the Zion Baptist Church in nearby Xenia, Ohio, for twelve years before moving to Harlem in 1925, where he became a pastor at the Salem Methodist Episcopal Church on 129th Street and Seventh Avenue. F. A. Cullen, father of the Harlem Renaissance poet Countee Cullen, headed this congregation, and it was here that Becton became one of the most popular preachers in Harlem. Becton would saunter onto the stage of the church attired in a fine pearl-gray suit, white silk gloves, and a top hat, followed by "twelve disciples," all the while being welcomed by the music of a jazz band consisting of anywhere from seven to fifteen players. He referred to his show as "The World's Gospel Feast Party," the primary component being the "consecrated dime." [14]

While most Harlemites loved Becton, Hughes could not stand this early proponent of the prosperity gospel. "Dr. Becton was a charlatan if there ever was one," he claims. But Becton put on a great show and was able to fill up a large church. One of Hughes's main criticisms was Becton's seeming duplicitousness in bilking money out of his congregation. "Dr. Becton had an envelope system, called 'The Consecrated Dime—A Dime a Day for God.' And every Sunday he would give out his envelopes. And every Sunday he would collect hundreds of them from the past week, each with seventy cents therein, from the poor working men and women who made up the bulk of his congregation. Every package of dimes was consecrated to God—but given to the Reverend Dr. Becton." To Hughes this practice was unconscionable, especially given the fact that it took place during the height of the Great Depression, when poor blacks in Harlem could not, in his view, afford to give away seventy cents a week.[15]

One day the good reverend invited Hughes to his home to talk a little business, a discussion that certainly did not raise Hughes's estimation of Becton nor, by extension, other ministers who employed similar methods. Becton revealed to him that he had been a student of behavioral psychology and knew how to keep his audience enthralled and giving more money. He also said that "he knew the effects of music and rhythm on the human emotions . . . and he knew how to handle them. Now, he was looking for someone who was clever with the written word to do with the people through the printed page what he could do with them in person. During his talk with me, never once did he mention God. In the quiet of his study, he talked business, God being, no doubt, for public consumption."[16]

Hughes would decline Becton's job offer, despite his interest in finding out whether or not Becton actually believed his own profession of religion. This experience was yet another in a long line of events that would turn Hughes away from Christianity and toward a form of secular humanism that posited the ineffectiveness of divine assistance in forwarding racial and economic justice in the United States. This is not to say that Hughes articulated a strong atheism, nor to say that he tried to completely separate himself from African American religious traditions. He would use religious language in his work for decades and continued to attend religious services throughout his life. But his professions of Christ's and God's weakness in a number of different works certainly undermined one of the key attributes of God's character, according to orthodox followers, namely omnipotence. His doubts about Jesus and about Christian ministers suggest he was an agnostic at least and certainly one of the foremost freethinkers of his era. And as the literary scholar Michael Lackey argues, Hughes's political critique of religion, when taken in tandem with those of other black secular writers, would provide one of the most "compelling arguments for turning our backs on God, religion, and theological 'thinking'"[17]

Nella Larsen was another well-known writer of the Harlem Renaissance who explored secular themes in her writing, although her explorations of freethought appeared in her fiction. While Larsen published just two books in her career, her literary acclaim nevertheless "helped establish the novel as a creative form for New Negro writers, and her success . . . focused attention on women as literary artists in a cultural movement of highly visible men, most of whom initially wrote poetry or short fiction," according to her biographer. Larsen was born in 1891 and spent most of her youth in Chicago before leaving to attend Fisk University in 1907. After graduating she moved to New York City to train as a nurse, went back down south to work at Tuskegee Institute for a year, then moved back to New York in 1916, where she married a physicist named Elmer Samuel Imes. She soon began writing and published her first essay in the *Brownies' Book* in 1920. It was after quitting her job as a nurse and taking a position as a library assistant at the 135th Street branch of the New York Public Library, now the Schomburg Center for Research in

Black Culture, that her career as a writer began to gain steam. She published her first novel, *Quicksand*, in March 1928, a novel that was unique in a number of ways, not the least of which is its treatment of religion and sexuality.[18]

The central character in the novel is twenty-two-year-old Helga Crane, and the story begins with her articulating her dissatisfaction with Naxos, a school that is a composite of Fisk and Tuskegee. From the start of the book, readers can see Helga feels out of place, and the primary reason for this feeling is religion. She was in her room and hoped to get a few minutes to rest and change, but instead "hundreds of students and teachers had been herded into the sun-baked chapel to listen to the banal, patronizing, and even the insulting remarks of one of the renowned white preachers of the state." The preacher discussed at length how Naxos Negroes were better than other blacks because they knew to stay in their place. He also said that he greatly admired blacks for their progress but urged them to know when and where to stop pushing for more. "And then he had spoken of contentment, embellishing his words with scriptural quotations and pointing out to them that it was their duty to be satisfied in the estate to which they had been called, hewers of wood and drawers of water. And then he had prayed." From the first three pages of the book, then, Larsen portrays Christianity as a stifling religion, one that whites skillfully employ to retard racial progress and that African Americans use to inhibit the expression of black culture. A little while later she talks to the school's dean of women, likely representative of Margaret Murray Washington, the wife of Booker T. Washington, who tells Helga that black women should never wear bright colors such as green, red, or yellow, but instead should wear brown, navy blue, and black. Helga cannot understand the purpose of this, thinking that bright colors are exactly what darker women should be wearing. "These people yapped loudly of race, race consciousness, of race pride," she pronounces. "And yet suppressed its delightful manifestations, love of color, joy of rhythmic motion, naïve, spontaneous laughter." Again, for Helga, the respectability that goes hand in hand with black Christianity is not helping African Americans but rather is stifling their individuality and repressing their beautiful culture. Because of this situation, Helga believes that Naxos is no longer a school or even a community. Instead "it had grown into a machine. It was now a show place in the black belt, exemplification of the white man's magnanimity. . . . Life had died out of it."[19]

Helga soon leaves to return to her hometown of Chicago, where she grows to distrust black Christianity even more. She spends weeks in Chicago looking for work, to no avail. Her education hurts her prospects, as most jobs available for women are for domestics, and employers do not want to hire a former teacher. So Helga turns to the Church, as many southern migrants did during the Great Migration, to help her find employment. Larsen writes, "Helga Crane was not religious. She took nothing on trust. Nevertheless, on Sundays she attended the very fashionable, very high services in the Negro Episcopal church on Michigan Avenue. She hoped that some good Christian would speak to her, invite her to return, or inquire kindly if she was a stranger in the city. None did, and she became bitter, distrusting religion more than ever." Once again Helga feels betrayed by black Christians. It is not just her inability to find a job that vexes her, but also the lack of acceptance from the community. In this scene we can also glimpse Larsen's own views on religion. A short biography of Larsen published in the New York *Amsterdam News* said that she was "a modern woman, for she smokes, does not believe in religion, churches and the like." As we saw with Hughes, however, even those who did not personally believe themselves still had ideas on the function that churches should serve in society. For Larsen, if one was going to attend church and participate in religious communities, there should be some practical benefit for life on Earth rather than simply otherworldly rewards.[20]

Helga soon travels to Harlem, where she stays for a few months. She is unhappy there, especially with what she considers the pretentious black middle class copying the mannerisms of middle-class whites, and she travels to Denmark to stay with family. She lives there for two years before coming back to Harlem, where she is spurned by the former principal of Naxos, after which she accidentally stumbles into a storefront church, an experience that would profoundly shape the course of her life. The church members and the minister pray for her, calling her a Jezebel and hoping for her salvation. "Helga Crane was amused, angry, disdainful, as she sat there, listening to the preacher praying for her soul. But though she was contemptuous, she was being too well entertained to leave. And it was, at least, warm and dry." So Helga stays and listens to the passionate prayers to God for her salvation, accompanied by intense shouting and groaning of the church members. "Particularly she was interested in the writhings and weepings of the feminine portion which seemed to predominate," Larsen writes. "Little by little the performance took on an almost Bacchic vehemence. Behind her, before her, beside her, frenzied women gesticulated, screamed, wept, and tottered to the praying of the preacher." Larsen's portrayal of the church service contains a not-so-subtle critique of African American religious practices. Black church-women are portrayed as "frenzied" and out of control. Elsewhere she refers to the service as a "weird orgy" and says the congregation seemed possessed by madness. Helga is enthralled, however, "possessed by the same madness," and eventually accepts Jesus and is saved.[21]

The next day Helga makes a rash decision to marry the revival preacher from the night before, a man from Alabama named Pleasant Green. She does this partly because the conversion experience was the only nonmaterial thing she had ever had in her life, even though she is already starting to feel the ecstasy and spiritual release from the previous day slipping away. The two move to Alabama, where Helga quickly adapts to life as a preacher's wife, starting a sewing circle, attempting to help other women, and having children in quick succession. In one twenty-month period she has three children, a set of twin boys and a girl, and after having a fourth child she becomes incredibly sick and is confined to bed for weeks. Larsen writes that during Helga's sickness she "had learned what passion and credulity could do to one. In her was born angry bitterness and enormous disgust. The cruel, unrelieved suffering had beaten down her protective wall of artificial faith in the infinite wisdom, in the mercy, of God. For had she not called in her agony on Him? And He had not heard. Why? Because, she knew, He wasn't there. Didn't exist." Here we see a theme that Hughes mentions in his autobiography, namely the inability or unwillingness of God to respond to the problems of human beings. Larsen likewise picks up on another theme Hughes would mention, the idea that if there is a god, this deity cares only about white people. "With the obscuring curtain of religion rent," Larsen writes of Helga, "she was able to look about her and see with shocked eyes this thing she had done to herself. She couldn't, she thought ironically, even blame God for it, now that she knew he didn't exist. No. No more than she could pray to him for the death of her husband, the Reverend Mr. Pleasant Green. The white man's God. And his great love for all people regardless of race! What idiotic nonsense she had allowed herself to believe. How could she, how could anyone, have been so deluded. How could ten million black folk credit it when daily before their eyes was enacted its contradiction?" As Hughes's father did, Larsen equates religion with backwardness and argues that blacks would be better off without the church.[22]

Helga soon realizes that in marrying Green, a choice that symbolizes her conversion to Christianity, she has ruined her life. This decision "made it impossible ever again to do the things she wanted, have the things that she loved, mingle with the people she liked. She had, to put it as brutally as anyone could, been a fool. The damnedest kind of fool." Even with this realization, however, she almost wishes that religion had not failed her. She now realizes it is an illusion; however, it is "better, far better, than this terrible reality. Religion had, after all, its uses. It blunted the perceptions. Robbed life of its crudest truths. Especially it had its uses for the poor—and the blacks." Larsen's critique of religion here was common one among black freethinkers, namely that faith in god is useful for the weak and downtrodden but unnecessary for those with the strength to navigate life's challenges. She further reinforces her earlier argument that Christianity is an appropriation of white culture and meant to keep blacks in a subordinate place in America's racial hierarchy.[23]

Larsen's *Quicksand* contains probably the most extensive exploration of religious skepticism in African American literature to that point. This fact alone does not mark Larsen as a freethinker in her own right, but contemporary evidence points to her lack of religious belief. We have already seen the newspaper biography reference her as a modern woman who rejected churches and religion. Further, in a letter to her literary patron Carl Van Vechten, she wrote that she was no fan of the black church and that the Imes family she married into was "tiresome" and "ultra religious." Like her character Helga Crane, Larsen's experiences at both Fisk and Tuskegee turned her away from religion, as the various missionary endeavors she was forced to participate in seemed to exaggerate "the negative stereotypes of the needy, backward, and downtrodden race," according to Thadious Davis.[24]

Contemporary reviewers quickly recognized the affinities between Helga Crane and Larsen. For some, this was positive. E. Merril Root wrote, "The book, in so far as it is Miss Larsen herself, is excellent. She has, in so far as she has simply bared a modern soul, race-divided and disillusioned by our current misophosy, done us a service." For others, the affinities between fiction and real life were nothing to be praised. Thadious Davis notes that many blacks were offended by "the portrait of the unwashed minister and his primitive Alabama congregation. Religious African Americans saw it as an affront to the church." And the Imes family, which had been prominent in the black church and Alabama missionary work for decades, took the novel as a personal insult. The fact that she could write such negative portrayals of their family heritage was a shameful betrayal.[25]

Quicksand is a key text in the history of black freethought because it intimately ties gender inequality and sexual oppression to religion. Heterosexual marriage is not celebrated in the text but rather decried as a symbol of oppression and serves "as the focal point of at times biting critiques of bourgeois black society and so-called middle-class black values," according to Ann duCille. Cheryl Wall supports this point, noting that the novel "exposes the sham that is middle-class security, especially for women whose dependence is morally debilitating." Furthermore Larsen shows that patriarchy is not the preserve of white men alone but something that black men employ to oppress black women. And Larsen recasts the bedrock of the black community, the black family, as something that constrains black women and keeps them from achieving their dreams. While African American literature to that point had celebrated child rearing and the creation of a stable family life, Larsen challenges this depiction and forces us to consider the ways in which traditional family values disrupt rather than strengthen community. This work is thus one of the first black feminist novels and helped inaugurate the intimate ties between feminism and African American freethought.[26]

Langston Hughes and Nella Larsen are just two of the many writers, artists, and intellectuals of the New Negro Renaissance to embrace freethought and secularism. They were joined by Claude McKay, Zora Neale Hurston, Louise Thompson Patterson, Hubert Harrison, and W. E. B. Du Bois, among others. As it did with Hughes, religious skepticism seemed to go hand in hand with radical politics, as many black communists in the North were freethinkers. And just as it did for Larsen, freethought provided black women with an opportunity to protest against respectability politics and patriarchy, protests that occurred both in everyday life and in novels such as *Their Eyes Were Watching God*. The presence of secular themes in so much of the literary and artistic output of this era demonstrates the critical importance of the Harlem Renaissance in fostering this new development in black religious thought.

This presence likewise points to the previously unrecognized importance of secularism in twentieth-century African American intellectual life.[27]

Notes

1. *Executive Sessions of the Senate Permanent Subcommittee on Investigations of the Committee on Government Operations*, vol. 2, Eighty-third Congress, First Session, 1953 (Washington, D.C.: US Government Printing Office, 2003), 980.

2. Wallace D. Best, *Passionately Human, No Less Divine: Religion and Culture in Black Chicago, 1915–1952* (Princeton, N.J.: Princeton University Press, 2005), 2, 51, 83–86, 100; Anthony B. Pinn, *Introducing African American Religion* (London: Routledge, 2013), 71, 88–89; Cheryl J. Sanders, *Saints in Exile: The Holiness-Pentecostal Experience in African American Religion and Culture* (New York: Oxford University Press, 1996); Jill Watts, *God, Harlem U.S.A.: The Father Divine Story* (Berkeley: University of California Press, 1992).

3. James Turner, *Without God, without Creed: The Origins of Unbelief in America* (Baltimore: Johns Hopkins University Press, 1985), 119.

4. Mark Solomon, *The Cry Was Unity: Communists and African Americans, 1917–1936* (Jackson: University Press of Mississippi, 1998), 4, 86–87; Joyce Moore Turner, *Caribbean Crusaders and the Harlem Renaissance* (Urbana: University of Illinois Press, 2005), 28.

5. Arnold Rampersad, *The Life of Langston Hughes*, vol. 1: *1902–1941, I, Too, Sing America* (New York: Oxford University Press, 1986), 13–17.

6. Langston Hughes, *The Big Sea* (New York: Hill and Wang, 1940), 19, 20.

7. Hughes, *The Big Sea*, 20, 21.

8. For Kierkegaard's fideism, the argument that religious truth is subjective and should not be subject to the same types of proofs as other kinds of truth, see his "Truth Is Subjectivity," in Michael Paterson et al., *Philosophy of Religion: Selected Readings* (New York: Oxford University Press, 2001), 95–98.

9. Hughes, *The Big Sea*, 77; Rampersad, *The Life of Langston Hughes*, 50–51.

10. Langston Hughes, "Song for a Dark Girl," *The Crisis* 25 (October 1922): 267; Ferguson, *The Harlem Renaissance*, 95.

11. Langston Hughes, "Litany," in *Selected Poems of Langston Hughes* (New York: Vintage, 1990), 24.

12. Hughes, "Who But the Lord?," in *Selected Poems*, 196; Qiana J. Whitted, *"A God of Justice?" The Problem of Evil in Twentieth-Century Black Literature* (Charlottesville: University of Virginia Press, 2009), 22.

13. Rampersad, *The Life of Langston Hughes*, 252, 309; Langston Hughes, "Goodbye Christ," in *The Collected Poems of Langston Hughes*, edited by Arnold Rampersad and David Roessel (New York: Vintage, 1994), 166–67.

14. Cary D. Wintz and Paul Finkelman, eds., *Encyclopedia of the Harlem Renaissance*, vol. 1: *A–J* (New York: Routledge, 2004), 110–11.

15. Hughes, *The Big Sea*, 275, 276–77. For the riot at Becton's funeral, see "5,000 Riot to See Harlem Funeral," *New York Times*, May 31, 1933.

16. Hughes, *The Big Sea*, 277–78.

17. Michael Lackey, *African American Atheists and Political Liberation: A Study of the Sociocultural Dynamics of Faith* (Gainesville: University Press of Florida, 2008), 16. In a recent article on "Goodbye, Christ," the religious historian Wallace Best argues that Hughes should be characterized as a religious liberal rather than an atheist or agnostic. While Hughes certainly articulated many tenets of religious liberalism, the dichotomy Best posits is a false one, as one can be both an agnostic and a religious liberal, one who believes that if you are going to adhere to a religion, whether or not you believe in God, that religion must be compatible with reason and must work to address the needs of people in this world. See Wallace Best, "Concerning 'Goodbye, Christ': Langston Hughes, Political Poetry, and African American Religion," *Religion & Politics*, November 26, 2013, http:// religionandpolitics.org/2013/11/26/concerning-goodbye-christ-langston-hughes -political-poetry-and-african-american-religion/.

18. Thadious M. Davis, *Nella Larsen, Novelist of the Harlem Renaissance: A Woman's Life Unveiled* (Baton Rouge: Louisiana State University Press, 1994), xiii, 51–89, 121–22.

19. Nella Larsen, *Quicksand* (1928; Mineola, N.Y.: Dover, 2006), 2, 3, 16, 17, 4.

20. Larsen, *Quicksand*, 31; Thelma E. Berlack, "New Author Unearthed Right Here in Harlem," *Amsterdam News* (New York), May 23, 1928.

21. Larsen, *Quicksand*, 105, 106.

22. Larsen, *Quicksand*, 120, 121.

23. Larsen, *Quicksand*, 123.

24. Davis, *Nella Larsen*, 172, 59; Nella Larsen Imes to Carl Van Vechten, November 12, 1926, James Weldon Johnson Collection, Beinecke Rare Book and Manuscript Library, Yale University.

25. E. Merril Root, "Ebony Hour-Hand, Pointing to Midnight," *Christian Century*, October 18, 1928, 1262; Davis, *Nella Larsen*, 280.

26. Ann duCille, *The Coupling Convention: Sex, Text, and Tradition in Black Women's Fiction* (New York: Oxford University Press, 1993), 87; Cheryl Wall, "Passing for What? Aspects of Identity in Nella Larsen's Novels," *Black American Literature Forum* 20, nos. 1–2 (1986): 109; Thadious M. Davis, introduction to Nella Larsen, *The Gender of Modernism: A Critical Anthology*, edited by Bonnie Kime Scott (Bloomington: Indiana University Press, 1990), 211.

27. For more on Hurston's secularism, see Christopher Cameron, "Zora Neale Hurston, Freethought, and African American Religion," *Journal of Africana Religions* 4, no. 2 (2016): 236–44.

"I Had a Praying Grandmother"

Religion, Prophetic Witness, and Black Women's Herstories

LeRhonda S. Manigault-Bryant

The Spirit, or spirituality, defies definition. . . . Like the wind, it cannot be seen, and yet, like the wind, it is surely there, and we bear witness to its presence, its power. We cannot hold it in our hands and put it on a scale, but we feel the weight, the force, of its influence in our lives. We cannot hear it, but we hear ourselves speaking and testifying because it moves, inspires, and directs us to do so.

> —Gloria Wade-Gayles, *My Soul Is a Witness:*
> *African-American Women's Spirituality*

But I had a praying grandmother!

> —Helen Baylor, "Helen's Testimony,"
> *WOW Gospel*, EMI Records, 1998

Framing the Grandmaternal

Within black intellectual history there has been a long-standing practice of drawing upon the words, experiences, and knowledge of black female forebears. Black women scholars have relied upon Sojourner Truth's now contested "Arn't I a Woman" speech (1851) to account for black women's deep engagement with the "first wave" of American feminism. They have also engaged the critical call for gender equality raised by Anna Julia Cooper's *A Voice from the South* (1892) and utilized Ida Wells Barnett's antilynching crusade to demonstrate black women's broad activism, civic mindedness, and pursuit of black liberation. Relatedly they have examined the perspectives espoused by Maria Stewart, Jarena Lee, and Julia Foote to unearth the faith systems black women have drawn upon to sustain their communities while seeking freedom from their own intersecting oppressions.[1] In short, black women have always been active participants in the black American intellectual tradition and have used their standpoints as activists, writers, leaders, artists, sages, and intellectuals to cultivate the simultaneous result of gender equality and black liberation.

Since the mid-twentieth century, greater scholarly attention has been paid to the particular role of black maternal figures in the construction of black religious life and identity.[2] While negative representations of black womanhood popularized by the now infamous Moynihan Report loomed large in the American imagination,[3] increased academic focus on the complex spiritual lives of black women actively disrupted a damaging metanarrative about the inferiority of black women (and their bodies) that had existed since the dawn of the transatlantic slave trade. Instrumental to this dismantling has been the debunking of what Hortense Spillers calls the "American Grammar Book," the idea that American patriarchal familial patterns are a prevailing social fiction (with their own accompanying, hierarchical language) imposed upon black communities and are antithetical to the inherently nonpatriarchal structures that exist between black women and men.[4] Also pivotal to this dismantling has been the intentional emphasis—whether through the lens of reproduction, labor, ethics, social history, or literature—on the ways black women's religious identities explicitly inform the broadest contours of black life.

Efforts to reveal the varied ways black women contribute to the development of black life writ large have also refuted the harmful tropes associated with black womanhood broadly, and black motherhood in particular. Because mother-child bonds were continually at risk within plantation systems, and continue to be precarious due to the creation of a global racial hierarchy that has placed black people at the bottom, motherhood has been simultaneously viewed as one of the most dangerous and selfless decisions black women can make. In her seminal text, *Black Feminist Thought* (1990), Patricia Hill Collins lifts up the ways concepts of motherhood have been central to the philosophies of black people and characterizes black mothering as a form of radical activism that constructs dialectical relationships with other black mothers, communities, children, and the self. By taking seriously ideas about black motherhood that emanate from within black communities, Collins broadens the landscape in which we imagine black motherhood and parses important distinctions among blood mothers, other mothers, and women-centered networks.[5]

Similarly Gloria Wade-Gayles makes an explicit case for considering "our mothers' faith" as a means of celebrating ancestral connections via music, rituals, symbols, and belief systems in *My Soul Is a Witness*. These systems augment the ways that culture, race, gender, religion, and spirituality are foundational to black women's identities. Notably Wade-Gayles relies on two oral formats for communication of black women's rich stories of spirituality: storytelling and testimony. Layli Maparyan's *The Womanist Idea* extends our understanding of black women's diverse spirituality and suggests that rather than being limited to the assumed biological origins, mothering is open and available to anyone. Maparyan contends that care for other humans and other black women invokes an ethic or spirit of caretaking or "motherly stewardship."[6] In short, recent considerations of the broadly applicable nature of mothering as led by Collins, Wade-Gayles, and Maparyan have resulted in a broader celebration of women's cultures while disrupting associations of motherhood as exclusive to femaleness (biology).

Whether treated as a radical form of activism, a sacred mode for communicating spirituality, or as enacting an ethic of caretaking, black mothering has become a largely accepted means for considering how knowledge is passed on within and among black women. Less, however, has been documented about how black women appropriate the knowledge they receive specifically from their grandmothers.[7] Yet critical reflection on modes of black intellectual and cultural production—literature, the arts, dance, religion, and music—reveal the numerous ways that black women rely upon the insights and instruction passed on from other black women, especially from their grandmother figures. Take music, for example. At the beginning of the 1995 gospel hit "If It Had Not Been for the Lord on My Side," Helen Baylor opens with a powerful testimony—the recounting of her experiences with substance abuse, sexual promiscuity, a veering away from her Christian upbringing, and the role that God played in her deliverance from those travails and her return to the Christian faith.[8] Essential to Baylor's testimony is her grandmother, who took on the pivotal role of intercessor during the most difficult moments of her life. Baylor's grandmother, in fact, "prayed her through" her addiction to drugs and alcohol and was instrumental to Baylor's subsequent devotion to an explicitly Christian life.

Baylor's testimony is significant for five reasons: first, it exemplifies—in a very public way—a black woman's most intimate religious sentiments and experiences; second, her story reveals black women's complex (and at times contradictory) relationship to formal religion; third, it centers the importance of community-led notions of faith; fourth, it models the efficacy of testimony as an instrumental, poetic form for communicating religious identity, hallowed relationality, and sacred temporality; and fifth, it positions the role of the spiritual intercessor-ancestor in that of the grand-maternal figure. This essay uses Baylor's story, with particular emphasis on her relationship with her grandmother, as a framing device for considering how testimony communicates black women's varied experiences of spirituality, becomes a means of navigating the past and the present, and functions as a mode for connecting women to ancestral and intergenerational understandings of faith.

In addition to interrogating the image, significance, and role of "the praying grandmother," this chapter uses the South as exemplified in the life and work of Zora Neale Hurston, my personal relationships with my own grandmothers (which, like Hurston's, are directly impacted by my upbringing as a southerner), and my research in the South Carolina low country as a backdrop for investigating how black women negotiate and reconcile instruction received from their grandmothers with their own experiences. My reliance on these examples—the legacy of Hurston, my research in South Carolina, and my relationships with my grandmothers—serves a twofold purpose. On the one hand, using these illustrations takes seriously all of the features laid bare in Baylor's story and positions testimony as a legitimate rhetorical device that also bears real-life, intergenerational implications for black women. On the other hand, it reflects an intentional methodology that considers the ways that I too am a beneficiary of the knowledge forms that continue to be passed on to, by, and for black women. Essential to this chapter is the following question: How do "grandmother wits" become a means for understanding black women's religious "herstories"?[9]

I contend that grand-matrilineal ways of knowing take on four particular forms: *perspective knowledge*, the ways of knowing directly influenced by one's particular point of view and location; *experiential knowledge*, the awareness that comes from what one actually lives and observes (versus imagines or hypothesizes); *faith knowledge*, the understanding that derives from a deep belief in something greater than oneself (which may or may not be explicitly tied to a deity); and *conjure knowledge*, the reliance upon intuitive, ancestral traditions that contest Western notions of reason. These forms of knowledge are as valid a historical source as more traditional (written) forms of archival information because of how they are internalized and experientially drawn upon by black women, and because of how they have historical implications comparable to those of written sources. By utilizing grand-maternal knowledge(s) of faith and their testimonial forms of transmission, we can reimagine and expand the archives of black women's herstories.

Grandma Zora: "All Good Traits and Leanings Come from the Mother's Side"

From the mid- to the late twentieth century, a proliferation of acclaimed black women's writings resulted in a public affirmation of black women's perspectives as a legitimate narrative standpoint.[10] In addition to an increase in nuanced expressions of black women's experiences, literary contributions in nonfiction, poetry, and fiction established black women's stories as valid sources of historical knowledge. Although there were numerous black women writers who paved the way for these popularized insertions of black women's stories, writings by Maya Angelou, Ntozake Shange, Toni Cade, Gloria Naylor, Toni Morrison, and Alice Walker solidified the growing lineage of black women's poetics.[11] Instrumental to this development was the reclamation of the life and work of the folklorist, anthropologist, and storyteller Zora Neale Hurston (1891–1960), which was fueled in great part by Walker.[12] The reversal of Hurston's relative obscurity in the annals of the American literary imagination, and the declaration of Hurston as a formidable anthropological collector and literary, scholarly, folk tour de force, has led to an array of

Zora Neale Hurston beating the *hountar*, or mama drum, 1937. Library of Congress Prints and Photographs Division.

scholarship that engages Hurston's writings and invokes her unprecedented panache, unfettered individualism, undeniable artistry, and boundless imagination.[13] Notably the increased attention to Hurston's life and work has resulted in her subsequent veneration to that of a sacred ancestor figure. It is thus fitting that any foray into the realm of testimony-as-archive begin with Hurston, who has become, by all contemporary accounts, a black literary grand-matriarch.[14]

In Hurston's award-winning but "controversial" autobiography *Dust Tracks on a Road* (1942), she offers a brief but important testimonial phrase that guides her life from the time she is a child and throughout her adulthood: "All good traits and leanings come from the mother's side."[15] This "universal female gospel" was offered at a time in Hurston's life when differences between her and her siblings (including that her father treated her much more harshly than her sister Sarah) crystallized in her memory. Hurston learned this adage from her mother, Lucy, who offered it to Hurston as a means of letting her know exactly which behaviors were appropriate and which were not. Included in those deemed inappropriate was behaving "like no-count Negroes and poor-white trash—too poor to sit in the house—[and] had to come outdoors for any pleasure, or hang around somebody else's house."[16]

Even as Hurston loved playing at home, she often, much to her family's dismay (and her father's reproach), had a traveling spirit, and she roamed the streets of her town looking for adventure. Worse, she used her active imagination to conjure elaborate stories that were deemed unsuitable to verbalize, let alone think. She enjoyed wrestling and fighting with boys, was notoriously impudent, and earned a reputation for being too outspoken for her own good. The antithesis of a passive, timid, "mealy mouthed rag doll,"[17] Hurston refused to comply with the gendered norms of her time, was punished (by her father) often, and was relegated to the life of a young loner.

The irony of Hurston's claim about "good traits" is that she internalized it, even as it countered her well-known precociousness. Why would Hurston rely on a "mother wit" when it collided with what she came to know about herself, which was that she was more like her father, John, than anyone wanted to acknowledge? (Perhaps some good traits do in fact come from the father's side?) I contend that it is because of the perspective knowledge of her location and point of view as a young woman in the Hurston family that she made sense of the joys, pains, truths, and contradictions she experienced, and acted accordingly. The reality for Hurston was that even as her mother admonished her to "jump at de sun" and explore every opportunity made available, she would spend her life fighting against those who would rather limit her opportunities.[18] Katie Cannon has suggested, "As a Black woman artist, subjected to the violence of whites, of male superiority, and of poverty, Zora Neale Hurston offered an especially concrete frame of reference for understanding the Black woman as moral agent."[19] Hurston's knowledge of black womanhood did not occur in a vacuum; she was influenced by her mother, Lucy Potts Hurston, who encouraged her daughter's spiritedness, and by her maternal grandmother, Sarah Potts, who discouraged it.

Hurston's relationship with her maternal grandmother was complicated by her mother's choice to marry John, who was considered to be from the wrong side of the tracks.[20] Their relationship was also fraught with tension because Grandma Potts's expectations for young black women often ran in opposition to Zora's precociousness and ambition. Sarah (and her husband, Richard) were by all accounts well off for their time, but were also experientially rooted in the legacies of enslavement and Reconstruction. As such, "Grandma Potts offered moral counsel in light of events and their possible consequence. She tried to warn Hurston of how her actions would offset the prospects of her survival."[21] The counsel Sarah offered was steeped in strategies that would allow Zora to survive injury, sexual assault, lynching, and other horrors that frequently peppered black southern life.[22] It was thus "through the Black community's oral tradition [that] Hurston learned how to live on Black terms—how to resist, to oppose, and to endure the immediate struggles over and against terrifying circumstances."[23]

We can see how Hurston deployed what Delores Williams has called "lifeline politics," the strategies informed by faith, ritual, experience, and thoughts about God to sustain black women as they face various forms of oppression, and used to "hold on to traditional supportive alliances while they struggle to create new relational forms of independence for themselves in the present."[24] These lifeline politics, which I call perspective knowledge, are informed by a black woman's unique experiential lens and develop into a set of beliefs that subsequently guide black women's actions. Critical to perspective knowledge is the cultivation of spaces within a given belief system that accommodates change. In Hurston's case, the lifeline politics that emerged throughout her writings were inherited from deep maternal and grandmaternal ties, were augmented by strategies that would ensure her survival without crushing her spiritedness, were steeped in oral tradition (especially folklore, folk religions, and testimony), and were spirit-driven survival strategies reinforced by practical, moral wisdom.[25] From Grandma Zora's testimony, black women have learned not only how to survive against layered and competing oppressions but how to prevail against these subjugations without suppressing our spirits.

Grandma Annie Mae and Grandma Phyllis: "Humble Pie Is Meant to Be Eaten; Pride Is Meant to Be Swallowed"

By all accounts, Hurston's efforts to reconcile competing and at times conflicting information with her experience was not easy. My life and location as a black woman from the South complements and complicates what we have learned from Grandma Zora. My development as a young woman revolved around competing claims from two grandmaternal figures—my maternal grandmother, Annie Mae, and my paternal grandmother, Phyllis. Their instruction, which was passed down to me directly and via the intermediary role my mother, Gwendolyn, at times served, had everything to do with how to survive as a black woman in the South, how to maintain "the Faith" in the God of Christianity, and how to do so by way of developing a healthy relationship with pride and humility.

Born on September 20, 1929, Annie Mae Brown was a fiercely religious woman. She taught Sunday school at the Methodist church in the town where I grew up and, as far as I know, was always a serious woman of faith, even in her youngest years. Grandma Annie Mae had three siblings and was very close to her grandmother and my great-grandmother, Caroline, who upon meeting the man who would become my grandfather Sanford, immediately turned to her and said, "This one is the man for you. He'll bring you heartache, but more love and joy than you can stand." With that blessing, my grandparents married and moved from upstate South Carolina and began their life in the low country (Moncks Corner) in the all-black neighborhood called West End. According to my grandmother, their life together was largely happy, and she was, in her own words, "blessed with three healthy children, including that baby girl of mine, Gwendolyn." Over the nearly fifty years of their marriage, they faced significant losses, including the death of a fourth child during childbirth, the sudden aneurysm that killed my uncle Roy (the youngest son) at the age of forty-two, the trauma of losing their oldest son, W.C., who returned from Vietnam "shell shocked" and who disappeared and never returned, and seeing my mother wrestle with addictions to various substances. My grandfather—whom I remember as a serious man who rarely spoke, loved country music, and almost always carried around a fifth of liquor—began drinking shortly after the passing of their unnamed child (though, let my grandmother tell it, it had everything to do with "the burdens he brought back with him from the [Korean] War"), and never stopped until the day he died.

When my mother returned to work after having me, it was Grandma Annie Mae who looked after my older brother, Maurice, and me until we reached school age, and every Sunday Grandma Annie Mae took us to church. I spent nearly every day of my life with Grandma Annie Mae, from the time I was born until I left for college, and we were extremely close. I learned almost everything I know about cooking, "turning a hot house cool," greasing my scalp, removing odors from a house (a dish of vinegar), and how to "send up my timber" in such a way that God would know that I was serious. It was also from her that I inherited the knowledge of how to "cut my eyes" to convey exactly what words could not—a survival strategy I continue to use today. Our closeness never seemed to be impeded by the distance in age and time between us or the differences that would eventually emerge between us in regard to how to live one's faith in God. Even as I was grateful to be present when she transitioned in 2007, I was devastated, not only because of the loss of someone who seemed to love me unconditionally but because she was the person who knew me best, and she never tried to control me or thwart my outspokenness and penchant for truth-telling.

My fond memories of and experience with Grandma Annie Mae stood in direct opposition to my relationship with my paternal grandmother. Phyllis Brown, who was also born in 1929 (January 21), was one of fourteen children and walked with a steady limp all of her life due to an early bout with polio. Grandma Phyllis has left my family with what has arguably been two of its biggest scandals: first, that at age fourteen she gave birth to my father and, with my paternal family's help, sustained the lie that my father was her youngest sibling; second, that she had an illicit affair with a married man half her age. Grandma Phyllis was notoriously mean, and it was hard to listen to her because she fussed and because her words always contained an underlying sting, edge, and grating quality. Whether it was about how to properly wash dishes, how to pray, the importance of going to church, or how to behave, Grandma Phyllis was always scolding me about some thing or another. When I now consider the time and circumstances in which she was born (and the conditions under which she gave birth to my father), I understand why she might have been so prone to rage during her lifetime. And, despite her meanness, she had a wicked sense of humor and was deeply religious, and her devotion to God was peppered with all of those elements: fierceness, wit, and devotion. Regardless of how easy it would have been not to do so, my father tried his best to maintain a relationship with her, which meant that we spent many weeks during the summer with her in her Charleston home.[26] This resulted in my having to consistently make sense, at a fairly young age, of what to do with two grandmothers, who were so very different but who offered advice, instruction, and prayers and did their best to show their love for me and their hopes that I would always stay "in the will of God."

Despite their differences, Phyllis and Annie Mae shared a profound sense of righteousness, with clear parameters for what constituted right and wrong and where a young black girl's place was within those structures. Their shared perspective knowledge was informed by a deep moral consciousness and faith in God. Their expressions of Christianity were fairly conservative (though not fundamentalist), for even as their own lives offered them plenty of reason to do so, they could never imagine questioning God. And questioning God was something that I was especially adept at and an aspect of my personality that perpetually vexed them both. My formative years with my grandmothers were framed by a refrain they shared: "I won't stop praying for you, LeRhonda." Prayer was a way of ensuring ongoing and open lines of communication between us and God, and a way for them to intervene on my behalf when I did not and could not know better for myself. Like Baylor, my grandmothers believed in the power of prayer to change circumstances for anyone, especially me.

Their grandmother wits, then, were their own form of faith knowledge and were informed explicitly by what they knew about God and how they lived their lives as a result of that knowledge. Their advice was a form of intercessory prayer for me and, like prayer, was a constant reminder of the greater sights upon which I should set my focus. I vividly recall the day Grandma Annie Mae offered her proverbial wisdom about humility. I was giddy about having won the competition for best essay in the entire second grade. I rode the bus to my grandmother's house unable to contain my excitement. I burst in the door, exclaimed my greeting, and launched into my newest achievement. My grandmother, who was in the kitchen preparing my biscuits, removed her hands from the dough, wiped them on her apron, and stared at me, and for several moments did not utter a word. I did not know what she was going to say, but I knew it was something I would not like. "LeRhonda"—she paused for effect—"humble pie is meant to be eaten. Shall I cut you a slice?" My huge grin, which had already dissipated, morphed into a grimace. "Grandmaaaaaa! What did I do wrong? I thought I did good!" She then explained, with the utmost calm, that I had done something that should be celebrated, but that *how* I marked my accomplishments was what mattered most. The lesson, though, came not in a lecture about achievement but about making biscuits for those who are hungry. Even in that moment, her focus on doing for others—a key marker of her faith in God—remained at the forefront of her instruction. And in that exchange I learned the importance of staying humble and remaining grounded not only in spite of but also *because* of my successes. "Humble pie is meant to be eaten" thus became a reminder of Grandma Annie Mae's wisdom, inasmuch as it was a reminder of how she always hoped, expected, and prayed that I would do the right thing for myself and for others.

My recall of Grandma Phyllis's lesson is not as distinct or clear, but it is memorable for how it became a refrain she would randomly offer. When I completed my chores, including the painstaking task of hand-washing laundry, rather than congratulate me or suggest that I did well, she would proffer, "Pride is meant to be swallowed!" If I got an attitude because of being asked to do something I did not like (which happened more times than I could count), she would chime, "Pride is meant to be swallowed!" When I was accepted to Duke University, I remember calling her with the news. She told me, "Good for you! Now don't forget: pride is meant to be swallowed!" Grandma Phyllis's catchphrase became so common in my family that whenever my brother or members of my maternal family would mock or imitate Grandma Phyllis, we would parrot, "Pride is meant to be swallowed!" and laugh hysterically. There even came a time when Grandma Annie Mae would combine my grandmother wits, saying, "Humble pie is meant to be eaten; pride is meant to be swallowed, LeRhonda."

Grandma Phyllis's and Grandma Annie Mae's admonishments to me regarding pride and humility emerged from their experiences of growing up in an era when poverty, segregation, and racial caste practices limited young black women's access. Their grandmother wits thus communicated to me the principles they saw as essential to survival as a young black woman in South Carolina. They were reminders and lessons about how to survive such circumstances, and how to do so with one's humanity intact. Moreover, rooted in these principles was their own form of "womanist god-talk,"[27] whereby their experiential knowledge fashioned from day-to-day lived experience and observations informed their faith knowledge generated from their testimonies and encounters with God, and vice versa. My subsequent internalization of their adages is an ongoing reminder that my grandmothers were praying for me and that their hopes for me surpassed the constrictions of time and geography. Through my grandmothers' efforts to positively intervene in my life, they sowed the seeds of a rooted, survivalist pragmatism informed by belief in something greater than myself.

"But I Had a Praying Grandmother"

Through Grandma Zora, Grandma Annie Mae, and Grandma Phyllis, we see how grand-maternal wisdom—when passed on to granddaughters—becomes a mechanism for black women to draw upon the past in order to inform their present. These women, and the grandmother wits they shared, connect women to three forms of grand-maternal knowledge: (1) perspective knowledge, which is informed by a black woman's specific context and location and develops over time into a set of principles that guides her actions; (2) experiential knowledge, whereby a woman's life directs what she knows about, how she sees, and how she engages with the world; and (3) faith knowledge, so that what women know and believe about God and/or Spirit guides their rituals, choices, and actions. These three ways of knowing overlap and work together to structure black women's sense of self. They have also been a long-standing part of black intellectual histories, even when they have not always been named or identified as such. In addition to my own experience as a young woman growing up in the South, my scholarly work about Gullah/Geechee women and black women's responses to representations in popular film has revealed that intergenerational understandings are not only important to faith and religion but are imperative to how black women see themselves in and how they navigate this world.[28]

A closer look at the lives of Grandma Zora, Grandma Phyllis, and Grandma Annie Mae, the wisdoms they have passed on, and the black women to whom they have passed said insights reveals an equally important fourth category: conjure knowledge, or the reliance upon folkways that explicitly draw from ancestral traditions, experiences, and narratives and, as such, explicitly counter Western practices of rationality. As conjure knowledge contests the linear notions of time and space espoused within Western traditions, it also most explicitly connects black women's ways of knowing to global, diasporic knowledge, which Sheila Smith McKoy calls "diaspora temporality."[29] Black women's dependence upon cultural folkways as evidenced here readily places them in a global, transnational conversation where strategies are created to disrupt the various matrices of domination that seek to oppress black women.

Conjure knowledge is thus a cyclical wisdom that permeates the foundations of black intellectual thought. Conjure knowledge is the aspect of black women's wisdom traditions that is most comparable to faith knowledge because of its emphasis on belief, but is distinct because that belief is not connected to a divinity. Rather it is expressly tied to an inner voice, intuition, or inner power that draws directly from ancestors, ancestral traditions, and ancestral powers. Conjure knowledge inhabits the spaces where, as Grandmother Toni (Morrison) explains, the ancestor is foundation, and two worlds of knowing where superstition and magic (the supernatural) blend in enhancing (versus limiting) acceptance of a real-world rootedness.[30]

Conjure knowledge is also the feature of grand-maternal wisdom that allows younger generations of women—myself included—to reconcile competing claims that emerge when our experiences run up against the knowledge that we have heard and internalized from our grandmothers and, more important, to create our own knowledge anew. This helps us understand, in part, why Grandma Zora constructed her faith knowledge from an amalgamation of "certain things that seemed to her to be true."[31] It also explains, in part, why Grandma Zora had an affinity with, was initiated into, and readily applied folk and non-Christian religious systems, including voodoo, hoodoo, and superstition, alongside her Christian upbringing.[32] My grandmothers, who were similar to the women I describe in *Talking to the Dead*, were open to folkways like dreams and visions that communicated ancestral expectations, accepted the belief in second sight, or the ability to foresee the future, and respected the work of local conjurers. Whether through the image of the praying grandmother, as espoused by Baylor, or the lives of Grandma Zora, Grandma Annie Mae, and Grandma Phyllis, conjure knowledge has always been an undercurrent in black women's testimonies. Black women, as James Manigault-Bryant and I have argued, "effectively call upon conjure to face the very real effects of modernity and, more importantly, to configure strategies on which they draw to help move *beyond* the effects of modernity. Conjure becomes the mystical, metaphysical course that Black women summon to survive with their bodies, minds, and souls intact."[33] When considering the multiple and layered sources of black women's spirituality, one must always consider the role of ancestors and folk traditions and how they are represented in the form of conjure knowledge.[34]

Finally, conjure knowledge, like the other three knowledge forms presented in this essay, inform and shape each other and is also present in the image upon which this essay is framed—that of Baylor's praying grandmother. Baylor's testimony calls upon her grandmother, and the phrase "But I had a praying grandmother" becomes a repeated, sung trope. In that practice of repeating a musical phrase, Baylor in essence conjures her grandmother's spirit within the space of her testimony. Baylor says it was at her grandmother's encouragement that she began singing as a child, that it was her grandmother who first told her that "God would use her" one day, and she identifies her grandmother as the person who fasted and prayed on her behalf. Baylor's initial relationship with God derived from what she learned through her grandmother's experiential knowledge and faith knowledge. After all, it was the learning that she attained from her grandmother that Baylor, in her own words, "knew enough to call on the name of Jesus" for her salvation and deliverance from substance abuse. At the same time, Baylor constructed her own faith, experiential, and perspective knowledge from her ability to use conjure knowledge to invoke her grandmother's wisdom. This cyclical process of drawing from her grandmother's experience to inform her own ensured that she constructed a life she deemed suitable for herself.

Throughout this essay I have made a case for considering the information passed on by black grandmothers as a continuation of black women's intellectual traditions. Even though they are not all public figures, these four grandmothers—Helen Baylor's grandmother, Grandma Zora, Grandma Phyllis, and Grandma Annie Mae—have left extraordinary testaments to their granddaughters, but also are sources of archival knowledge upon which we may draw. These narratives reveal that historically, black women have negotiated in-between spaces, where they strive to reconcile the knowledge they inherit from the women in their lives with what they know and see to be experientially true for themselves—especially contradictory information. These stories also expose the ways that black women's spiritual identities are deeply tied to nearly four centuries of a black intellectual tradition where black women's voices have been "transmitted orally and in writing, through religious teachings, speeches and tests, domestic arts and everyday activities."[35] The four forms of knowledge described here are also intimately connected to black women's theoretical and intellectual traditions, even as they may go unrecognized.

Through our grandmothers' testimonies, black women can actively wrestle with how we hold on to or even reclaim the intergenerational understandings of faith, religion, and spirituality that shaped our grandmothers. We are also empowered to decide whether or not many of those intergenerational understandings are advantageous for black women today. This is an important ability to have, especially as black women navigate similarly complex, tumultuous, and contradictory terrains that are against, even hostile toward black women's well-being and survival. In the end the image of the praying grandmother and the wisdom she passes on to her granddaughters are robust ways to consider black women's archives anew. These are, in fact, stories to be passed on.

Notes

1. For a more extensive review of black women's contributions to black American intellectual history, see Beverly Guy-Sheftall, ed., *Words of Fire: An Anthology of African-American Feminist Thought* (New York: New Press, 1995); Mia Bay, Farah J. Griffin, Martha S. Jones, and Barbara D. Savage, eds., *Toward an Intellectual History of Black Women* (Chapel Hill: University of North Carolina Press, 2015).

2. See especially Alice Walker, *In Search of Our Mother's Gardens: Womanist Prose* (New York: Harcourt Brace, 1983); Cheryl Townsend Gilkes, "The Roles of Church and Community Mothers: Ambivalent American Sexism of Fragmented American Familyhood?," *Journal of Feminist Studies in Religion* 2, no. 1 (1986): 41–59; Delores S. Williams, *Sisters in the Wilderness: The Challenge of Womanist God-Talk* (Maryknoll, N.Y.: Orbis Books, 1993); Katie Geneva Cannon, *Katie's Cannon: Womanism and the Soul of the Black Community* (New York: Continuum, 1995); Gloria Wade-Gayles, *My Soul Is a Witness: African-American Women's Spirituality* (Boston: Beacon Press, 1995).

3. Daniel Patrick Moynihan, *The Negro Family: The Case for National Action* (Washington, D.C.: US Department of Labor, 1965).

4. Hortense Spillers, "Mama's Baby, Papa's Maybe: An American Grammar Book," *Diacritics* 17, no. 2 (1987): 64–81.

5. Patricia Hill Collins, *Black Feminist Thought*, Classics edition (New York: Routledge, 2009). See especially chapter 8, "Black Women and Motherhood."

6. Layli Maparyan, *The Womanist Idea* (New York: Routledge, 2011), 62–65.

7. See Mamie Garvin Fields and Karen Fields, *Lemon Swamp and Other Places* (New York: Free Press, 1983), which centers dialogue and partnership between a black grandmother and granddaughter; Karen Fields, "What One Cannot Remember Mistakenly," in *History and Memory in African-American Culture*, edited by Geneviève Fabre and Robert O' Meally (New York: Oxford University Press, 1994), 150–63; Aishah Shahidah Simmons, "Celebrating the Extraordinary Who Are Relegated to Ordinary: A Tribute to Rebecca White Simmons Chapman and Juanita Cranford Robinson Watson," *Feminist Wire* May 12, 2013, http://www.thefeministwire.com/2013/05/celebrating-the-extraordinary-who-are-relegated-to-ordinary-a-tribute-to-rebecca-white-simmons-chapman-and-juanita-cranford-robinson-watson/.

8. I am indebted to James Manigault-Bryant's articulation of testimony as a "confessional rhythmic style that articulates the philosophical meaning of the cry for the individual and the community" in "The Poetics of Testimony and Blackness in the Theology of James H. Cone," *CLR James Journal* 10, no. 1 (2004): 48.

9. Lucinda H. MacKethan, "Mother Wit: Humor in Afro-American Women's Autobiography" *Studies in American Humor*, new series 2, 4, nos. 1–2 (1985): 51–61, presents mother wit as a vernacular, humorous, yet pragmatic collection conveying commonsense expectations passed on within African American women's communities. See also Alan Dundes, *Mother Wit from the Laughing Barrel* (Englewood Cliffs, N.J.: Prentice-Hall, 1973); Geneva Smitherman, *Talkin and Testifyin: The Language of Black America* (Boston: Houghton Mifflin, 1977).

10. Mari Evans, *Black Women Writers (1950–1980): A Critical Evaluation* (New York: Anchor Press/Doubleday, 1984); Marjorie Pryse and Hortense J. Spillers, *Conjuring: Black Women, Fiction, and Literary Tradition* (Bloomington: Indiana University Press, 1985); Houston A. Baker Jr., *Workings of the Spirit: The Poetics of Afro-American Women's Writing* (Chicago: University of Chicago Press, 1991).

11. Maya Angelou, *I Know Why the Caged Bird Sings* (New York: Random House, 1970); Ntozake Shange, *for colored girls who have considered suicide when the rainbow is enuf: a choreopoem* (New York: Collier Books, 1977); Toni Cade Bambara, *The Salt Eaters* (New York: Random House, 1980); Gloria Naylor, *The Women of Brewster Place* (New York: Penguin Books, 1982); Toni Morrison, *Beloved* (New York: Knopf, 1987) and *The Bluest Eye* (New York: Knopf, 1993); Alice Walker, *The Color Purple* (New York: Harcourt, Brace, Jovanovich, 1992).

12. Walker's efforts to seek Hurston out as a model led to the monumental identification of Hurston's unmarked grave in Fort Pierce, Florida, as well as an intense reclamation of Hurston's literary contributions. See Walker, *In Search of Our Mothers' Gardens*; Zora Neale Hurston, *I Love Myself When I Am Laughing . . . And Then Again When I Am Looking Mean and Impressive* (New York: Feminist Press, 1979); Thadious M. Davis, "The Polarities of Space: Segregation and Alice Walker's Intervention in Southern Studies," in Bay et al., *Toward an Intellectual History of Black Women*, 160–77.

13. A brief selection of these sources includes Robert Hemenway, *Zora Neale Hurston: A Literary Biography* (Urbana: University of Illinois Press, 1977); Katie Geneva

Cannon, "Resources for a Constructive Ethic in the Life and Work of Zora Neale Hurston," *Journal of Feminist Studies in Religion* 1, no. 1 (1985): 37–51; Delores S. Williams, "Women's Oppression and Lifeline Politics in Black Women's Religious Narratives," *Journal of Feminist Studies in Religion* 1, no. 2 (1985): 59–71; Valerie Boyd, *Wrapped in Rainbows: The Life of Zora Neale Hurston* (New York: Scribner, 2003); Karla Caplan, *Zora Neale Hurston: A Life in Letters* (New York: Anchor Books, 2003); Tiffany Patterson, *Zora Neale Hurston and a History of Southern Life* (Philadelphia: Temple University Press, 2005); James A. Manigault-Byrant and LeRhonda S. Manigault-Bryant, "Conjuring Pasts and Ethnographic Presents in Zora Neale Hurston's Modernity," *Journal of Africana Religions* 4, no. 2 (2016): 225–35.

14. Jennifer Jordan, "Feminist Fantasies: Zora Neale Hurston's *Their Eyes Were Watching God*," *Tulsa Studies in Women's Literature* 7, no. 1 (1988): 104–17.

15. Hurston, *Dust Tracks on a Road* (New York: HarperCollins, 1996), 20. Biographer Robert Hemenway has noted that *Dust Tracks on a Road* omits important information, including Hurston's date of birth, place of birth, the name of her first husband, and details regarding her second marriage; ignores the public record; and avoids placing personal events within a historical framework.

16. Hurston, *Dust Tracks on a Road*, 20.

17. Hurston, *Dust Tracks on a Road*, 21.

18. Hurston, *Dust Tracks on a Road*, 21.

19. Cannon, "Resources for a Constructive Ethic," 39.

20. Hurston's biographers Robert Hemenway and Valerie Boyd have done a masterful job of capturing the fraught relational nature of the between the Hurston and Potts families. See chapter 1 of Hemenway's *Zora Neale Hurston* and chapters 4 and 5 of Boyd's *Wrapped in Rainbows*.

21. Cannon, "Resources for a Constructive Ethic in Hurston," 40.

22. Hurston, *Dust Tracks on a Road*, 46.

23. Cannon, "Resources for a Constructive Ethic in Hurston," 39.

24. Williams, "Women's Oppression and Lifeline Politics," 68.

25. Hurston's rootedness in and valuing of oral tradition was intimately tied to the power of testimony as an oral form and her relationship with her father, who was well known throughout central Florida for the impressive sound of his voice and his oratory skills. See chapter 3 of Boyd's *Wrapped in Rainbows*. In "Resources for a Constructive Ethic," Katie Cannon reveals how the deathbed speech of the character Lucy in *Jonah's Gourd Vine* (which is based on Hurston's mother) accounts for the deep proverbial wisdoms that marked Hurston's transition from childhood into adulthood.

26. I have previously written about my summers with Grandma Phyllis, including the time I spent at Emanuel African Methodist Episcopal Church. See "#prayforcharleston," *Black Perspectives*, June 19, 2015, http://www.aaihs.org/prayforcharleston/.

27. See Williams, *Sisters in the Wilderness*, preface.

28. See LeRhonda S. Manigault-Bryant, *Talking to the Dead: Religion, Music, and Lived Memory among Gullah/Geechee Women* (Durham, N.C.: Duke University Press, 2014); LeRhonda S. Manigault-Bryant, Tamura A. Lomax, and Carol B. Duncan, eds., *Womanist and Black Feminist Responses to Tyler Perry's Productions* (New York: Palgrave Macmillan, 2014).

29. Sheila Smith McKoy, "The Limbo Contest: Diaspora Temporality and Its Reflection in *Praisesong for the Widow* and *Daughters of the Dust*," *Callaloo* 22, no. 1 (1999): 208–22.

30. Toni Morrison, "Rootedness: The Ancestor as Foundation," in *Black Women Writers, 1950–1980*, edited by Mari Evans (New York: Anchor/Doubleday, 1983), 342.

31. Hurston, *Dust Tracks on a Road*, 277.

32. See especially chapters 16, 17, 26, and 27 in Boyd's *Wrapped in Rainbows*.

33. Manigault-Bryant and Manigault-Bryant, "Conjuring Pasts and Ethnographic Presents," 230.

34. I discuss the power and use of conjure at length in chapter 2 of *Talking to the Dead* (66–103). See also Delores S. Williams, "Sources of Black Female Spirituality: The Ways of 'the Old Folks' and 'Women Writers,'" in *My Soul Is a Witness: African-American Women's Spirituality*, edited by Gloria Wade-Gayles (Boston: Beacon Press, 1995), 187–91; Tracey Hucks, "'Burning with a Flame in America': African American Women in African-Derived Traditions," *Journal of Feminist Studies in Religion* 17, no. 2 (2001): 89–106; Yvonne Chireau, *Black Magic: Religion and the African American Conjuring Tradition* (Berkeley: University of California Press, 2006).

35. Kristin Waters and Carol B. Conaway, *Black Women's Intellectual Traditions: Speaking Their Minds* (Lebanon, N.H.: University Press of New England, 2007), 2. See also the framing of this vast history of black women's intellectual traditions as espoused in Bay et al., *Toward an Intellectual History of Black Women*.

Part III

✦

Racial Politics and Struggles for Social Justice

Introduction

Pero Gaglo Dagbovie

Though the "black intellectual tradition" has existed since the birth of African American intellectual culture (and even earlier for Afrocentric theorists), this specific term was arguably first popularized within certain black studies circles by the historian Manning Marable in the 1980s and 1990s.[1] In his 2000 *Souls* essay "Black Studies and the Racial Mountain" that also appeared his state-of-the-field edited volume, *Dispatches from the Ebony Tower: Intellectuals Confront the African American Experience*, Marable further refined his conceptualization of the "black intellectual tradition." For him, this praxis- and time-honored ideological institution is simply defined as "the critical thought and perspectives of intellectuals of African descent and scholars of black America and Africa and the African diaspora" that are descriptive, corrective, and prescriptive in orientation.[2] While the three thought-provoking essays in this section focus on different subject matter and, as scholarly writings, are potentially prescriptive in quite limiting terms, they do indeed, in their own ways, belong to what Marable broadly envisioned as the black intellectual tradition and certainly speak to the black intellectual traditions that the philosopher Lewis R. Gordon has more recently outlined.[3] At the most basic level, each essay is also an expression of the loosely defined field of black intellectual history. Each author practices "thinking historically" (i.e., situating and analyzing their subject matter within their appropriate historical contexts) and rereads and/or uncovers and dissects telling primary source documents. More concretely, in their own distinct ways all of the authors address overarching issues of racial politics, black political thought, wars of words, and notions of the enduring quest for social justice, a key—although often vaguely defined—ingredient of the black intellectual tradition. The authors are also revisionist historians. They strive to explicitly challenge the canonical interpretations and predominant, orthodox historiographical trends in their respective subspecialties. Guy Emerson Mount argues that amateur and professionally trained historians have, with few exceptions, drastically misinterpreted Frederick Douglass's controversial 1884 marriage to Helen Pitts. Ibram X. Kendi disputes the "prevailing historiography" on the evolution of antiracist and assimilationist ideas in the middle of the twentieth century. And Ashley Farmer challenges the historiography on Black Power–era cultural nationalism as well as women's and gender studies scholarship that has tended to frame black female cultural nationalists as "victims of sexism" who were "unable to theoretically or organizationally challenge the patriarchal gender constructs of cultural nationalist groups."

In "Historical Ventriloquy: Black Thought and Sexual Politics in the Interracial Marriage of Frederick Douglass," Mount argues that the historic and highly politicized interracial union between Douglass and Pitts during the "nadir" of black life has been misinterpreted by generations of writers and historians since the late nineteenth century. Mount asserts that his essay is the first serious, in-depth, and objective treatment of how this abolitionist icon's black and white contemporaries viewed his marriage to Pitts, a union that Mount dubs "a pivotal test case" for race relations and black progress during the late nineteenth century. His analysis is multifaceted. Not only does he share with his readers what Douglass himself said about his marriage in newspapers like the widely read *Washington Post*, Douglass's vision of race relations and of "a widespread mixed race America," and how Douglass reacted to the mainstream contemporary press's sometimes disparaging coverage of this notable matrimony, but he also excavates how the black press and leading African American spokespersons perceived and judged his decision to marry a white woman at a time when Ida B. Wells resolutely insisted that more than a few black men were lynched for supposedly raping white women. Mount criticizes generations of Douglass biographers for failing to objectively and accurately portray Douglass's interracial marriage by, among other miscalculations, ignoring the diversity of Douglass's black contemporaries' reactions and by citing only those who criticized Douglass's commitment to his second wife. In fact Mount maintains that even professionally trained historians, beginning with Benjamin Quarles—who authored the first scholarly biography on Douglass, in 1948—grossly misinterpreted the Douglass-Pitts union. "At the very least, the scholarship on the Douglass marriage represents a glaring historiographical blunder," Mount surmises. "The Douglass marriage also demonstrates what can go wrong when we unquestionably follow a single, codified black intellectual tradition." Mount concludes his essay with a call to arms and a warning of some sort to historians like the Pulitzer Prize winner William S. McFeely, proclaiming that black millennial historians will not fall victims to "historical ventriloquy."

In "Reigning Assimilationists and Defiant Black Power: The Struggle to Define and Regulate Racist Ideas," Kendi expands upon arguments that he raised in his exhaustive National Book Award–winning *Stamped from the Beginning: The Definitive History of Racist Ideas* (2016) by scrutinizing how the ideologies of assimilationist thinkers—who claimed to debunk the racial discourse of past and contemporary eugenicists—were forthrightly challenged by a diverse group of Black Power–era theorists. According to Kendi, Black Power–era activists' and intellectuals' decentralized efforts to redefine, deconstruct, and reconceptualize racism and assimilationists' complex and misleading racial discourse were "one of the most important developments in the long history of the Black intellectual tradition." Implicit in this assertion is Kendi's contention that, with the exception of Malcolm X, who was assassinated on the eve of the Black Power movement and was one of the campaign's chief progenitors, antiracist theorists during the modern civil rights movement did not effectively dispute or even recognize assimilationists' reactionary racial/racist discourse. Instead, Kendi argues, more conservative civil rights activists were preoccupied with discrediting their more militant ideological foes. After outlining the racist, pseudo-scientific theories of leading eugenicists and, more important, the beliefs and convictions of cultural assimilationists such as Franz Boas, Ruth Benedict (who in 1940 offered the first consensual, scholarly definition of racism), E. Franklin Frazier, Gunnar Myrdal, Theodosius Dobzhansky, Ashley Montagu, Daniel Patrick Moynihan, and Nathan Glazer, among others, Kendi chronicles how a range of leaders, spokespersons, and scholars challenged "America's domineering assimilationist ideas" and also identified assimilationists as racists. This antiracist and anti-assimilationist camp is indeed a diverse group of scholars and activists, including, among others, Andrew Billingsley, Joyce Ladner, Black Panther Party theorists, a post-1967 Martin Luther King Jr., Stokely Carmichael and Charles V. Hamilton, and black feminists like Frances Beal. In Kendi's estimation, following the assassination of King in 1968, Black Power intellectuals vigorously challenged assimilationism from both inside and outside of the academy. Kendi's sweeping reading of a wide array of primary sources is compelling, convincing, and unambiguous. In the end he draws attention to the fact that Black Power intellectuals were not able to totally dismantle assimilationists' racial discourse, which "carries on to this day." A staunch, old-school-minded black studies practitioner, Kendi concludes his essay by insinuating that future African Americanists must still challenge detrimental assimilationist ideas, however subtle and veiled they might be.

Unlike Mount and Kendi, Ashley D. Farmer focuses on a group of black women's political thought and intellectual innovation. Specifically she complicates the normative interpretations of black women's so-called submissive positions in popular and impactful Black Power–era cultural nationalist organizations. In "Becoming African Women: Women's Cultural Nationalist Theorizing in the US Organization and the Committee for Unified Newark," by positioning various previously overlooked black women cultural nationalists as ideologues, leaders, fault-finders, and catalysts of change, Farmer contributes to what she calls scholarship on "Black Power intellectualism." She treats Kawaidist women's writings and philosophies as revealing and legitimate sources of black intellectual history and highlights that these cultural nationalist women struck a balance between what the male leadership expected them to do and what they wanted to accomplish. In particular she analyzes how black women in Maulana Karenga's short-lived Los Angeles–based organization, the Committee for Unified Newark (CFUN)—a black cultural nationalist organization composed of activists from United Sisters, Sisters of Black Culture, United Brothers, the Spirit House, and the Black Community and Development who espoused, qualified, and modified Karenga's Kawaida Defense theory—and Amiri Baraka's Congress of Afrikan People strategically reconceptualized the conventional and traditional roles of black women in their scores of publications and hands-on activities, such as CFUN's well-attended three-day 1974 Afrikan Women's Conference. Farmer coherently frames her analysis by briefly recounting the history of US and by describing how they originally delineated gender-specific roles that marginalized and limited women's participation. While women in US may have initially bought more into the organization's restrictive gender constructs, in the late 1960s black women theorists in the Malaika (US's female auxiliary) began to artic-ulate new roles for women, challenge restrictive Kawaidist gender constructs and hierarchies, negotiate and expand the notion of "women's work," rede-fine the politics of black liberation, and institutionalize the "African woman ideal" in discursive spaces, such as US's news organ, *Harambee*. Effective in their delivery, Kawaidist women even inspired Karenga to rethink and revise his gender outlook. Farmer explores female cultural nationalists' activities and thought that are rarely discussed by Black Power studies scholars. For instance, in analyzing CFUN, whose day-to-day operations were led by the organization's high-ranking women, the Muminina, and those active in the Women's Division, she examines CFUN's treatise "Mwanamke Nwanandi," also known as the "Nationalist Women's Handbook." According to Farmer, this document became "an integral part of the organization's intellectual pro-duction" that underscored "the importance of cultural nationalism and wom-en's roles within it." Moreover she argues that women in CFUN, "Kawaidist women," adhered to parts of Karenga's and US's masculinist framing of black women's roles in the struggle for black liberation while also championing "progressive" ideas about black women's positions (i.e., challenging black women's roles in the domestic sphere). Because much scholarship has been published on Baraka, Farmer's exploration of his thought is refreshing. In the end Farmer's subjects crafted notions of "the African woman ideal" and deliberately yet prudently altered conventional gender constructs of their times. Like Kendi, Farmer acknowledges change over time, noting that by 1969 black women in CFUN had joined the leadership ranks, engaged in the public sphere, exercised more autonomy, and expanded the notion of "what a woman ought to be and to do."[4]

Notes

1. For Marable's early definitions of the "black intellectual tradition," see Man-ning Marable, "Black Studies: Marxism and the Black Intellectual Tradition," in *The Left Academy: Marxist Scholarship on American Campuses*, edited by Bertell Oilman and Edward Vernoff (New York: Praeger, 1986) , 35–66; Marable, "Black Studies and the Black Intellectual Tradition," *Race and Reason* 4 (1997–98): 3.

2. Manning Marable, "Black Studies and the Racial Mountain," *Souls: A Critical Journal of Black Politics, Culture, and Society* 2 (Summer 2000): 17–36.

3. Simon J. Bronner, ed., *Encyclopedia of American Studies* (Baltimore: Johns Hopkins University Press, 2017), s.v. "Black Intellectual Tradition" (by Lewis R. Gordon), http://eas-ref.press.jhu.edu/view?aid=780 (accessed March 14, 2017).

4. This idiom comes from Stephanie Shaw, *What a Woman Ought to Be and to Do: Black Professional Women during the Jim Crow Era* (Chicago: University of Chicago Press, 1996). Fruitful comparisons could be drawn between the subjects of Farmer's study and black women activists from previous eras, such as the "nadir" period and the vast era of Jim Crow segregation.

Historical Ventriloquy

Black Thought and Sexual Politics in the Interracial Marriage of Frederick Douglass

Guy Emerson Mount

Ongoing struggles for social justice have informed nearly every iteration of the black intellectual tradition. Indeed if there is a single thread that ties together the diverse strands of black intellectual scholarship, it is that present-day political concerns in any given era have always driven, shaped, and animated black historical inquiry. While such a strategy can be powerful and productive in linking diverse black freedom struggles across space and time, it also contains a potential downside: historical ventriloquy.

When the voices of prior black thinkers are ignored, marginalized, or even altered to meet the demands of a present-day political project, however noble its aims may be, historical ventriloquy has taken place. Presentism distorts interpretations of the past. Historical ventriloquy changes the facts. It asks us to believe that black thinkers and black communities said things they never said and thought things they never thought. Sometimes this involves one historian putting words in the mouth of a single black thinker, and other times it involves entire historiographical canons attributing thoughts to a wide segment of prior black populations. Similar to the tendencies uncovered by Barbara Dianne Savage in regard to "the black church" and Hazel Carby in regard to "race men," historical ventriloquy is an ahistorical temptation to project contemporary black thought and politics backward in a way that misrepresents the existential realities of prior black subjects on the ground.[1]

This chapter traces a prime case study in historical ventriloquy. It uncovers how the interracial marriage of Frederick Douglass to Helen Pitts in 1884 has been ignored, distorted, and miswritten over time. Tellingly this is the first article-length exploration of what black thinkers, including Douglass himself, thought about the nineteenth century's most prominent interracial marriage. This fact alone is nothing short of an erasure—an archival silencing. As the famed Haitian anthropologist Michel-Rolph Trouillot asserts, such omissions are rarely accidents.[2] By juxtaposing the limited professional scholarship that exists on this topic against the actual reactions of everyday black people in 1884, it becomes clear that what black people thought about interracial marriage in 1884 bears almost no resemblance to what scholars today think they thought about it.

"A Practical Exemplification of His Views"

Frederick Douglass and Helen Pitts exchanged wedding vows on January 24, 1884.[3] It was not just another marriage. The *Washington Post* proclaimed, "Next to the Emancipation proclamation it is the most important event in the history of the race on this continent." The editors were careful to note that "the late decision of the Supreme court against the constitutionality of the Civil Rights bill" was no exception.[4] Just one year after the Supreme Court dismantled the Civil Rights Acts of 1875 and allowed states to ban interracial marriage, the most prominent black man in America married interracially.[5] His union became a pivotal test case—a national referendum on the meaning of emancipation.

"I have simply exercised the right which the laws accord every citizen," Douglass declared. While identifying as a feminist, he was asserting his patriarchal sovereignty in the one institution that "every man holds most dear and sacred, the affairs of the family."[6] In Douglass's view, shared by many African Americans, the freedom to determine the membership of one's own family was not a special, ancillary privilege to be exercised after all others were secured. Forming a family of one's choosing was a basic, fundamental right of citizenship. Interracial marriages were simply an assumed consequence of emancipation. Marriage equality, in this light, was the starting point, and not the finish line for black people emerging from slavery. It was, in many ways, the cornerstone of emancipation. As one black Civil War veteran said in 1866, "The Marriage Covenant is at the foundation of all our rights."[7]

One of the many other such rights that derived from marriage equality was the protection of family members from a still evolving public sphere and its relentless consumer marketplace. This often took the form of a right to privacy in the so-called domestic sphere. Emboldened by the sanctity of his legal contract, a device crucial to navigating postemancipation market capitalism, Douglass lambasted the press after his marriage.[8] He insisted that they should not "present to the eye of the public curiosity my private affairs."[9] Yet while appealing to privacy, Douglass knew that marriage was also a very public political institution. Any divisions between the public and the private sphere were rhetorical, not ontological.[10] Therefore, in the same breath, Douglass observed, "What the American people object to is not the mixture of the races, but honorable marriage between them."[11] Marriage (in contrast to sexual relationships outside of it) involved a very public claim to equal citizenship and full protection under the law.[12] Marriage in general, and the right of interracial marriage specifically, was also a political demand for absolute equality. Because marriage helped secure a basket of legal rights (contract, inheritance, etc.) and was part of a comprehensive claim to equal citizenship, any attempt made by either the state or social convention to force black people into marriages with exclusively black partners was a restriction on full citizenship. Antimiscegenation laws were consequently the very core of the Jim Crow regime.

Douglass's view of family as "the most dear and sacred" space to exercise the rights of citizenship aligned perfectly with his larger racial theology and overall vision for an America without slavery. When asked to explain the interracial character of his marriage, Douglass flatly rejected the question. The Sage of Anacostia preached, "I conceive that there is no division of races" because "God Almighty made but one race," and "you may say that Frederick Douglass considers himself a member of the one race which exists." Not coincidentally, for Douglass, that "one race" was a long continuum of mixed-race people—with himself standing firmly in the middle. "I am not an African, as may be seen from my features and hair, and it is equally easy to discern that I am not a Caucasian." "All this excitement, then, is caused by my marriage with a woman a few shades lighter than myself. If I had married a black woman there would have been nothing said about it. Yet the disparity in our complexions would have been the same."[13] This appeal to his own multiracial body, and to phenotypic intraracial difference, was much more than a mocking refrain. It was a challenge to the very idea of race itself and its potential future in the wider American polity.

Along with many religiously minded black and white Americans anticipating God's plan for a postemancipation America, Douglass further prophesied that the increased presence of mixed-race people (like himself) and interracial marriages (like his own) meant that "in time the varieties of races will be blended into one."[14] According to Douglass, the future was clear. There were already "a million of intermediate [mixed-race African Americans]. And this will continue."[15] Douglass had promoted a similar position for much of his public career in calling for a new "composite nationality" in America.[16] His words took on an entirely new meaning, however, in light of his own marriage. White and black Americans would now have to seriously consider the social and theological ramifications of his stance. Several newspapers in 1884 wondered how the nation would respond now that Douglass had "put into practice the theories of his life" and given "the country a practical exemplification of his views."[17]

For his part, Douglass doubled down on this position in an 1886 essay titled "The Future of the Colored Race." He dismissed the ideas of segregation, colonization abroad, and even a multicultural integration whereby black people would "forever remain a separate and distinct race." Instead he reiterated that "an intermediate race has arisen, which is neither white nor black," and that "this intermediate race is constantly increasing." The African diaspora was destined to follow the model of the ancient Phoenicians in Europe, spreading far and wide until white and black people were both subsumed into one "blended race." He insisted, however, "I am not a propagandist, but a prophet." Widespread interracial families and mixed-race children were not "what I say *should* come to pass, but what I think is likely to come to pass, and what is inevitable."[18]

While this inevitability may seem strange to historians today—now fully aware of the virulent racial segregation that occurred—it made perfect sense for a generation of newly emancipated former slaves with an entirely different set of expectations. Their future had not yet been written. Consequently Douglass continued to believe in the inevitability of a widespread mixed-race America, underwritten by interracial marriage, until 1895, when he took his final breath on this earth. Even after the rise of Jim Crow and lynch mob rule—when colonization seemed like an increasingly attractive option to many African Americans—Douglass continued to insist that his marriage was a harbinger of things to come. To the advocates of colonization and black nationalism in 1894 he asked a pointed question: "where the people of this mixed race are to go, for their ancestors are white and black, and it will be difficult to find their native land anywhere outside the United States."[19]

"It Means Progress!"

Douglass was not alone in his vision. He was articulating the majority position of African Americans in the 1880s. Interracial marriage was, in fact, part of the larger collective black consciousness that was informing a newly emergent, nationwide, imagined black community. Bolstered by the rise of print capitalism, the black press overwhelming supported Douglass's interracial marriage.[20] One black newspaper in Indiana declared, "Mr. Douglass has simply put into practice the theories of his life," while another in Philadelphia connected Douglass's marriage to his fight against slavery, stating that through his marriage "old man eloquent only shows that the fire of liberty still burns within him as when, in his younger days, he braved the physical despotisms of his old master."[21] Many saw the marriage as a symbolic turning point in the political destiny of black America, one paper saying, "It means progress!" and asserting that it was the next logical step toward "wiping out the lines of racial distinctions, caste and prejudice!"[22] Another asked, "Is it not time these prejudices against race should cease? Are they not out of place in a republican government in which all men are now happily considered 'free and equal?'"[23] Extending this connection between nation and family, one black observer characterized the marriage as "a benevolent and patriotic enterprise."[24]

Most African Americans clearly assumed that in 1884 the acceptance of interracial marriage should be taken as a given. Captain O. S. B. Wall, brother-in-law of the noted black politician John Mercer Langston, nonchalantly conveyed this sentiment in his reaction to the Douglass marriage. Invoking the language and ideology of contract, Wall insisted that such decisions regarding the black family should be "determined alone by the high contracting parties." Wall's reading was supported publicly by a black stockbroker, William E. Matthews.[25] Blanche K. Bruce, a former senator who, along with his wife, Josephine, accompanied the Douglasses to their wedding, also claimed to see no cause for alarm as "Mr. Douglass has only exercised a right that thousands of others have done, in that he has married the woman of his choice." Bruce also invoked the right to privacy, saying, "This is not a question which the public are properly interested in."[26] A *Washington Post* reporter named L. A. Wood argued that the marriage was not "by any means unprecedented," which was confirmed by a descendant of abolitionist royalty, Dr. Charles B. Purvis. Purvis, with white skin and interracial unions running throughout his family tree, rattled off a list of similar marriages while claiming that "at least two hundred families of the best colored people" in Washington, D.C., were "interwoven by ties of blood with the best white families of the land." According to Purvis, any alarm over the Douglass marriage "seems like making a mountain out of a mole hill." Such family arrangements should be "nobody's business than that of the parties to the marriage themselves."[27]

The nation's most prominent African American newspaper editor, T. Thomas Fortune, whom many viewed as a potential successor to Douglass, mirrored Douglass's position almost exactly.[28] Fortune declared in the most widely read black newspaper at the time that interracial unions like Douglass's "are not only natural but are likely to be of more frequent occurrence in the future." Fortune, who, like Douglass, was expressing the genuine spirit of the age, was "surprised at the amount of gush which intermarriage inspires in this country."[29] He proclaimed, "We regard the American people as one people, and the artificial barriers which now divide them into races, with more or less of odium." Like Douglass, Fortune believed that race itself "will eventually succumb to the march of time and the triumph of Christian enlightenment" and that "like all the narrow prejudices of the American people, it is doomed."[30]

In the 1880s Fortune, Douglass, and their cohort were not outliers. They might more accurately be described as the embodiments of a postemancipation black intellectual tradition—where the radical, transformative dreams of Reconstruction had not yet faded. In addition to framing interracial marriage as the "inalienable" and "undisputed right of every individual,"[31] many black newspapers explicitly supported this grander, long-term perspective on interracial marriage as part of an increasingly multiracial black political identity. In response to Douglass's marriage, the New Orleans–based *Southwestern Christian Advocate* spoke of the "progressive spirit of the age" wherein "the divine doctrines" of "the fatherhood of God, the brotherhood of man, and the unity of the races" will lead to the "utter anuihilation [*sic*]" of "American color line heresy."[32] The editor also embedded his claim within Douglass's mixed-race body. He asserted that Douglass "belongs to both races" and that "it is too late to cry out against the intermingling of the races." Interracial unions were

Frederick Douglass, 1870.
Photographer: George Francis
Schreiber. Library of Congress
Prints and Photographs
Division.

something that "no power on earth can prevent." The marriage contract was
further destined to replace the "illegitimate miscegenation" perpetrated by
Douglass's white "Southern ancestors" against black women.[33] The *New York
Independent* concurred, saying, "Decency of morals requires honest, sanctified
wedlock to take the place of thousands of illegitimate unions." The Douglass
marriage, for the *Independent*, was "one of the best things that could happen
for the race in America" and "an example which will be followed, and which
must be followed before the prejudice against color will die out."[34] Despite the
Victorian attachment to heteronormative marriages and the highly gendered
overtones infusing the protection of black women from white sexual assault,
the underlying drive was clear: new labor relations meant new familial and
sexual relations as well.

"Discord into Our Social Family[?]"

A small minority of African Americans, however, foreshadowing the later
position of Booker T. Washington, seemed to disagree, not with interracial
marriage per se but rather with its timing. The *People's Advocate*, for example,
questioned the directionality of "absorption" as a political strategy, arguing
that "the policy of marriages between the races *as a means*" of eliminating

prejudice was backward. The paper instead offered that *"intermarriages will come as a sequence,* not as an expedient" to equality."[35] This position was echoed by another paper, which claimed that interracial marriages should not be seen as a social prescription but rather as a "weather-cock" marking the winds of prejudice and the direction of change at any given moment.[36] In a line that might have appeared verbatim in the Atlanta Compromise a decade later, one cautious editor claimed that black people should "not force ourselves where we are not wanted socially, until race prejudice is extinct."[37]

A few early black nationalists also critiqued Douglass's wisdom (but rarely his right) to marry interracially. Bruce Grit—who along with Edward Wilmont Blyden and Alexander Crummell stanchly opposed any whiff of absorption—called the marriage "a national calamity."[38] Another black newspaper threatened that although currently Douglass's "picture hangs in our parlor," they would now "hang it in the stable."[39] Several black patriarchs asserted that the marriage was a poor "reflection upon the colored ladies of the country" and constituted "malicious libel" against them.[40] Black women themselves, however, including Ida B. Wells and Mary Church Terrell, said no such thing and sided with Douglass.[41]

Still, other black men went so far as to claim that Douglass "branded us by his own act as inferior to the white race; which reverses the labors of his life."[42] Invoking the language of family and fictive kinship, one anonymous writer, who called himself "Africanus," said that black people looked to Douglass "to keep peace in our social family," and "any attempt to prefer another race is to bring discord into our social family."[43] Several black observers took this logic to its natural conclusion. The upstart *Georgia Weekly* argued that Douglass should be expelled from the black community altogether because his marriage covered him in "the dust of humiliation" and that black people with white spouses should "lose their hold upon identification with the race and the benefits accruing therefrom."[44] These expressions of an early form of cultural black nationalism were part of a much larger battle. Often lining up along intraracial distinctions of class, color, and mixed-race identity, these debates were effectively defining the normative boundaries of blackness in a postemancipation world.

While many of the historians discussed below would later pick up on these bombastic statements and generalize them into a near universal black condemnation of the marriage, astute observers at the time (along with Douglass's own family) recognized such attacks for what they were: politically expedient attempts to discredit Douglass. The fact that they did not work further indicated that the black public overwhelmingly supported Douglass and his vision of marriage equality. The white *Washington Post* reported that many of those who opposed Douglass's marriage did so for personal political gain. It noted that "every colored man whom Mr. Douglass had rebuffed at any time . . . rolled this declaration around in his mouth like a delicate morsel and then evolved it among his fellows with great gusto."[45] Douglass's son Charles, from his first marriage, told his father in a private letter that these voices came from opportunists who wanted "to alienate you from your children" by spreading rumors that "your children are against you because of your marriage." Charles assured his father that this was a "mistaken idea": "I have no prejudice against anybody because of color. I took no stock in the opposition to your marriage because your wife is white." Charles believed his siblings felt the same and that "not one would turn against you in any emergency."[46]

After Douglass's appointment to the ambassadorship of Haiti in 1889 his political rivals, hoping to land this prized patronage job, tried to undermine his position by claiming his marriage was harming his country abroad. Again it did not work. His interracial union supposedly represented a "bad piece of diplomacy" that would earn him an "objectionable social reputation" among both white US Navy officers and Haitian statecrafters.[47] Douglass's unlikely redeemer was the former ambassador to Haiti and Douglass's bitter rival, John Mercer Langston. Arguing that the Haitians would not reject Douglass "on the ground of his having a white wife," Langston pointed out, "Not a few of the most noted people on the island are blacks who have white wives." Interracial black families in the postemancipation era were a global, diasporic practice as well as a future expectation. According to Langston, any objections the Haitian people may have had to Douglass would be because he was part of the American colonial project in Haiti and not because of his marital status or choice of sexual partners. According to Langston, everyday Haitians were anxious about "the annexation or sale of any part of their island to the United States" and "may associate Douglass with such schemes."[48] With the transnational and geopolitical implications of the Douglass marriage in full view, black critics found little solid ground to stand on in the era before Jim Crow.

Yet soon these self-serving critics—always in the minority—would have their voices amplified by historians. Consequently the anomalies of 1884 are wrongly imagined today as the flag-bearers of their era. Most modern-day historians and Douglass biographers simply assume that the "criticism was loud and clear" and that "the marriage pleased no one but the bride and groom."[49] A very basic survey of black political thought from the time, however, shows us otherwise. How the supportive voices described earlier were forgotten and manipulated speaks volumes about the political tensions within the black intellectual tradition itself.

The Emergence of Historical Ventriloquists

The Douglass-led zeitgeist that was building around interracial black families in 1884 did not last. The Douglass marriage, in fact, may have been its apex. The slow dissent into the American nightmare of Jim Crow increasingly took hold in a post-Douglass America. Black folk circled the wagons in response to a system that forced their wagons into a circle. Thoughts about interracial marriage shifted accordingly. Initially, however, early biographies tried to keep Douglass's hope alive and refused to fall directly into the abyss of segregation. Published in 1891, *Frederick Douglass: The Colored Orator* by Frederic May Holland suggested that Douglass's "marriage with Miss Helen Pitts, early in 1884, has done much to make his later years bright and happy."[50] Foreshadowing the affective turn in contemporary scholarship and the work of Treva B. Lindsey and Jessica Marie Johnson, Holland was essentially asking, "What did ecstasy look like for newly emancipated blacks?"[51] The answer, at least for Douglass, was a companionate, romantic marriage with a woman he loved irrespective of her racial background. Black newspapers from the 1880s also invoked this language of affective emotion, asking, "Why should they not be happy?"[52]

Charles Chesnutt would follow this characterization of a happy marriage in 1899 with a Douglass biography that drew out the marriage's political implications. Chesnutt acknowledged that there was "some criticism . . . by colored persons who thought their leader had slighted his own people," but overall he offered a full-throated endorsement of Douglass's model for an interracial black family. Chesnutt, like Fortune, Langston, and Purvis, experienced Douglass's marriage through his own white-skinned mixed-race black body—a body increasingly being lost to the larger visual regime of Jim Crow. Chesnutt insisted that Douglass had "devoted his life to breaking down the color line" and "did not know any more effectual way to accomplish it" than through his marriage.[53] Several twenty-first-century scholars, in assessing Chesnutt's portrayal, seemed shocked at his refusal to endorse their twenty-first-century version of a fallen, disgraced Douglass. The scholars Ernestine Williams Pickens and William L. Andrews claimed in 2001 that Douglass was somehow cast out by "his own people" for marrying a white woman. They expressed a dumbfounded displeasure that "Chesnutt unlike more recent biographers of Douglass, did not ask whether the aging Douglass became disconnected from the African American rank and file."[54] Perhaps this was because Chesnutt was closer to the events at hand and knew that interracial marriage did not make Douglass "disconnected" from "his own people" but, in fact, placed him perfectly in line with their still resonant, radical thoughts for Reconstruction.

This hope waned, however, as America began mimicking abroad the spectacular violence it was already unleashing upon internally colonized peoples at home. By 1907 the tide had turned, and Booker T. Washington was at the helm. As part of his strategy to pacify white America and limit the brutal lynchings that were taking place all over the nation, Washington began the process of misrepresenting and forgetting the Douglass marriage. Dutifully playing his part in the Atlanta Compromise, Washington assured white audiences that black families should contain only black members. Interracial marriages and social equality were neither desired by nor beneficial to black people. The happy interracial families of Douglass, Holland, Fortune, Purvis,

Langston, and Chesnutt quickly became the dogmatically black-only families of Washington (who, ironically, was mixed-race himself). Not wanting to stir up trouble, Washington faithfully rewrote history in an attempt to keep the peace that Jim Crow never delivered.

In this new rendering Washington promised that Douglass was "severely criticized" for his interracial marriage. "The fact that his second wife, Miss Helen Pitts, was a white woman caused something like a revulsion of feeling throughout the entire country," according to the Wizard of Tuskegee's alternate reality. Supposedly Douglass's "own race especially condemned him, and the notion seemed to be quite general that he had made the most serious mistake of his life." Parroting the white segregationists of his age, Washington imagined that the Douglass marriage demonstrated "just how deep-seated was the sentiment of white and black people alike against amalgamation," adding that it "has never been so clearly demonstrated as in this case."[55] The fact that these statements were in complete contradiction to the historical record did not matter. They served Washington's political project, which was more concerned with minimizing the immediate lynching of black men on the pretext of rape than the more long-term dismantling of race that had driven Douglass.

Washington's newly imagined history was probably also a direct response to the world-class racist and misanthrope extraordinaire Thomas Dixon. In a 1905 article published in the *Saturday Evening Post* Dixon accused Washington of being a closeted integrationist and miscegenationist while arguing that black colonization to Africa was still the only solution to America's racial woes. Dixon chastised Washington for his "worship" of Douglass, who, by marrying Pitts, had "at last achieved the climax of Negro sainthood."[56] Dixon and Douglass's "climax" quickly became Washington's dread. He ran from the fight. And the segregationists won.

For the next three decades any mention of Douglass's interracial marriage largely disappeared from the historical record. As Jim Crow normalized, regulated, and brutalized the all-black black family, the intellectual and political possibilities of Reconstruction narrowed as well. Two black women in the 1940s, however, made one last attempt to recapture the original narrative of the Douglass marriage even as many of Washington's distortions survived. Mary Church Terrell in her 1940 autobiography remembered reading the editorials on the Douglass marriage back in 1884. She was "then and there convinced that no sound argument could be produced to prove that there is anything inherently wrong in the intermarriage of the races." Terrell railed at the hypocrisy of black leaders who "were continuously clamoring for equality—absolute equality along all lines," and yet condemned Douglass "for practicing what they themselves have preached long and loud."[57] Despite her support for Douglass, however, Terrell, as a proud race woman, could not resist the new hegemony against interracial marriage—vowing herself, despite several interracial romances and marriage proposals, to marry only a black man.

One of the most sensitive portrayals of the Douglass marriage came in 1947 from Shirley Graham, the second wife of W. E. B. Du Bois. Interestingly presented as a work of historical fiction, *There Was Once a Slave* is perhaps the last time the Douglass marriage was remembered as it actually happened. Graham's novel recalled a heroic romance of two star-crossed lovers. Returning to the themes of joy, ecstasy, and happiness, Graham said that as a result of his interracial marriage "a warm peace filled [Douglass's] heart. He knew that all the years of his living had not been barren." Seeing no contradiction been Douglass's romantic and sexual fulfillment and his political commitments, Graham staged a telling scene between Douglass and his minister. Douglass was cautioned against interracial marriage by this anointed man of God, who insisted, "You can't! It's suicide!" Douglass "smiled quietly" and defiantly replied, "I am a free man."[58]

Yet Graham was already a dinosaur by the late 1940s. Benjamin Quarles, part of a new generation of professional black historians, emerged on the scene in 1948 with a Douglass biography that would continue to spin the new orthodoxy that had been started by Washington. Quarles predictably wrote, "The majority of Negroes . . . were downright shocked by his second marriage." It was "a risky step for a race spokesman," cautioned Quarles, no doubt reflecting more on his own time than Douglass's. Interestingly Quarles also cited Terrell's reaction to the marriage but left out her initial approval and instead positioned her as an "acutely race-conscious" woman who wisely avoided marrying a white man herself. Quarles projected the political talking point of his day, that "intermarriage was highly questionable." He may also have been the original source for the error that "the unpopularity of the marriage extended to Douglass's own children," a claim Quarles offers without evidence or citation. He concluded by painting Douglass as an out-of-touch old man as he sarcastically mocked, "Elder Statesman that he was, though his people reprove him, yet would he deliver them!"[59]

Following Quarles, Philip Foner published the fourth volume of his *Life and Writings of Frederick Douglass* in 1955. As a white Marxist, Foner was particularly sensitive and receptive to the idea of the black proletariat being betrayed by a supposedly bourgeois leader. He consequently reads the Douglass marriage as a moment wherein "the overwhelming majority of the Negroes were bitter and felt betrayed by their leader."[60] Foner ironically cites as his source Rev. Archibald Grimke, the black preacher who blessed the marriage, wrote glowingly about its significance, and absolutely adored Helen Pitts.[61] Foner dismissively portrays Douglass's commitment to interracial marriage and a multiracial black identity as tongue and cheek, claiming that Douglass would "laughingly remark" about his mixed-race identity and his commitment to marriage equality.[62] In this way Foner made a joke about what he should have taken seriously. The political project taking place among Douglass, Fortune, Chesnutt, and many other mixed-race black activists in the 1880s was no laughing matter. It was a crucial battleground—one of sexual, familial, and bodily survival.

With the publication of Stanley Elkin's *Slavery* in 1959, along with the more policy-inflected Moynihan Report in 1965, black intellectuals began to respond to the idea of damaged, broken black families. Unfortunately they rarely questioned the monoracial, heteronormative, patriarchal, nuclear model used in these studies. Instead they squabbled over the relative brokenness of "the black family" while assuming its supposedly singular and uniform composition. This state of affairs clearly came to bear on Rayford Logan's take on the Douglass marriage in 1962. Logan believed that Washington's biography overlooked Douglass's post-1884 years because Washington "blamed [Douglass] for taking for his second wife a white woman." [63] To Logan the marriage was indeed a scandalous distraction and a serious mistake but one that should not have caused so many to forget Douglass's legacy. Logan was willing to overlook the "sin" of Douglass's interracial marriage to focus on his many other virtues.

In a strange twist, Anne Weaver Teabeau, Douglass's great-granddaughter, confirmed this position in 1979 when she told *Jet* magazine, "His marriage to a white woman seemed to be the only thing his people knew about him." [64] Teabeau, like Logan, wanted black audiences in the Black Power era to overlook what was clearly an embarrassing taboo of sexual misconduct while disaggregating Douglass's sex life from his radical politics. Douglass, of course, saw the two as intimately connected.

Certainly, the most sophisticated post–Black Power rendering of Douglass came from Waldo Martin in 1985. In *The Mind of Frederick Douglass*, Martin positions Douglass's interracial marriage as part of a much wider critique of Douglass's vision for a "composite America." Martin scolds Douglass for "blending biologically with the white oppressor" and "jumping into the melting pot to conform to Anglo-European cultural norms." Douglass is portrayed as fighting tragically and naively for interracial marriage and mixed-race identities, "as two social heresies that offended black race pride in addition to white racism." While this was certainly true in 1985, it was just as certainly untrue in 1884. Reflecting his own political moment, Martin was quick to imagine that "the reaction among blacks was particularly intense." Douglass's "grandest hope" was treated as his greatest folly. [65]

The most renowned white biographer of Douglass, William McFeely, also appropriated this orthodoxy. In fact McFeely drove the narrative from simply misguided to downright bizarre. Without evidence or citation, he conjured an elaborate tale involving the feelings of Douglass's children to the marriage. Douglass's children supposedly thought that by marrying Pitts their father had "seemed formally to have repudiated his family—his children, their mother, and their mother's people—all black people." Projecting a certain narrow kind of black nationalism, McFeely assumed that "marriage to someone other than their mother, to someone who was not black, was anathema to them." McFeely's stated reason, again offered without citation, was that "marrying a white woman seemed a public confirmation of his children's hitherfore private grievance, their sense that they, being darker than he, were of less value." McFeely imagined that "in this feeling the Douglass children were joined by many black Americans." McFeely further paints Douglass as a selfish, detached father who "never quite understood how ill-equipped his children were for the emotional reach his way of life imposed on them."[66] McFeely believed the scourge of race mixing that Douglass "imposed" upon black people as a "way of life" damaged not only black families and black communities but the psyches of his black children as well.

This storyline even crossed the Atlantic and gained purchase with white historians internationally. Maria Diedrich seems to celebrate *Love across the Color Lines*, but, in the end, her pop psychoanalysis of Douglass was just as flawed as McFeely's. Dietrich reasoned that Douglass's sexual attraction to white women was a direct result of a mixed-race identity crisis. His interracial sexual desire was apparently part of a more general pathology of being "torn between two races, tortured by his double consciousness of being both and neither." After replaying this tragic mulatto motif, things somehow got worse. Dietrich's Freudian analysis prompted her to claim that Douglass's desire for white women was also a pathological urge brought on by his "childhood experiences." After the trauma of being abandoned by his mother and being torn away from his grandmother during slavery, he supposedly developed "an unconscious resentment of these black mothers." His desire to cheat on his dark-skinned black wife with a string of white women was therefore a way to get back at the black women in his life who could not protect him from the ravages of slavery.[67] Loving one white women meant that Douglass hated all black women—and himself. This pathologizing of interracial marriage, as part of a supposedly radical pro-black sexual politics, not only butchered the historical record but exposed its own compulsive overcompensation.

At the very least, the scholarship on the Douglass marriage represents a glaring historiographical blunder. Today's historians clearly got it wrong. But *how* they got it wrong is also important. Contained within the wrongness itself are a number of generative methodological lessons and cautionary tales for black intellectual traditions. While the marshalling of radical black politics to inform black intellectual history is one of the most potent and useful features of these traditions, it is not without its pitfalls. By reading current political positions and sexual politics backward into the historical record, we run the risk of misrepresenting our historical subjects—forcing long-dead former slaves to labor once more in an act of historical ventriloquy.

Additionally, when scholars codify "the black intellectual tradition" as a single, linear, perhaps even timeless tradition they further run the risk of obfuscating the richness and diversity of that tradition while imposing their shadow upon the past. Just as prior formulations of "the black family" and "the black church" have proven inadequate, coaxing historical actors to perform a canonized script of what "the" struggle for social justice should look like, or what a revolutionary black consciousness should sound like, will ultimately backfire. Radicalism, in this narrow rendering, becomes removed from the dynamic, contested, and dangerous terrain that informed it and is reduced instead to a static ahistorical constant. What we think is radical today may not have been what people thought was radical a hundred years ago. Likewise our views of radical thought in this moment will undoubtedly seem rather quaint, if not downright naive, a hundred years from now.

The Douglass marriage also demonstrates what can go wrong when we unquestionably follow a single, codified black intellectual tradition, even as articulated by our most brilliant secondary sources. Instead we must go back to the even deeper tradition waiting to be rediscovered in our primary sources. In this case the combination of Booker T. Washington's accommodationism and a crude caricature of a post–Black Power nationalism colluded to rob black thinkers in 1884 of one of their most powerful demands: marriage equality. Radical black politics, black pride, and black self-love were never incompatible with interracial love, marriage, solidarity, or sexuality for the vast majority of former slaves.

While the current ethos initiated by Black Lives Matter may signal a restrengthening of monoracial marriage sentiments within certain radical black political circles, a new generation of black millennials might also just as easily reverse this trend and affirm blackness in all its diverse, multihued, interracial complexity. In either case the days of the historical ventriloquists will hopefully come to an end. There is nothing pro-black about forcing ideas upon black people in the past who thought no such thing. We would do well to listen and learn from such ancestors rather than tell them what to think.

Notes

1. Hazel V. Carby, *Race Men* (Cambridge, Mass.: Harvard University Press, 2000); Barbara Dianne Savage, *Your Spirits Walk Beside Us* (Cambridge, Mass.: Belknap Press, 2009).

2. Michel-Rolph Trouillot, *Silencing the Past: Power and the Production of History* (Boston: Beacon Press, 1995).

3. For more on Helen Pitts, see Francis James Grimkè, *The Works of Francis J. Grimkè*, edited by Carter G. Woodson (Washington, D.C.: Associated Publishers, 1942), vol. 4, 52, 72–79; Francis James Grimkè, "The Second Marriage of Frederick Douglass," *Louisville* (Ky.) *Courier Journal*, January 26, 1884, reprinted in *Idaho Avalanche*, February 16, 1884; Georgiana Rose Simpson, "A Tribute to Helen Pitts Douglass," *Negro History Bulletin* 7, no. 6 (1944): 131–132. See also the Frederick Douglass Papers at the Library of Congress, Image 332, Scrapbook 2, Library of Congress, Manuscript Division, Washington, D.C., in what appears to be a newspaper clipping of the *Washington Evening Transcript*, April 2, 1886,

Washington Post, May 30, 1897; Douglass Papers, Image 332, Scrapbook 2, in what appears to be a newspaper clipping of the *Washington Evening Transcript*, April 2, 1886.

4. *Washington Post*, January 26, 1884.

5. *United States v. Stanley; United States v. Ryan; United States v. Nichols; United States v. Singleton; Robinson et ux. v. Memphis & Charleston R.R. Co.,* 109 U.S. 3 (1883) declared Congress's Civil Rights Act of 1875 unconstitutional. The US Supreme Court's *Pace v. Alabama,* 106 U.S. 583 (1883) decision upheld the Alabama Supreme Court's *Pace & Cox v. State,* 69 Ala 231, 233 (1882) decision, which held that bans on interracial marriage were deemed constitutional.

6. *Washington Post,* January 26, 1884.

7. Quoted in Thomas C. Holt, *Children of Fire: A History of African Americans* (New York: Hill and Wang, 2010), 175.

8. For more on the ambiguous ideological and legal functions of contracts more generally in postemancipation America, see Amy Dru Stanley, *From Bondage to Contract: Wage Labor, Marriage, and the Market in the Age of Slave Emancipation* (Cambridge, UK: Cambridge University Press, 1998).

9. *Washington Post*, January 26, 1884.

10. For more on the battle to define these postemancipation boundaries between public and private, see Kate Masur, *An Example for All the Land* (Chapel Hill: University of North Carolina Press, 2012), 71–77, 92–193.

11. *New Hampshire Sentinel*, February 27, 1884.

12. For more on the role of interracial marriage in the development of the American nation-state, see Peggy Pascoe, *What Comes Naturally: Miscegenation Law and the Making of Race in America* (Oxford: Oxford University Press, 2009).

13. *Washington Post*, January 26, 1884.

14. *Washington Post*, January 26, 1884. Here Douglass becomes part of a long tradition of public figures (extending to the present) who imagine a perpetually future mixed-race America in utopian terms. See Greg Carter, *The United States of the United Races: A Utopian History of Racial Mixing* (New York: NYU Press, 2013).

15. *Washington Post*, January 26, 1884.

16. For more on Douglass's longtime espousal of a "composite nationality," see Waldo Martin Jr., *The Mind of Frederick Douglass* (Chapel Hill: University of North Carolina Press, 1984), 197–250; Peter C. Myers, *Frederick Douglass: Race and Rebirth of American Liberalism* (Lawrence: University of Kansas Press, 2008), 151–94.

17. *Leader* (Indianapolis, Ind.), reprinted in *New York Globe*, February 9, 1884; *Leader* (Cleveland, Ohio), reprinted in *Boston Daily Globe*, January 31, 1884.

18. Frederick Douglass, "The Future of the Colored Race," *North American Review*, May 1886, 437–40.

19. Frederick Douglass, "Why the Negro Is Lynched," in *The Lesson of the Hour* (1894), quoted in *The Life and Writings of Frederick Douglass: Reconstruction and After*, edited by Philip S. Foner (New York: International, 1955), 4:513.

20. Of the thirty-nine black newspapers that addressed the marriage, only fourteen had anything at all negative to say about it, and the majority of those still upheld interracial marriage as a legal right that should be protected.

21. *Leader* (Indianapolis, Ind.), reprinted in *New York Globe,* February 9, 1884; *Christian Recorder* (Philadelphia), reprinted in *New York Globe,* February 9, 1884.

22. *Cleveland* (Ohio) *Gazette,* February 2, 1884.

23. *New York World,* reprinted in *Southwestern Christian Advocate* (New Orleans), February 14, 1884.

24. Unknown newspaper summarizing an article from the *Independent* (New York), reprinted in *Washington Post,* March 3, 1884.

25. *St. Louis* (Mo.) *Daily Globe-Democrat,* January 26, 1884.

26. *Washington Post,* January 26, 1884.

27. *Washington Post,* January 26, 1884.

28. *New Amsterdam News* (New York), June 13, 1928.

29. *New York Globe,* February 2, 1884.

30. *New York Globe,* February 16, 1884; Fortune in Douglass Papers, Scrapbook 1, Image 180, in what appears to be a newspaper clipping from an unknown newspaper dated circa January 27, 1884.

31. *Boston Hub,* reprinted in *New York Globe,* February 9, 1884; *Atlanta Pilot,* reprinted in *New York Globe,* February 9, 1884.

32. *Southwestern Christian Advocate* (New Orleans), February 7, 1884.

33. *Southwestern Christian Advocate* (New Orleans), February 14, 1884.

34. *New York Independent,* reprinted in *Southwestern Christian Advocate* (New Orleans), February 7, 1884.

35. *People's Advocate* (Washington, D.C.), February 9, 1884 (original emphasis).

36. *New York Globe,* March 29, 1884.

37. *Cleveland* (Ohio) *Gazette,* February 16, 1884.

38. *The Grit* (Washington, D.C.), January 26, 1884.

39. *Pittsburg* (Pa.) *Weekly News,* reprinted in *New York Globe,* February 9, 1884.

40. *Baptist* (Augusta, Ga.), reprinted in *New York Globe,* February 9, 1884; *Tribune* (Topeka, Kan.), reprinted in *New York Globe,* February 9, 1884

41. See Mary Church Terrell, *A Colored Woman in a White World,* Black Women Writers Series (Washington, D.C.: Ransdell, 1940), 92–94; Ida B. Wells, *Crusade for Justice: The Autobiography of Ida B. Wells,* Negro American Biographies and Autobiographies, edited by Alfreda Duster (Chicago: University of Chicago Press, 1970), 72–75.

42. *Arkansas Mansion* (Little Rock) February 2, 1884.

43. *Cleveland* (Ohio) *Gazette,* February 16, 1884.

44. *Georgia Weekly* (Athens), reprinted in *New York Globe,* February 9, 1884.

45. *Washington Post,* February 21, 1895.

46. Charles Douglass to Frederick Douglass, August 10, 1889, Douglass Papers.

47. Douglass Papers, Scrapbook 2, Item 38 appears to be a newspaper clipping from *New York Herald,* October 3, 1889.

48. Douglass Papers, Scrapbook 1, Image 44 appears to be a newspaper clipping from the *New York Tribune,* May 7, 1891.

49. William S. McFeely, *Frederick Douglass* (New York: Norton, 1991), 320; Mia Bay, *To Tell the Truth Freely: The Life of Ida B. Wells* (New York: Hill and Wang, 2009), 130.

50. Frederic May Holland, *Frederick Douglass: The Colored Orator* (New York: Funk & Wagnalls, 1891), 355.

51. Treva B. Lindsey and Jessica Marie Johnson, "Searching for Climax: Black Erotic Lives in Slavery and Freedom," *Meridians* 12, no. 2 (2014): 189.

52. *Charleston* (S.C.) *New Era*, February 9, 1884 as reprinted in *New York Globe*, February 9, 1884.

53. Charles W Chesnutt, *Frederick Douglass*, edited by Ernestine Williams Pickens and William L. Andrews (Atlanta, Ga.: Clark Atlanta University Press, 2001), 122.

54. Andrews in Chesnutt, *Frederick Douglass*, xxvii. See also Pickens's preface.

55. Booker T. Washington, *Frederick Douglass* (Philadelphia: G. W. Jacobs, 1907), 306.

56. Thomas Dixon Jr., "Booker T. Washington and the Negro: Some Dangerous Aspects of the Work of Tuskegee," *Saturday Evening Post*, August 19, 1905.

57. Terrell, *Colored Woman*, 92–93.

58. Shirley Graham (Du Bois), *There Was Once a Slave: The Heroic Story of Frederick Douglass* (New York: J. Messner, 1947), 291.

59. Benjamin Quarles, *Frederick Douglass* (Washington, D.C.: Associated Publishers, 1948), 297, 299, 300.

60. Philip S. Foner, *The Life and Writings of Frederick Douglass: Reconstruction and After* (New York: International, 1955), 4:115–16.

61. Francis J. Grimke, "The Second Marriage of Frederick Douglass," *The Journal of Negro History* 9, no. 3 (1934): 324–29.

62. Foner, *The Life and Writings of Frederick Douglass*, 116.

63. Frederick Douglass, *Life and Times of Frederick Douglass: His Early Life as a Slave, His Escape from Bondage, and His Complete History*, edited by Rayford Whittingham Logan (New York: Bonanza Books, 1962), 625.

64. *Jet*, November 22, 1979.

65. Martin, *The Mind of Frederick Douglass*, 224, 221, 99, 100.

66. McFeely, *Frederick Douglass*, 320, 321.

67. Maria Diedrich, *Love across Color Lines: Ottilie Assing and Frederick Douglass* (New York: Hill & Wang, 1999), 174, 173.

Reigning Assimilationists and Defiant Black Power

The Struggle to Define and Regulate Racist Ideas

Ibram X. Kendi

Since the early twentieth century, eugenicists have tried to make Americans believe that negative human traits were derived from genetics and certain peoples inherited superior genes and thereby superior traits—and thereby were superior people. Eugenicists had been on an intellectual mission to improve the genetic quality of Western populations, either through positive eugenics like mass-reproducing people with supposedly good genes, or negative eugenics like mass-murdering or sterilizing people with supposedly bad genes. Eugenicists had made advances, especially in the quiet sterilizing of thousands of southern black women and the louder programs in Nazi Germany.[1] But when Americans started reeling from reports of murders by Nazi eugenicists in 1939, the Carnegie Foundation pulled its funding from the headquarters of the eugenics movement, New York's Cold Spring Harbor Laboratory. It marked the end of the reign of eugenics as a politically correct idea and social policy.[2]

But what really sealed the fate of eugenics in 1939, pushing it from the legitimate foreground to the illegitimate background of the American racial discourse, was the same development that sealed the fate of the racial discourse for the next three decades—and ever since. The Columbia University anthropologist Ruth Benedict inserted the term *racism* into the American vocabulary in 1940. "To recognize race does not mean to recognize racism," Benedict told her readers in her groundbreaking monograph, *Race: Science and Politics.* The introducer of the term usually introduces the definition. Here was her definition: "Racism is an unproved assumption of the biological and perpetual superiority of one human group over another."[3]

Benedict had also helped to popularize the scientific construct of culture through her easily readable, scientifically laced, and straight-shooting 1934 best seller, *Patterns of Culture.* Hereditary determining of human behavior is nothing but "mythology," Benedict intoned. Human differences reflect different patterns of culture. "A culture, like an individual, is a more or less consistent pattern of thought and action," she wrote. It is wrong, she argued in antiracist fashion, for us to "set our own belief over against" the beliefs of a different culture—a notion that became known as cultural relativity. But Benedict did not follow her own theory when she identified in the book certain cultures as "primitive" and African American cultures as more or less assimilated, which to her signified racial progress. To her trained eye, northern black urbanites did not speak, eat, dress, worship, and groove differently from their white neighbors; neither was their culture primitive. "The culture of the American Negro in northern cities has come to approximate in detail that of the whites in the same cities," she wrote. And this assimilation would continue because "the vast proportion of all individuals who are born into any society always . . . assume . . . the behavior dictated by that society."[4]

Since the days of American slavery, proslavery and pro-segregation theorists, calling forth the biblical truth of the curse of Ham, the natural truth of polygenesis (separately created race-species), and the scientific truth of social Darwinism, had refused to be classed as biased and prejudiced. Eugenicists too had defined themselves outside of prejudice, looking upon their detractors as refusing to believe God's law, nature's law, and science's law of biological racial hierarchy in the early twentieth century. In the 1930s and 1940s, as assimilationists like Benedict gained the helm of racial thought, their racial ideas of biological *equality* and behavioral or cultural *hierarchy* became the new law of the land—of God, nature, and science. Their racial ideas became objective and antiracist, and they defined eugenicists and segregationists as the subjective racists (while dismissing as political extremists those *antiracists* suggesting biological, cultural, and behavioral racial equality). As this chapter shows, assimilationists could degrade, denigrate, and dismiss the behaviors and cultures of African people and project to the world that they were not racist since they did not root these behaviors in biology. Assimilationists denigrated people of African descent while claiming that they did not deem these negativities to be permanent. Instead they identified the supposed historical, environmental, and cultural causes of inferior black behaviors and argued that blacks were capable of being civilized and developed and assimilated.[5]

Assimilationists—and their definition of racism—regulated the racial discourse until Black Power ideas exposed their bigotry in the late 1960s. In the process Black Power intellectuals waged an intellectual struggle to redefine racist ideas. This chapter chronicles the rise and reign of postwar assimilationists and the challenge assimilationists faced for control of the racial discourse from Black Power intellectuals in the 1960s. This long intellectual struggle is still largely unknown and unrecorded. In the common narrative based on the prevailing historiography, antiracist ideas started to take hold in the 1930s and 1940s in reaction to the Great Migration, Great Depression, early civil rights activism, and especially the Nazi Holocaust.[6] But this chapter revises that history, showing that in fact it was assimilationist ideas that took hold in the 1930s and 1940s. This chapter, then, rewrites the history of racist ideas in the mid-twentieth century.

In the literature of racist ideas, this history of assimilationist ideas has rarely been identified, let alone chronicled, perhaps because so many historians of racism still abide by Benedict's definition.[7] Meanwhile historians of Black Power have presented and interrogated Black Power's resounding critiques of racism in the United States and abroad.[8] This chapter does not build on Black Power studies as much as it provides a firmer base for Black Power studies, further excavating the Black Power movement's intellectual foundation. This chapter offers a new perspective on the history of racist ideas and builds on the black intellectual tradition, which, like Black Power, has consistently rewritten the modern story of race and racism.

Before Black Power activists could critique racism, they first had to redefine racism. After all, the most popular and prevailing definition of racism during the emergence of Black Power in the mid-1960s was still Benedict's 1940 definition: "Racism is an unproved assumption of the biological and perpetual superiority of one human group over another."[9] Based on this definition, all those Americans believing that black residents brought neighborhoods down; believing black schools and colleges were inferior to white schools and colleges; believing black women were asexual Mammies, hypersexual Jezebels, emasculating Sapphires, or undeserving welfare recipients; believing black men had been emasculated; believing black rioters were mentally disordered; believing black politicians were incompetent; believing woman-led black families were pathological; believing black workers were lazy; believing the lighter the skin, the better; believing African American culture was defective or nonexistent—all these believers could not be cast as racist if they also believed in biological equality. As such, Black Power's overlooked and understudied redefinition campaign became the all-important ideological platform for the movement. This informal, leaderless, unorganized, indirect campaign primarily targeted Benedict's definition, redefining racist ideas as unproved assumptions of any sort of superiority of one racial group over another, perpetually or temporarily. This campaign was one of the most important developments in the long history of the black intellectual tradition, especially the black radical tradition and its challenging of American racism. But this chapter centrally contends that Black Power intellectuals did not just challenge American racism; they attempted to redefine American racism by redefining the reigning assimilationist ideas as racist.

The Reign of Assimilationists

Benedict studied under Columbia University's Franz Boas, the preeminent cultural anthropologist in the United States in the early 1920s. After earning her doctorate in 1923, she joined Columbia's Anthropology Department, where she remained extremely close, in more ways than one, to "Papa Franz," as she adoringly called Boas.[10] By then Boas had already laid down the creed of assimilationists in his magnum opus, *The Mind of Primitive Man* (1911)—the creed he would teach to Benedict. All of the principal antiracist and racist ideas of assimilationist thought were in *The Mind of Primitive Man*:

(1) rejection of the eugenicist "theory of hereditary inferiority," (2) black people are subjected to racial discrimination, (3) the oppression-inferiority thesis that the history of oppression had made black people inferior, (4) African American culture was either nonexistent or pathological, (5) "North American negroes . . . in culture and language" were "essentially European," and (6) the black race was capable of development "when given facility and opportunity." A decade later, in *The Yale Review*, Boas added, "The negro problem will not disappear in America until the negro blood has been so much diluted that it will no longer be recognized."[11]

The interlocking of racial progress and cultural assimilationists was a prominent theme of not only Boas's Columbia school of cultural anthropology but also Robert Park's school of urban sociology at the University of Chicago. "It is very difficult to find in the South today anything that can be traced directly back to Africa," Park had written in Carter G. Woodson's *Journal of Negro History* in 1919.[12] Since they had been stripped of their African culture, African Americans were socially disorganized. They would socially reorganize as they moved through what Park called the natural race relations cycle: "progressive and irreversible" periods of contact, competition, accommodation, and assimilation. He rejected eugenic notions of biological inequality but had much to say about black behaviors: the Negro shows "an interest and attachment to external, physical things rather than to subjective states and objects of introspection."[13]

Park's greatest black student, the Howard University sociologist E. Franklin Frazier, released a book in 1939 that standardized assimilationist ideas in the racial discourse as much—and as long—as Benedict's book that year regulated these ideas outside of racism. In *The Negro Family in the United States*, Frazier painted broad strokes of the urban black family as an ugly, disordered, matriarchal albatross: absent fathers and unmarried working mothers leaving their children alone; a paucity of role models; sons growing into criminals; daughters learning to imitate "the loose behavior of their mothers" and thus transmitting immoral "illegitimacy" from one generation to the next.[14]

Slaveholders and their ideological descendants had spent a century promoting the Mammy trope of black womanhood. Now the nation's second most famous black male scholar was doing it for them.[15] Citing "plenty of evidence" in *The Negro Family in the United States*, Frazier imagined that the Middle Passage and forced breeding resulted in the enslaved mother often showing "inhuman indifference towards her own offspring, and undying devotion to the children of the master race."[16] The Mammy trope received Frazier's scientific stamp in time for the theatrical release on December 15, 1939, of Hattie McDaniel's Academy Award–winning Mammy character in *Gone with the Wind*.[17]

This "disorganized family life" in black neighborhoods was not the result of barbaric black biology, Frazier argued, challenging eugenicists. He gendered the old oppression-inferiority thesis. The wretched family life was caused by racial discrimination, poverty, cultural pathology, and the introduction of the matriarchal black family during slavery with "timid" black men and "dominating" black women. But Frazier was hopeful. What he considered to be racial progress—black "assimilation of . . . the more formal aspects of white civilization"—was happening in "the urban area," he proclaimed. And black folk will pass on to future generations "the gains in civilization which result from participation in the white world."[18]

The Northwestern University anthropologist Melville Herskovits—another student of Boas—disputed Frazier's assimilationist theories in *The Myth of the Negro Past* in 1941, bringing on the critical wrath of Frazier. African culture was no less resilient than European culture, and the cultural exchange went two ways, Herskovits maintained. African Americans created a strong and complex culture of European "outward form while retaining inner [African] values," he insightfully argued. Those who cannot see the equality of cultures are suffering from "race prejudice."[19]

Herskovits's *The Myth of the Negro Past* was one of the rare antiracist books of the era (and a favorite of Black Power activists a generation later). It was the first publication of a landmark study of the Negro, financed by the Carnegie Foundation.[20] Back in 1936 the Carnegie Foundation's president Frederick P. Keppel briefly considered Herskovits when he decided to heed Cleveland mayor Newton Baker's recommendation for a study on the "infant race." Keppel drew up a list of *only* European scholars and colonial officials who could complete the study "in a wholly objective and dispassionate way." He selected Gunnar Myrdal, the Swedish Nobel laureate economist, and brought him to the United States in 1938. With $300,000 of Carnegie funds, Myrdal employed a classroom of leading black and white scholars, including Frazier and Herskovits. Myrdal employed seemingly everyone except W. E. B. Du Bois and Carter G. Woodson and the anthropologist Zora Neale Hurston—antiracist black scholars whom assimilationist scholars and benefactors were increasingly calling biased.[21]

In his two-volume, nearly fifteen-hundred-page study published in 1944, Myrdal shone an optimistic light on *An American Dilemma*. The tome provided a devastating assault on the rationales of segregationists and an encyclopedic analysis of racial discrimination. To Myrdal, neither eugenicists nor segregationists, with their "preconceptions about the Negroes' inherent inferiority," nor the scholarship of black antiracists, "basically an expression of the Negro protest," were objective like him, like assimilationists. He instead presented the basic expression of assimilationist thought. "In practically all its divergences, American Negro culture is . . . a distorted development, or a pathological condition, of the general American culture," Myrdal wrote. "It is to the advantage of American Negroes as individuals and as a group to become assimilated into American culture."[22]

Still beaming from the runaway success of *An American Dilemma* and the cold war mandate to launch area studies programs of decolonizing nations, the Carnegie Foundation granted Herskovits $30,000 over three years to establish the first interdisciplinary African studies program at Northwestern University in 1948. As the cold war ventured into decolonizing Africa in the 1950s, support for African studies grew, along with its corpus of white scholars. In 1957 Carnegie funded the founding conference of the African Studies Association (ASA), and the Ford Foundation provided $25,000 of start-up funds. Herskovits was named the ASA's first president. In his first presidential address in 1958, he claimed that Americans—read "white Americans"—were specially positioned to conduct detached studies of Africa since they were "removed in space from the African scene," which "bring[s] us naturally to a heightened degree of objectivity."[23]

Herskovits first proposed his African studies program during a landmark year in racial science. As the Howard University historian John Hope Franklin's *From Slavery to Freedom* marked the antiracist future of black historiography and the University of Georgia historian E. Merton Coulter's *The South During Reconstruction* of the Dunning School marked the racist past, two renowned scholars came together from different disciplines in 1947 to set the future course of social Darwinism, away from the past of eugenics.[24] The Ukraine-born biologist Theodosius Dobzhansky at Columbia University and the England-born anthropologist Ashley Montagu published their uniting and groundbreaking article in the all-powerful *Science* journal on June 6, 1947. "Race differences," Dobzhansky and Montagu wrote, "arise chiefly because of the differential action of natural selection on geographically separate populations." They rejected eugenic ideas of a fixed racial hierarchy. Human populations (or races) were evolving, they argued, changing genetically through two evolutionary processes: one biological, one cultural. It was not nature *or* nurture distinguishing humans, but nature *and* nurture. This became known as the dual-evolution theory, or the modern evolutionary consensus.[25]

Utilizing dual-evolution theory, eugenicists could argue that African populations contained the lowest frequencies of good genes. Assimilationists could argue that European populations had created the most complex and sophisticated societies and were the most culturally evolved. And so, as much as Dobzhansky and Montagu buried eugenic ideas, they ended up birthing new assimilationist ideas, as reflected in the globally reported United Nations Educational, Scientific, and Cultural Organization (UNESCO) Statements on Race in 1950 and 1951. UNESCO officials had assembled an international dream team of scholars in Paris in 1950 to draw up the final rebuttal to Nazism and eugenicists worldwide. Virtually all of the scholars, including Montagu, Dobzhansky, Frazier, and Myrdal, had expressed assimilationist ideas, giving assimilationists global control over the racial discourse, showcasing that the global intellectual community defined racism as eugenics. While claiming no human populations have any biological evolutionary achievements, these assimilationists did express the "cultural achievements" of certain human populations. And then in 1951 geneticists and physical anthropologists figured in their revised UNESCO statement: "It is possible, though not proved, that some types of innate capacity for intellectual and emotional responses are commoner in one human group than in another." Eugenicists set out to prove these innate racial differences in intelligence.[26]

At the end of the 1950s Henry E. Garrett helped organize the International Association for the Advancement of Ethnology and Eugenics (IAAEE). Funded by the benefactor of the Progress Fund, Wickliffe Draper, the IAAEE was an international body of scholars devoted to preserving eugenics and segregation. Garrett established the *Mankind Quarterly* in 1960 to be the "cornerstone" of the eugenic establishment. In the journal's first issue, in 1961, Garrett classed "the equalitarian dogma" of biological equality "the scientific hoax of the century."[27]

The renewed eugenics movement dovetailed with the massive resistance to the civil rights movement, compelling assimilationist scholars to encourage their professional associations to adopt statements deploring eugenicists and Jim Crow segregation.[28] Northern assimilationists did not consider themselves racist; racism was a southern and segregationist phenomenon. After his rousing inauguration speech as Alabama governor on January 14, 1963, George Wallace became the face of American racism, when he should have been rendered the face of segregation only.[29] That year the sociologists Nathan Glazer and Daniel Patrick Moynihan should have been deemed the academic face of assimilation when they published their widely acclaimed book, *Beyond the Melting Pot: The Negroes, Puerto Ricans, Jews, Italians, and Irish of New York City.*[30]

Glazer wrote the chapter on the Negro, claiming that "the problems that afflict so many Negroes" can be attributed to "prejudice" and poverty, as well as black behavioral inferiority, particularly the "weak" black family, as "the sociologist Franklin Frazier" had told us. "The Negro is only an American, and nothing else," Glazer surmised. "He has no values and culture to guard and protect. He insists that the white world deal with his problems because, he is so much the product of America, they are not *his* problems, but everyone's."[31]

According to Benedict's prevailing definition of racism, the views of Glazer and Moynihan in *Beyond the Melting Pot* were not racist since they both believed in the biological equality of the races. But in the early 1960s this prevailing definition was under assault, especially by one of the principal ideological fathers of Black Power: Malcolm X. He did not clearly define what he considered to be a racist idea, but he clearly considered the United States to be a racist nation with racist policies and racist people, despite the prevailing intellectual belief in biological equality. While abroad in Egypt, Malcolm wrote a scorching commentary in the *Egyptian Gazette* on August 25, 1964. Its headline: "Racism: The Cancer That Is Destroying America." His message: "This seed of racism has rooted itself so deeply in the subconsciousness of

Malcolm X at
Queens Court, 1964.
Photographer: Herman
Hiller. Library of Congress
Prints and Photographs
Division.

many American whites that they themselves oftentimes are not even aware of
its existence, but it can be easily detected in their thoughts, their words, and
in their deeds." He was speaking as much to assimilationists, whom he often
framed as racist foxes, as he was to Jim Crow segregationists, whom he often
framed as racist wolves.[32]

Malcolm did not spend most of his public career challenging eugenicists
and segregationists. He spent most of his legendary career challenging assimilationists, white and black. These challenges pervaded his best-selling mem-
oir that served as one of the major ideological manifestos for the coming
Black Power movement. *The Autobiography of Malcolm X* vividly portrayed
his transformation from assimilationist to antiwhite separatist to antiracist
humanist. He argued that white people are not born racist, that it's "the American political, economic and social *atmosphere* that automatically nourishes
a racist psychology in the white man." He suggested that black people could
hold racist ideas when he shared the painful story of when he was trying
to get his hair "looking 'white.'" He wrote, "I had joined that multitude of
Negro men and women in America who are brainwashed into believing that
the black people are 'inferior'—and white people 'superior'—that they will

even violate and mutilate their God-created bodies to try to look 'pretty' by white standards."[33]

But Malcolm did not have the time to develop his antiracist philosophy. He was assassinated on February 21, 1965, as the civil rights movement ran its final leg in Selma, Alabama, for the Voting Rights Act. During his commencement address at Howard University on June 4, 1965, President Lyndon Johnson predicted the imminent passage of the voting rights bill, "the latest, and among the most important, in a long series of victories." But when the bill passes, the United States will not be finished, Johnson declared. Racial progress has primarily come for "a growing middle class minority," while for poor blacks "the walls are rising and the gulf is widening." Income disparities have grown. Disparities in poverty rates have grown. Disparities in infant mortality have grown. Urban segregation has grown. Johnson gave two "broad basic reasons" to explain the predicament of the black poor: one antiracist, "inherited poverty" and discrimination, and one racist, "the breakdown of the Negro family structure."[34]

Assistant Secretary of Labor Daniel Patrick Moynihan, whose *Beyond the Melting Pot* still dominated urban sociology, composed Johnson's speech with the ideas still fresh from an unpublished government report he had just finished. *The Negro Family: The Case for National Action*, which had reached Johnson's desk in May 1965, statistically demonstrated that civil rights legislation over the previous ten years had not improved the living conditions of most African Americans. After all his antiracist revelations, Moynihan trekked into assimilationist ideas, into discrimination emasculating black men and creating "a matriarchal structure" to the black family, which he considered a "tangle of pathology."[35]

On August 9, 1965, three days after Johnson signed the Voting Rights Act, *Newsweek* alarmed Americans by disclosing the findings of the Moynihan Report: "the rising rate of non-white illegitimacy" and the "runaway curve in child welfare cases" and the "social roots" of the "American dilemma of race"—the "splintering Negro family." A photograph of Harlem kids tossing bottles contained the caption "A time bomb ticks in the ghetto." The time bomb exploded two days later in Los Angeles, when a police incident set off a violent six-day rebellion against racial discrimination.[36]

The Moynihan Report primarily fed the racist backlash to the urban rebellions of the mid-1960s, and the urban rebellions fed the racist backlash that backed the Moynihan Report. "The reverberations" from the Report "were disastrous," explained the historian Deborah Gray White.[37] A command in *Ebony* became popular: the "immediate goal" of black women should be to establish "a strong family unit in which the father is the dominant person."[38] No major civil rights organization challenged Moynihan's descriptions of the pathological black family, of pathological African American culture, of pathological black behaviors, of the emasculating black woman, of the emasculated black man.[39]

Black Power's Challenge

Beliefs in pathological black masculinity and femininity informed beliefs in the pathological black family that informed beliefs in pathological African American culture. They were like legs holding up the seat of America's domineering assimilationist ideas. The sociologist Andrew Billingsley was one of the first scholars to strike at those legs. His seminal study, *Black Families in White America*, broke ground on antiracist black family studies in 1968. He refused to analyze black families using the criteria of white families. "Unlike Moynihan and others, we do not view the Negro as a causal nexus in a 'tangle of pathologies,' which feeds on itself," Billingsley wrote. Instead "we view the Negro family" as an "absorbing, adaptive, and amazingly resilient mechanism for the socialization of its children." Billingsley also exposed the assimilationist consensus forged by Boas that African Americans had no culture worth embracing. "To say that a people have no culture is to say that they have no common history which has shaped and taught them," Billingsley argued. "And to deny the history of a people is to deny their humanity."[40]

Three years later Joyce Ladner, after acknowledging Billingsley's groundbreaking work, showcased in her seminal study, *Tomorrow's Tomorrow: The Black Woman*, the "African survivalisms" in African American culture (after everyone from Boas to Frazier had asserted that durable European culture had conquered fragile African culture). Ladner blasted the stereotypes of both the strong black matriarch and the weak black eunuch, rebuilding the actual history of the black women and men who had survived and resisted American racism.[41]

Billingsley and Ladner wrote these two seminal studies that repackaged assimilationists as racists during the climax years of the Black Power movement. But these antiracist scholars were classed as biased and racist. From the beginning of the movement, assimilationists called Black Power activists "racist" in their efforts to maintain their defining reign over the racial discourse. Almost from the June day in 1966 when the chairman of the Student Nonviolent Coordinating Committee (SNCC) and Malcolm disciple Stokely Carmichael mainstreamed the term *Black Power* during a rousing speech in Greenwood, Mississippi, assimilationists tagged Black Power as racist. "No matter how endlessly they try to explain it, the term 'Black Power' means anti-white power," the NAACP's executive secretary Roy Wilkins charged at the association's annual convention on July 5, 1966. "It is a reverse of Mississippi, a reverse Hitler, a reverse Ku Klux Klan." In his convention speech, Vice President Hubert Humphrey added, "Yes, racism is racism—and there is no room in America for racism of any color."[42]

Assimilationists could hardly stop the challenge of Black Power. In October 1966 two Oakland community college students were incensed that their peers were not living up to Malcolm X's directives. Huey P. Newton and Bobby Seale composed a ten-point platform for their new Black Panther Party for Self Defense, declaring what they wanted and what they believed. "We want power to determine the destiny of our black community," the platform began, almost directly critiquing *Beyond the Melting Pot*'s colonial statement that the Negro "insists that the white world deal with his problems." Newton and Seale expressed their belief "in an educational system that will give to our people a knowledge of self." Assimilationist education had never done that, especially since assimilationists from the days of Boas had maintained that the Negro "has no values and culture to guard and protect," as again stated in *Beyond the Melting Pot*.[43]

The growth of the Black Panther Party in 1967 reflected the growth of the Black Power movement and its antiracist challenge to assimilationist ideas. The series of violent urban rebellions that summer of 1967 seemed to win the nation's most famous activist to the poor peoples' struggle and Black Power. Martin Luther King Jr. began planning the Poor People's Campaign, and he came out to Black Power at the Southern Christian Leadership Conference's annual convention on August 16, 1967. He encouraged his black listeners to shed their assimilationist ideas, echoing Malcolm X. "We must not longer be ashamed of being black," he boomed. The Negro "must stand up and say, 'I'm black, but I'm black and beautiful,'" King proclaimed to an exhilarating applause, to waving Afros and waving signs that read "Black Is Beautiful and It Is So Beautiful to Be Black."[44]

The title of King's speech was the title of the book he released in the fall of 1967: *Where Do We Go from Here?* "When a people are mired in oppression, they realize deliverance only when they have accumulated the power to enforce change," King wrote. "Power is not the white man's birthright; it will not be legislated for us and delivered in neat government packages." Having written King off, most Black Power activists did not read his book nearly as closely as the widely anticipated *Black Power: The Politics of Liberation in America*, published shortly after *Where Do We Go from Here?* Carmichael and the political scientist Charles Hamilton contrasted "individual racism" as less harmful than "institutional racism," a term they introduced to clarify the collective manners of discrimination that led to racial disparities. "The distinction was a crucial one," explained the historian Peniel Joseph. They turned "at least a generation of reputable social science scholarship on its head—most notably Gunnar Myrdal's classic *An American Dilemma*."[45]

Like Malcolm before him, King did not have the opportunity to develop his antiracist challenge to the prevailing assimilationist ideas or clarify his definition of racism. He was assassinated on April 4, 1968. In the following week more than 125 cities experienced another wave of urban rebellions. If the calamity of the Nazi Holocaust devastated the legitimacy of eugenics, then the death of King devastated the legitimacy of assimilationism, especially since King's death triggered Black Power's growth into one of the largest antiracist mass mobilizations in American history.[46]

After King's death, Black Power intellectuals inside and outside of the academy increasingly challenged assimilationists from nearly ever vantage point, including the vantage point of gender. Assimilationist theory had been built on the back of the black matriarch trope since at least the days of Frazier, and many male Black Power activists reinforced this theory. Black feminists challenged white assimilationists and those Moynihan Report–reading black men fantasizing about their emasculation. Frances Beal, who helped found the Black Women's Liberation Committee in SNCC, wrote the black feminist manifesto, "Double Jeopardy: to Be Black and Female," which she circulated in 1969. America has held up child-rearing homemakers as the "middle class white model," and then forced black women to work away from their children in "degrading and dehumanizing jobs" and browbeat them as inferior for not assimilating into "this mirage of 'womanhood.'" Beal also lamented that "since the advent of Black Power, black men are maintaining that they have been castrated by society but that black women somehow escaped this persecution and even contributed to this emasculation." Actually "the black woman in America can justly be described as a 'slave of a slave.'"[47] (Two years later the sociologist Robert Staples published "The Myth of the Impotent Black Male," setting the record straight.)[48]

As Beal's "Double Jeopardy" circulated in 1969, the Black Power challenge to all those dominating assimilationist ideas and scholars on campuses crested. Black students and their faculty allies looked upon nearly all the traditional disciplines—history, sociology, psychology, anthropology, disciplines dominated by assimilationist ideas—as racist. These black students conjured and started requesting, demanding, and protesting something completely new, which they called black studies. Between 1967 and 1970 black students and their allies compelled nearly a thousand colleges and universities to introduce black studies departments, programs, and courses.[49]

On March 1, 1967, junior Jimmy Garrett issued the first known black studies proposal to his faculty at San Francisco State. "For a black student the typical liberal education at San Francisco State College is a destructive one," Garrett wrote.[50] In requesting black studies at Mount Holyoke College in 1968, Barbara Smith informed her professors, "When the focus in these classrooms is almost exclusively . . . white . . . and almost never black, dissatisfaction among those students with historical and cultural roots which are not white and European is inevitable."[51] On December 23, 1968, black students issued a clarification of their demands at Swarthmore College. They rebuked those who insisted on "clinging to his 'integrationist ethic,'" which "is the most dangerous kind of paternalist racism, that kind which would deny the legitimacy of their self-definition, while at the same time seeking to impose its own viewpoint and the viewpoint of the few negroes who agree with it."[52]

The student and founding faculty push for black studies primarily confronted assimilationist scholars, who negated the uniqueness of the African American experience, who negated the uniqueness of African American culture, who negated the equality of cultures, who thought and taught from what the famous Kerner Commission report on the urban rebellions called the "white perspective" in 1968.[53] These founders of black studies classed assimilationist professors as racist, bringing forth one of the first intellectual achievements of the discipline of black studies: the redefinition of racist ideas to include assimilationists.[54]

By the mid-1970s the Black Power movement had ended. And yet the challenge of Black Power proved unable to completely marginalize assimilationists in the racial discourse as profoundly as assimilationists did eugenicists after World War II. The assimilationist definition continued to prevail into the 1980s and 1990s. Assimilationists continued to identify themselves as the chief antiracists, while rejecting any suggestion otherwise. In 1993 the historian Herbert Aptheker's *Anti-Racism in U.S. History* framed many of the assimilationists in this chapter as antiracists. And this framing was based on his definition: "Belief in the superiority of one's particular culture or nation or class or sex is not the same as belief in the inherent, immutable, and significant inferiority of an entire physically characterized people." He considered the latter to be "racism." Aptheker refused to consider that culture and nationality and class and sex had intersected with race, allowing assimilationists and segregationists to consider African American culture, black nations, black poor people, black elites, black women, and black men to be inferior to European American culture, white nations, white poor people, white elites, white women, and white men.[55]

Even as assimilationists and their definition prevailed long after Black Power, black studies and other intellectual enterprises critical of assimilationist theories and definitions found their own niche in the racial discourse of the 1980s and beyond. The battle for the racial discourse hardly ended after Black Power ended in the 1970s. It carried on. It carries on to this day.

Notes

1. For the history and context of sterilization programs, see Dorothy Roberts, *Killing the Black Body: Race, Reproduction, and the Meaning of Liberty* (New York: Knopf Doubleday, 2014); Harriet A. Washington, *Medical Apartheid: The Dark History of Medical Experiment on Black Americans from Colonial Times to the Present* (New York: Knopf Doubleday, 2008).

2. See Harry Hamilton Laughlin, *Official Records in the History of the Eugenics Record Office, Cold Spring Harbor, Long Island, New York* (Cold Spring Harbor, N.Y.: The Office, 1939). There has been a wealth of studies on the eugenics movement. Here is a small sampling: Robert W. Sussman, *The Myth of Race: The Troubling Persistence of an Unscientific Idea* (Cambridge, Mass.: Harvard University Press, 2014); Randall Hansen and Desmond S. King, *Sterilized by the State: Eugenics, Race, and the Population Scare in Twentieth-Century North America* (Cambridge, UK: Cambridge University Press, 2013); Robert C. Bannister, *Social*

Darwinism: Science and Myth in Anglo-American Social Thought (Philadelphia: Temple University Press, 1979).

3. Ruth Benedict, *Race: Science and Politics* (New York: Viking, 1940), v–vi.

4. Ruth Benedict, *Patterns of Culture* (New York: Mariner Books, 2005), 13–15, 50.

5. For a history of assimilationist ideas, see Ibram X. Kendi, *Stamped from the Beginning: The Definitive History of Racist Ideas in America* (New York: Nation, 2016); George M. Fredrickson, *The Black Image in the White Mind: The Debate on Afro-American Character and Destiny, 1817–1914* (New York: Harper & Row, 1971).

6. See, for example, Elazar Barkan, *The Retreat of Scientific Racism: Changing Concepts of Race in Britain and the United States between the World Wars* (New York: Cambridge University Press, 1992).

7. See, for example, George M. Fredrickson, *Racism: A Short History* (Princeton, N.J.: Princeton University Press, 2002); Stanley Feldstein, *The Poisoned Tongue: A Documentary History of American Racism and Prejudice* (New York: Morrow, 1972); Pat Shipman, *The Evolution of Racism: Human Differences and the Use and Abuse of Science* (New York: Simon & Schuster, 1994).

8. For a good overview of voices and ideas of Black Power studies, see Peniel Joseph, ed., *The Black Power Movement: Rethinking the Civil Rights–Black Power Era* (New York: Routledge, 2013).

9. See Thomas F. Gossett, *Race: The History of an Idea in America* (Dallas, Tex.: Southern Methodist University Press, 1963).

10. For information on Benedict's life, see Margaret Mead, *Ruth Benedict* (New York: Columbia University Press, 1974); Judith Schachter, *Ruth Benedict: Patters of Life* (Philadelphia: University of Pennsylvania Press, 1983).

11. Franz Boas, *The Mind of Primitive Man* (New York: Macmillan, 1921), 127–28, 272–73; Franz Boas, "The Problem of the American Negro," *Yale Review* 10 (January 1921): 395.

12. Robert E. Park, "The Conflict and Fusion of Cultures with Special Reference to the Negro," *Journal of Negro History* 4, no. 2 (1919): 116.

13. For more on Park's race relations cycle, see Robert E. Park, "Behind Our Masks" and "Our Racial Frontier on the Pacific," *Survey Graphic*, May 1, 1926, 135–39 and 192–96; Robert E. Park, *Race and Culture: Essays in the Sociology of Contemporary Man* (New York: Free Press, 1950); Stanford M. Lyman, "The Race Relations Cycle of Robert E. Park," *Pacific Sociology Review* 11 (1968): 16–21; Winifred Raushenbush, *Robert E. Park: Biography of a Sociologist* (Durham, N.C.: Duke University Press, 1979), 107–18.

14. E. Franklin Frazier, *The Negro Family in the United States* (Chicago: University of Chicago Press, 1939), 355–57.

15. See Patricia Morton, *Disfigured Images: The Historical Assault on Afro-American Women* (Westport, Conn.: Greenwood Press, 1991); Melissa Harris-Perry, *Sister Citizen: Shame, Stereotypes, and Black Women in America* (New Haven, Conn.: Yale University Press, 2011).

16. Frazier, *The Negro Family*, 42.

17. See Tara McPherson, *Reconstructing Dixie: Race, Gender, and Nostalgia in the Imagined South* (Durham, N.C.: Duke University Press, 2003).

18. Frazier, *The Negro Family*, 58, 290, 488–89.

19. Melville Jean Herskovits, *The Myth of the Negro Past* (Boston: Beacon, 1990), 19, 298.

20. Donna Murch, "A Campus Where Black Power Won: Merritt College and the Hidden History of Oakland's Black Panther Party," in *Neighborhood Rebels: Black Power at the Local Level*, edited by Peniel Joseph (New York: Palgrave, 2010), 97.

21. Jerry Gershenhorn, *Melville J. Herskovits and the Racial Politics of Knowledge* (Lincoln: University of Nebraska Press, 2004), 94, 156–67; David Levering Lewis, *W. E. B. Du Bois, 1919–1963: The Fight for Equality and the American Century* (New York: Henry Holt, 2001), 435–50.

22. Gunnar Myrdal, *An American Dilemma: The Negro Problem and Modern Democracy* (New York: Harper & Row, 1944), 751–52, 928–29.

23. Melville J. Herskovits, "Some Thoughts on American Research in Africa," *African Studies Bulletin* 1 (November 1958): 1–11. For a good overview of the early development of African studies, see Gershenhorn, *Melville J. Herskovits*, 169–200.

24. John Hope Franklin, *From Slavery to Freedom: A History of Negroes Americans* (New York: Knopf, 1947); E. Merton Coulter, *The South During Reconstruction, 1865–1877* (Baton Rouge: Louisiana State University Press, 1947).

25. Theodosius Dobzhansky and Ashley Montagu, "Natural Selection and the Mental Capacities of Mankind," *Science* 105, no. 2736 (1947): 587–90; Hamilton Cravens, "What's New in Science and Race since the 1930s? Anthropologists and Racial Essentialism," *The Historian* 72, no. 2 (2010): 315–18; Michael Yudell, *Race Unmasked: Biology and Race in the Twentieth Century* (New York: Columbia University Press, 2014), 111–32, 201–2.

26. UNESCO, *Four Statements on the Race Question*, UNESCO and Its Programme (Paris: UNESCO, 1969), 30–43; Yudell, *Race Unmasked*, 148–67.

27. Edward Garrett, "The Equalitarian Dogma," *Mankind Quarterly* 1, no. 1 (1961): 253–57. Also see William H. Tucker, *The Funding of Scientific Racism: Wickliffe Draper and the Pioneer Fund* (Urbana: University of Illinois Press, 2007).

28. I. A. Newby, *The Development of Segregationist Thought* (Homewood, Ill.: Dorsey Press), 169–70; S. L. Washburn, "The Study of Race," *American Anthropologist* 65 (June 1963): 521–31.

29. Francis D. Adams and Barry Sanders, *Alienable Rights: The Exclusion of African Americans in a White Man's Land, 1619–2000* (New York: Harper Collins, 2004), 289.

30. Nathan Glazer and Daniel P. Moynihan, *Beyond the Melting Pot: The Negroes, Puerto Ricans, Jews, Italians, and Irish of New York City* (Cambridge, Mass.: MIT Press, 1963). For a hailing review, see Oscar Handlin, "All Colors, All Creeds, All Nationalities, All New Yorkers," *New York Times*, September 22, 1963.

31. Glazer and Moynihan, *Beyond the Melting Pot*, 11, 35, 50–53, 84–85.

32. "Racism: The Cancer That Is Destroying America," *Egyptian Gazette*, August 25, 1964.

33. Malcolm X and Alex Haley, *The Autobiography of Malcolm X* (New York: Ballantine Books, 1965), 54–55, 371.

34. Lyndon B. Johnson, "To Fulfill These Rights" (1965), in *The 1960s: A Documentary Reader*, edited by Brian Ward (New York: Wiley-Blackwell), 83–89.

35. Daniel P. Moynihan, *The Negro Family: The Case of Nation Action* (Washington D.C.: US Government Printing Office, 1965).

36. "New Crisis: The Negro Family," *Newsweek*, August 9, 1965.

37. Deborah G. White, *Too Heavy a Load : Black Women in Defense of Themselves, 1894–1994* (New York: Norton, 1999), 198–203.

38. "For a Better Future," *Ebony*, August 1966, 150.

39. Morton, *Disfigured Images*, 3–5, 125.

40. Andrew Billingsley, *Black Families in White America* (New York: Simon and Schuster, 1968), 33, 37.

41. See Joyce A. Ladner, *Tomorrow's Tomorrow: The Black Woman* (Garden City, N.Y.: Doubleday, 1971).

42. Peniel E. Joseph, *Waiting 'til the Midnight Hour: A Narrative History of Black Power in America* (New York: Henry Holt, 2006), 141–46.

43. Huey P. Newton, *Revolutionary Suicide* (New York: Harcourt Brace Jovanovich, 1973), 116–19; Glazer and Moynihan, *Beyond the Melting Pot*, 52–54.

44. Martin Luther King Jr., "Where Do We Go from Here?," in *Say It Loud: Great Speeches on Civil Rights and African American Identity*, edited by Catherine Ellis and Stephen Smith (New York: New Press, 2013), 41.

45. Joseph, *Waiting 'til the Midnight Hour*, 197–201; Martin Luther King Jr., *Where Do We Go from Here?* (New York: Harper & Row, 1967); Stokely Carmichael and Charles V. Hamilton, *Black Power: The Politics of Liberation in America* (New York: Random House, 1967).

46. See Clay Risen, *A Nation on Fire: America in the Wake of the King Assassination* (Hoboken, N.J.: John Wiley & Sons, 2009).

47. Frances Beale, "Double Jeopardy: To Be Black and Female," in *The Black Woman: An Anthology*, edited by Toni Cade Bambara (New York: Washington Square Press, 2005), 109–22.

48. Robert Staples, "The Myth of the Impotent Black Male," *Black Scholar* 2, no. 10 (1971): 2–9.

49. For the origins of black studies, see Ibram H. Rogers, *The Black Campus Movement: Black Students and the Racial Reconstitution of Higher Education, 1965–1972* (New York: Palgrave, 2012); Martha Biondi, *Black Revolution on Campus* (Berkeley: University of California Press, 2012).

50. William Barlow and Peter Shapiro, *An End to Silence: The San Francisco College Student Movement in the '60s* (New York: Pegasus, 1971), 124–26.

51. "Commentary: Black Studies—The Things We Need to Know," *Choragos*, November 14, 1968, Mount Holyoke College Archives and Special Collections, South Hadley, Massachusetts.

52. Swarthmore Afro-American Students' Society, "Demands," *Black Liberation 1969 Archive*, December 23, 1968, accessed January 15, 2017, http://blacklib1969.swarthmore.edu/items/show/445.

53. National Advisory Commission on Civil Disorders, *The Kerner Report: The 1968 Report on the National Advisory Commission on Civil Disorders* (New York: Pantheon Books, 1968).

54. For some early perspectives on the mission of black studies, see Armstead L. Robinson, Craig C. Foster, and Donald H. Ogilvie, *Black Studies in the University: A Symposium* (New Haven, Conn.: Yale University Press, 1969); Jacqueline Bobo, Cynthia Hudley, and Claudine Michel, *The Black Studies Reader* (New York: Routledge, 2004); Nick Aaron Ford, *Black Studies: Threat-or-Challenge* (Port Washington, N.Y.: Kennikat Press, 1973).

55. Herbert Aptheker, *Anti-Racism in U.S. History: The First Two Hundred Years* (New York: Greenwood Press, 1992), xiii–xiv.

Becoming African Women

Women's Cultural Nationalist Theorizing in the US Organization and the Committee for Unified Newark

Ashley D. Farmer

In 1971 women in the Committee for Unified Newark (CFUN), a New Jersey–based organization, published a guide for its female members called "Mwanamke Mwananchi," or "Nationalist Woman." One of the many organizations that developed during the Black Power movement of the late 1960s, CFUN members practiced Kawaida, a cultural nationalist philosophy based on the idea that culture was the "crucible in which black liberation takes form."[1] Marketing the handbook as an "outline for sisters to pick up and use," the authors envisioned it as guide for female members in their daily practice of Kawaida.[2] In it they provided directives for how women could embody and enact the ideal of the "African woman," a political identity based on a set of core cultural nationalist beliefs. One of the many documents that women in CFUN produced, the guide became an integral part of the organization's intellectual production that was aimed at convincing audiences of the importance of cultural nationalism and women's roles within it.

CFUN women published the handbook during a period of intense public debate about gender roles. The resurgence of black nationalism in the late 1960s revitalized discussions about how black activists could best organize against oppressive systems. Articles and essays proliferated in which activists and analysts offered their opinion on the "correct" understanding of men's and women's responsibilities in political organizing. By the early 1970s a clear narrative developed. Black Power could best be achieved when black men adopted leadership positions and women embraced marginal rank-and-file roles. Black women challenged these discourses, producing newspaper articles, anthologies, and artwork that countered this narrative and redefined ideas of revolution and women's roles within it.[3] The result was a vibrant intellectual and political culture that fostered new ideas about gender roles in black political organizing.

These conversations had important implications for women in CFUN precisely because many variants of cultural nationalist ideology prescribed marginal roles for women. The Kawaida doctrine, as originally conceived by a

Los Angeles–based activist, Maulana Karenga, assigned women to traditional roles in political organizing. However, as texts like "Nationalist Woman" show, women in Kawaidist organizations developed a body of writings that reframed this characterization of their responsibilities within these groups. Although they did not entirely break with the cultural nationalist ideology, they proffered progressive ideas about women's political participation that altered organizers' perspectives about gender roles within this faction of the movement.

This chapter explores Kawaidist women's redefinition of the African woman ideal and its effects on cultural nationalist organizations and practices. In doing so it joins a growing body of literature on male activists within these organizations.[4] It also contributes to activists' and scholars' analyses of women's roles in these groups, particularly ones that pinpoint how Kawaidist gender constructs could be both "liberating and confining" for women.[5] Yet both the historiography of cultural nationalist organizing and critiques of it have not adequately explored female adherents' positions on gender roles in cultural nationalist organizing. Instead both scholarly and popular accounts frame these women as victims of sexism, unable to theoretically or organizationally challenge the patriarchal gender constructs of cultural nationalist groups.

This chapter offers a new approach for understanding women's organizing and theorizing within CFUN and the US Organization, a California-based black nationalist group established by Maulana Karenga. Rather than assuming that the women in these groups ascribed to or were muted by conservative gender mandates, it explores how they reshaped these conversations through their writings about the Kawaida doctrine and the African woman ideal. The chapter illuminates how women's reconfiguration of this political identity played a key role in pushing organizational leaders to adopt more equitable organizing frameworks. It also documents how their renegotiation of gender roles produced more expansive interpretations of the Kawaida doctrine.

Foregrounding Kawaidist women's intellectual production simultaneously advances debates about cultural nationalist organizing and Black Power intellectualism. The conservative nature of these organizations often negates substantial scholarly engagement with members' beliefs and values.[6] However, cultural nationalist ideals were popular during this period, and their practices and ceremonies, including the Kwanzaa celebration, are part of the cultural fabric of today. Moreover activists in these groups engaged in conversations about gender roles within Kawaidist organizing because they believed these debates to be central to developing effective forms of political opposition to white hegemony and a vital component of their personal and collective self-liberation. As a result we must treat the complexities of cultural nationalist organizing with the same seriousness that we examine other forms of Black Power activism and theorizing. Examining Kawaidist women's ideas can reveal the progressive and insurgent aspects of their organizing even within groups that espoused conservative gender politics. It can also offer a fuller picture of the spectrum of Black Power ideologies of the 1960s and 1970s and the myriad ways in which black women navigated them.

Additionally, excavating and assembling women's writings about the African woman transforms the body of evidence on which much of this scholarship has been written. The history of cultural nationalism has primarily been told through the voices and sources of black men. Not only does this reflect a historical bias in who is considered a practitioner or theorist; it also shows a predisposition for the exclusion of women-authored texts—including handbooks and advice columns—as valued sources in the black intellectual tradition. In reading women's writings as central sources about cultural nationalist ideology, this chapter challenges dominant archival practices in the study of cultural nationalism and foregrounds female Kawaidists' vibrant tradition of political thought.

The US Organization, Modern Cultural Nationalism, and Kawaida

Karenga's US Organization popularized the ideal of the African woman. This group developed out of the vortex of racism and black nationalism that characterized black life in Los Angeles in the 1960s. In the second half of the twentieth century, black Angelenos, like their counterparts across the country, endured ongoing housing, workplace, and law enforcement discrimination along with urban poverty.[7] This repression came to a head when California highway patrolmen stopped a black man, Marquette Frye, on the suspicion of driving under the influence. What began as a traffic stop on August 11, 1965, turned into a full-scale revolt after an argument among Frye, his mother, and police officers turned violent. Word of the altercation spread throughout the city. By nightfall Los Angeles was in the midst of a full-scale riot now known as the Watts revolt.[8]

US developed out of the haze of the rebellion in Watts. On September 7, 1965, Karenga, along with local activists Dorothy Jamal, Brenda Haiba Karenga, and Hakim Jamal, transformed a local study group into the cultural nationalist organization.[9] US designated both the organization and the black community versus the implied *them*, their white oppressors.[10] Founding member Hakim Jamal, a close associate of Malcolm X, originally led the group. In early 1966 leadership of the group transferred to Karenga.[11]

US organizers' goal was to bring about revolution through cultural education and coalition building.[12] Rather than developing a mass organization, members, or advocates as they were called, functioned as a small band of organizers intent on reorienting black Americans' cultural compass using the Kawaida doctrine. The philosophy called for the reclamation of an African past and identity through a set of cultural, social, and political practices based on an African value system, the Nguzo Saba. Advocates changed their names, dressed in traditional West African clothing, and developed traditions like Kwanzaa that fostered core Kawaidist principles.

Kawaida contained gender-specific roles for advocates. The primary roles of the African woman were to "inspire her man, educate her children, and participate in social development."[13] The organization's patriarchal approach to cultural reinvention also extended to the private sphere. The African woman was to openly accept and participate in polygamous relationships. US leadership argued that adopting the practice was a way to refute white, Eurocentric familial constructs and mirror social relationships found in African societies. US was not the only group to espouse this patriarchal approach to gender politics. However, the Los Angeles group garnered attention and criticism because of members' declarations of men's supremacy and their use of African culture to support their male-dominated practices. Both contemporaneous and post hoc assessments noted that US's gender constructs were predicated on ahistorical ideas of Africa and emulated white rather than African societal gender roles. Critics suggested that the group's structure reinforced the 1965 Moynihan Report, a government-sponsored document that labeled black women as "emasculating" matriarchs and blamed them for the race problem in America. Far from emulating African practices, they argued, US reinforced hegemonic gender constructs and fortified the Moynihan-inspired argument that black families suffered from a shortage of black men.[14]

Even with its controversial stance on gender roles, US enjoyed widespread community support until several factors weakened the group. The FBI and local law enforcement tried to dismantle the organization through office raids and arrests of individual members.[15] The Bureau also exacerbated feuds between US and the Black Panther Party, eventually leading to a shootout and the deaths of two Panthers in 1969.[16] Fearing retaliation, US members curtailed their community work. They also developed a paramilitary structure to ward off future attacks.

Women emerged as leaders amid this organizational restructuring. They began to take on roles in the group's administration and security sectors. Female advocates' new responsibilities included intelligence gathering and security detailing. This new division of labor meant that women worked alongside men and, at times, headed US initiatives. It also created opportunities for women advocates to reshape the group's perceptions of gender roles.[17]

US women introduced their progressive conceptualization of the African woman in such newspaper articles as "View from the Womans' [sic] Side of the Circle" (1969), published in their news organ, *Harambee*. In it, the Malaika (women's subunit) defined the African woman as an activist who was committed to the gendered directives of Kawaida but not circumscribed by them. US women based their new conceptualization of African womanhood in the Kawaidist principle Ujima, or collective work and responsibility. They argued that, by 1969, men and women in US were practicing the principle

of Ujima "together in a oneness that verge[d] on symbiosis." They credited
this organizational and ideological unity with advocates' adherence to the
Kawaida doctrine. However, the Malaika also argued that the group had
achieved a higher level of consciousness and organizing because women had
moved from a "minimum" to a "maximum practice" of gender-specific cultural nationalist tenets and objectives.[18]

The Malaika envisioned the African woman as an activist who engaged
in the "maximum" practice of the doctrine's directives for women: inspiration, education, and social development. Male leadership's interpretations
of inspiration were predicated on women's support of men and community
education. The Malaika expanded this definition of inspiration to include
women's public acts of political struggle. "We inspired our men in the past,
and we are still continuing to inspire them in these ways today, but we have
also found new ways to inspire them," they explained. US leadership taught
female advocates that "Black men [were] inspired by Black women who are
capable of carrying on the revolution in their absence." The Malaika argued
that black men were "inspired even more by Black women who can carry on
the revolution in their presence." Female advocates did "not have to wait for
the future in order to make a positive contribution" to black political struggle.
Instead they should reformulate the African woman ideal to reflect an understanding of inspiration predicated on women's public political activism alongside and, if needed, in lieu of black men.[19]

US women also challenged limiting interpretations of women's roles in
education and social development. They argued that, in 1969, "the revolution
being fought" was a "revolution to win the minds of [their] people." Given
the urgency of the political moment, the African woman could no longer
limit herself to simply educating children in the home or the school. She
had a responsibility to reach beyond traditional spheres of domestic influence and "educate the people by forming an unbroken circle between [their]
education and the social development of [their] community." This reciprocal
relationship between education and social development meant that women
also had to reconceptualize their roles in community organizing and move
beyond archetypal spaces of women's work. The Malaika advanced a vision
of the African woman as an activist who enhanced the cultural growth of the
black community by setting a "good example" of "complementarity" in the
public sphere by "attend[ing] community meetings," teaching about "Black
Cultural nationalism," and appearing at and leading public events alongside
black men.[20]

US women ended the article by establishing their own vision of the African
woman. They declared that the "US organization ha[d] produced the first
truly revolutionary woman" of the Black Power movement, a woman who
was "submissive yet vocal, who [was] revolutionary yet feminine, who [was]
complimentary [*sic*] not equal." The African woman did not seek independence but a more balanced interdependence with her male counterpart. She

contributed to the struggle not by "changing [her] role, but by broadening the scope of [her] role."[21]

The Malaika's article reflected their critical engagement with the intersection of womanhood, political struggle, and the Kawaida doctrine. US women claimed that the quotidian practice of cultural nationalism—particularly in the face of government repression—required a complete commitment to Kawaidist principles. Engaging in this practice at the highest level necessitated a collective redefinition of the African woman ideal. Accordingly the Malaika envisioned the African woman as an activist who found parity with her male counterpart in her inspirational and educational work and who took on a leading role in shaping cultural nationalists' political projects. Their reformulation of this political identity advanced a progressive and politically responsive interpretation of Kawaida. It also challenged the ideological basis on which gender roles within the US Organization rested by suggesting that advocates' conceptions of gendered political organizing were more porous than previously thought.

In theorizing their version of the African woman, the Malaika bent the gender-specific pillars of the Kawaida doctrine to better fit their needs but did not break with them. Kawaida doctrine held that equality between men and women was a false concept.[22] The women's division reinforced this point. They continually sought to broaden the definition of what constituted "women's work." However, they remained invested in a gendered division of labor and distinctly masculine and feminine political identities. This set them apart from their contemporaries in other Black Power organizations. For the Malaika, the radical aspect of their gendered theorizing and organizing lay in their rejection of Eurocentric cultural and political models and their progressive interpretation of the gendered directives of the Kawaida doctrine.

The Malaika's statement, and other internal debates within the US Organization, significantly shaped the group's perception of gender roles. In particular it caused male leaders, including Karenga, to abandon limited understandings of male-female relationships and adopt more progressive conceptualizations of the African woman. In subsequent publications the US leader remarked that black men must "stop denying [their] women the full and heroic role in the history and development of [the black] struggle" and argued that African Americans will "never liberate [themselves] as a people" until they rid themselves of "behavioral patterns like sexism" and "male chauvinism."[23] Karenga credited women with fostering his revised perspective, revealing the importance of women's theorizing within the organization's ranks.

Despite these inroads, Malaika had little time to enact its progressive vision of the African woman. Following the 1969 shootout, US's organizational structure broke down and its influence declined. During this period there was a mass exodus of advocates from the US leadership and the paramilitary subunits.[24] Some advocates abandoned the organization completely. Others joined the ranks of the CFUN in Newark, New Jersey.[25]

CFUN and the Spread of Cultural Nationalism

US advocates who ventured east encountered an activist community that developed coevally and, at times, in conjunction with nationalist organizing in Los Angeles. In Newark, as in other major cities, black activists created a dynamic organizing culture that included political protests, independent black community schools, and a vibrant black arts scene.[26] Local institutions like Amiri and Amina Baraka's Spirit House epitomized activists' conjoining of cultural and political mobilization. Both Newark natives, Amiri Baraka had found success as a poet and playwright in New York before returning to his hometown, while Amina, a talented dancer and painter, fostered the city's growing black art scene. Around 1965 the pair began organizing together and eventually married.[27] Nestled in Newark's largely black Central Ward, the Spirit House hosted the Baraka-led theater group, the Spirit House Players; it also functioned as a community meeting space and eventually was the site of an independent black elementary school.[28]

The Spirit House attracted Karenga's attention. In 1966 he visited the Barakas' cultural center and introduced the Newark activists to Kawaida. The trio met again in spring 1967, when Amiri was a visiting professor at San Francisco State University. While in California, he visited US's headquarters in Los Angeles. He found Karenga's organization and philosophy impressive as it seemed to him to be the "next-higher stage of commitment" to cultural organizing.[29] The Barakas returned to Newark in June 1967, armed with Karenga's doctrine and prepared to implement it at Spirit House.[30]

The Barakas returned home on the eve of the Newark Rebellion and the National Black Power Conference, two events that accelerated the development of cultural nationalism in Newark. Like the Watts uprising, the July 1967 Newark rebellion began with an incident of police brutality and catalyzed local residents' interest in black nationalism. The Black Power Conference, held eight days later, codified this sentiment and spurred the creation of new local organizations. Women were key organizers in Newark's burgeoning Black Power scene. Amina Baraka created the United Sisters, a women's study group that analyzed women's roles in education, community control, and African culture.[31] Other women joined the Sisters of Black Culture, an organization dedicated to encouraging black women to "go out in [their] neighborhoods and help black children learn to be ready to take over."[32] These groups became part of a network of organizations that fostered cultural nationalism in Newark. They also fostered vital conversations about women's roles in Kawaidist organizing.

Members of the United Sisters and the Sisters of Black Culture also helped build a black political front in Newark. In 1968, at Karenga's behest, both groups joined forces with three other local organizations—the United Brothers, the Spirit House, and Black Community Defense and Development—to create the Committee for Unified Newark.[33] Women oversaw the daily functions of the organization, running CFUN's restaurant, poverty programs, day care organizations, and community initiatives. Higher-ranking women, called the Mumininas, served as the women's social, intellectual, and cultural council. This circle included Amina Baraka, who headed CFUN's Social Division, and Malaika Akiba, who taught at CFUN's Political School of Kawaida.[34] The Women's Division became the largest and most diverse unit within CFUN. It was also responsible for devising the administrative structures that increased the functionality and reach of the group.[35]

Due in large part to the work of the Women's Division, CFUN became an exemplar of Black Power organizing. Amiri Baraka argued that the Newark model could translate into wholesale liberation if actualized on a bigger scale, envisioning an organization "whose function would be to struggle for Black Power wherever black people were in the world."[36] He called activists together for a 1970 Labor Day weekend conference, during which attendees created the Congress of African People (CAP). A federation of leftist organizations designed to achieve black power and empowerment on a global scale, CAP augmented Baraka's political power and injected cultural nationalism into black politics at the national level.[37]

CFUN served as the Congress's headquarters; the Women's Division formulated CAP's position on gender roles. Women in Newark used this position to their advantage, constantly encouraging Amiri Baraka to denounce sexism and to use his influence to eradicate it within CAP's ranks.[38] Not content to let male leadership determine their roles and responsibilities, women in CFUN also developed a body of literature aimed at reconceptualizing the African woman ideal. In their handbooks and advice columns they challenged male leadership's patriarchy and conservatism. They also produced some of the group's most progressive and gender-inclusive interpretations of the Kawaida doctrine.

The "Necessary" Roles of the African Woman in CFUN

Like their US Organization counterparts, CFUN women argued that the practical implementation of Kawaida required a fundamental reconceptualization of gender roles. Accordingly the Mumininas, a group that included Jaribu Hill, Salimu Rodgers, Jalia Woods, and Staarabisha Barrett, sought to reformulate CFUN's gender constructs through their organizational writings.[39] They created the "Nationalist Woman" handbook to publicize their progressive vision of the African woman. In line with Kawaidist women's literature, the manual reinforced doctrinal prescriptions for the African woman. However, CFUN women broke new ground by using the guide to challenge gender hierarchies within the organization and to redefine the axis on which members measured the African woman's political legitimacy and contribution to political struggle.

In the first section of the guide the Mumininas combined praise for the Kawaida doctrine with criticism of practitioners' patriarchal interpretations of its principles. They began by recapitulating Kawaida's catechisms on the "natural" roles of women and men. The women affirmed that "women can not do the same things as men. . . . They are made by nature to function differently." They also confirmed that men and women's "natural" differences translated to different responsibilities in political organizing. However, the Mumininas were unwilling to accept that these "natural" differences justified gendered hierarchies within the cultural nationalist community. Departing from typical interpretations of the doctrine, they asserted, "Nature has made women [sic] submissive—she must submit to man's creation in order for it to exist. This does not mean that she has to follow for the sake of following or be subservient to him." Instead they framed men's and women's roles as coeval components of a holistic emancipatory practice: "To speak of roles is to be concerned with completion—the balance of nature. . . . Roles do not mean that one is superior or inferior to the other, but necessary—complementary to the whole."[40]

The Mumininas brought this same perspective to bear on their assessment of their assigned roles in inspiration, education, and social development. They affirmed that these areas were guiding tenets of the African woman's activism. However, CFUN women pushed their readership to expand their perspectives on the ways in which women could and should enact these principles. Male advocates often argued that women were inspirational by submitting to their will. CFUN women reinterpreted this tenet based on their personal, political, and ideological interests. "By *being* African (color, culture, consciousness) woman is inspirational," they wrote. "By having an emotional commitment to Nationalism the Black Woman is inspirational. . . . By having a sincere undying faith in our leaders, our people and our righteousness and victory of our struggle is inspirational."[41] Their instructions for the African woman's practice of education and social development followed a similar pattern, emphasizing how women could embody and enact these principles in politically and emotionally motivated ways. If US Organization women defined the African woman as an activist who "broadened" her practice of gender-specific roles, then CFUN women argued that her practice of these principles need not rely on gender hierarchies or centralize black men.

Women in CFUN also established a new dimension of African womanhood: necessary roles. They explained that the "African woman ha[d] a natural and necessary role to play in the building of [the] nation." Inspiration, education, and social development were "natural" roles that she "would have to preform . . . even if [she] were free." Necessary roles were the functions that African women preformed because black Americans were still oppressed, "still slaves—a nation without political, institutional or coercive power." The Mumininas argued that political struggle required black women to be active members in all aspects of organizing. As a result, women had "to learn such things as secretarial skills, weaponry, first aid, driving, [and] administrative skills," in addition and sometimes in lieu of performing their "natural" tasks. They warned readers that it was "'nice' (but harmful) to think that women should just sit at home—sewing, cooking, taking care of the house and children." They needed to face the fact that they were a "BLACK AND POWERLESS PEOPLE" who had to do all they could to attain "self-determination, self-respect, self defense." The Mumininas summarized their argument by stressing the futility of divisions of labor in the political trenches: "All who can work will have to *work hard* until we have liberated ourselves then and only then—when we are free can we again decide whatever new roles women must have."[42]

The "Nationalist Woman" handbook revealed CFUN women's preoccupation with creating a viable model of African womanhood rooted in the realities of their lived experiences and the needs of the black liberation struggle. They argued that their definitions of black womanhood had to be predicated on contemporaneous political struggle instead of ahistorical ideas about men's and women's roles. Rather than completely reject the Kawaida doctrine, the Mumininas developed a new axis on which to measure black women's organizing. Taking their cue from their US Organization predecessors who called for women to move from a "minimum" to a "maximum" role, CFUN women redefined the African woman as an activist who eventually fulfilled her "natural" roles by enacting her "necessary" ones. Ultimately the Mumininas reimagined the African woman as an organizer who practiced a gender-inclusive form of cultural nationalism and tailored her activism to fit the needs of the political moment. She was also an activist who renounced ideological rigidity in favor of an evolving view of cultural revolution and women's roles within it.

More than simply a women's handbook, "Mwanamke Mwananchi" was a guide for reconceptualizing Kawaida and the black liberation struggle. According to the Mumininas, the African woman could exclusively preform her "natural" roles if, and only if, black Americans were free. Absent the realization of black liberation, both men and women needed to take on whatever "natural" and "necessary" roles the struggle demanded. To relegate the African woman solely to her "natural" roles was to fundamentally misunderstand the current state of the black struggle. It was also to proffer a static conception of revolution. As they explained, the African woman's "necessary roles will change as the needs of the nation change," and she should "be conscious enough to know what skills are needed at a particular time—what to do and when and where to do it."[43] The Mumininas generated a new interpretation of Kawaida, one that used the doctrine's culturally restorative qualities in service of developing a dynamic political praxis.

The Mumininas' call for egalitarian gender relationships also anticipated the changing ideological orientation of CAP and the larger Black Power movement. In 1972 members elected Amiri Baraka as chairman, solidifying Kawaida as CAP's official ideology. Baraka's new position coincided with a resurgence of Pan-African organizing among Black Power organizations and activists' increased contact with African liberation movements and leaders.[44] Under his leadership CAP members began to study and emulate African liberation groups such as Julius Nyerere's Tanzanian African Nationalist Union.[45] CAP members did not completely abandon their commitment to cultural liberation amid these changes. However, they did begin to adhere to a broader conceptualization of cultural nationalism that rejected the rigidity of Kawaida for a multifaceted, internationalist, and class-conscious political frame.[46]

As CAP refined its ideological position, female advocates developed more nuanced definitions of the African woman. Their articles in *Black NewArk* and *Unity and Struggle*, CFUN's and CAP's newspapers, respectively, documented this evolution. In particular Amina Baraka's "Social Organization" column served as a space in which the Women's Division leader articulated progressive conceptualizations of gender roles. She projected a model of the African woman that was steeped in CAP's expanding, Pan-African perspective and driven by the claim that black liberation could be achieved only through women's full political and ideological participation in political struggle.

In "On Afrikan Women" (1973), Amina Baraka framed the African woman as a progressive, culturally driven activist intent on bringing about global black liberation. She began by emphasizing black women's educational, cultural, and inspirational roles. "All of our children are being miseducated or uneducated, especially where we Afrikan women have not found it necessary to struggle to help create alternative institutions for ourselves," she wrote. "We must take an active role in the National and World Liberation of Afrikan people. We must become skilled in all areas. . . . We must work and study without complaint. . . . Push and support and develop Afrikan Culture based on tradition and reason. Let our lives and ways inspire Afrikan People to reject European culture and values."[47]

In the second half of the article, however, Baraka diverged from CAP's standard characterizations of women's roles by encouraging her female readership to envision themselves as consummate political thinkers. As "Afrikan Women," she told them, "we must seek political clarity and educate ourselves so we can support and help make revolution for Afrikan people all over this World." The leader called on women in CAP to "begin to study the scientific politics of revolutionaries so that [they could] understand the revolutionary nature of [their] work" and "provide the world of Afrikan children with an identity, purpose, direction."[48]

Amina Baraka presented a version of African womanhood that reified and reconfigured CAP's political outlook and organizing structure. She located the crux of the African woman's activism in Kawaidist directives of inspiration, education, and social development. By situating the African woman's activism in the global context, Baraka also mirrored CAP's growing Pan-Africanist orientation. The CFUN leader departed from traditional Kawaidist discourses, however, in her framing of black women as studied political activists. She envisioned the African woman as an organizer who inspired and educated men, women, and children through an ideologically grounded political agenda rather than philosophical abstraction. To be sure, her emphasis on social scientific reasoning reflected a broader trend within CAP, whereby leadership encouraged members to study the political theory of African liberation leaders. Yet Baraka's emphasis on women's ideological grounding had important implications for gender roles within CAP. Activists' previous interpretations of Kawaida maintained that political theory was the purview of men. By calling on CAP women to develop a political identity based on the "scientific politics of revolutionaries" rather than the hermetic interpretations of black men, Baraka charged black women with eradicating the remaining vestiges of Kawaidist conservatism. She also portrayed them as the progenitors of progressive forms of cultural nationalist thought and challenged the anti-intellectual characterizations of female cultural nationalists.

"On Afrikan Women" was emblematic of CFUN women's writings, which, by the early 1970s, had helped transform the organization into a locus of women's activism and theorizing. Looking to move their debates from printed pages to public forums, CFUN women created the Afrikan Women's Conference. Organizers billed the meeting as "an important step toward heightening the political awareness and educational development of Afrikan Women."[49] The July 1974 meeting consisted of workshops dedicated to traditional forms of women's organizing, including education, health, and social organization. It also included seminars in politics, communications, and institutional development, as well as lectures from "Afrikan women from America's liberation movements, West Indies, and progressive Afrikan countries."[50]

More than seven hundred people attended the three-day conference held at Rutgers University. Participants included women from multiple chapters of CAP and representatives from the Congress of Racial Equality and the Socialist Workers Party. The conference also attracted international attention. Students from Ethiopia and women ambassadors from Guinea were also in attendance.[51] Throughout the meeting, participants emphasized the integral role black women could play in bringing about self-determination throughout the diaspora.[52] Political workshop participants "generally agreed that women suffer triple oppression, that of race, class, and sex," while social organization workshop attendees focused on "the total development of healthy, revolutionary relationships." Hundreds of women debated the merits of independent schools in the education meeting, and the health and wellness workshop participants focused on the toll of racism on black women. Ultimately attendees were in "unanimous agreement that [they] should put forth an anti-capitalist, anti-imperialist, and anti neo-colonialist position" that challenged patriarchy and advanced black women's liberation.[53]

The Afrikan Women's Conference hastened key ideological shifts within CAP. Following the meeting, Amiri Baraka formally rejected traditional interpretations of Kawaida and its patriarchal maxims. He called on CAP members to adopt Revolutionary Kawaida, a political position that combined the best practices from Karenga's philosophy with principles and frameworks put forth by African liberation leaders.[54] A central tenet of Revolutionary Kawaida was the disavowal of the patriarchal practices of the original doctrine. CAP members now "rejected the interpretations of Kawaida as a form of reactionary chauvinism either racial or sexual." They also repudiated the practice of "extended famil[ies]," or polygamy.[55]

Male members credited women's theorizing with accelerating CAP's leftward ideological turn. Amiri Baraka asserted that the Afrikan Women's Conference was a "concrete step onward and upward in the ideological development of the Black Liberation Movement in North America." The conference, he argued, foregrounded the "need to draw Black Women not only into the liberation movement" but also "directly into the struggle against capitalism and imperialism."[56] The following year he rejected the remaining ideological remnants of Kawaida and embraced the gender-inclusive, anti-imperialist, and socialist platform akin to the one Afrikan Women's Conference participants espoused. He also made it the official political position of the Congress of African People.

In 1975 CAP became a socialist organization.[57] Before this point CAP members' interest in anticapitalism and socialism had been tempered by their ongoing belief in black cultural particularity. They now identified class struggle as the primary animator of black liberation. CAP women found the socialist turn to be a productive space for theorizing more radical conceptualizations of their roles. They created the Black Women's United Front (BWUF), an "anti-racist, anti-imperialist, and anti-capitalist" group dedicated to ending the "triple oppression" of black women.[58] The BWUF functioned as a collective within CAP, with members hosting meetings and assemblies to develop a women-centered, socialist agenda throughout 1976.[59] CAP's Marxist turn marked the end of female members' investment in reshaping the African woman ideal. However, CAP's embrace of the BWUF reflected black women's organizational and theoretical impact, as well as how they adopted, transformed, and applied CAP's "Black Power ends" to meet their gender-specific needs and goals.

New Perspectives on Black Power Intellectualism

Kawaidist women's efforts to reimagine the African woman were a testament to the importance of cultural nationalism in the Black Power era. Activists across the political spectrum often lamented the detrimental effects of white cultural hegemony, but few organizations provided tangible frameworks for rebuilding black cultural heritage. The Kawaida doctrine, and the ceremonies and rituals that cultural nationalists developed, offered black Americans a way to repair real and imagined connections to their African homeland, foster new forms of Black Power, and develop counterhegemonic models of manhood and womanhood. As a result Kawaida had mass appeal, even as it reproduced the white, heteropatriarchal social constructs and practices that advocates sought to subvert. The holiday Kwanzaa is one example of Kawaida's lasting influence, as it has been appropriated outside of the nationalist community and is still widely practiced today.

Black women's interpretations and applications of Kawaida were key catalysts behind its evolution and popularity. As members of the US Organization, CFUN, and CAP, they transformed, modernized, and popularized cultural nationalist organizing. Women in these groups continually developed accessible ways to implement Kawaida's core principles. They also redefined the African woman ideal, transforming it from a conservative, male-serving concept into a political identity rooted in their gender-specific interpretations of cultural nationalism and their lived experiences as activists. Armed with this more expansive understanding of their political and cultural roles, black women were leading organizers of grassroots initiatives in Los Angeles and Newark. After the formation of CAP in 1970, they expanded their reach and influence, helping to transform the federation of organizations into the preeminent black nationalist group.

By renegotiating the African woman ideal, women activists influenced the ideological and organizational trajectory of cultural nationalist groups. They created an evolving definition of gender roles that was steeped in the goals of cultural revolution but that also critiqued the practice of separate spheres of organizing. Their strategy was not one of blatant accusation and criticism; rather it challenged practitioners of the philosophy to adhere to its most emancipatory elements and work toward the liberation of *all* black Americans. This methodology allowed them to shape the debate in favor of more egalitarian interpretations of Kawaida, influence the organizational and ideological trajectories of US and CFUN, and inaugurate "period[s] of tremendous transformation in the consciousness of the men."[60] Karenga and Amiri Baraka may have been the spokesmen of cultural nationalism, but black women were important theorists of this tradition, refining and advancing the philosophy through their reconceptualization of their roles. Their impact illustrates the importance of studying cultural nationalist groups and viewing Kawaidist women as intellectuals in their own rights. Most important, their intellectual production is a reminder that black women's ideological and organizational engagement with cultural nationalist ideals was, and remains, a critical and generative component of the Black Power movement and its legacy.

Notes

1. Maulana Karenga, "Kawaida Philosophy and Practice: Questions of Life and Struggle," *Los Angeles Sentinel*, August 2, 2007.
2. Mumininas of the Committee for Unified Newark, "Mwanamke Mwananchi: The Nationalist Woman Handbook," "Books Available thru Jihad Productions,"

Reel 2, The Black Power Movement Part 1, hereafter referred to as the Baraka Papers.

3. See, for example, Toni Cade Bambara, ed., *The Black Woman: An Anthology* (New York: New American Library, 1970); Linda Greene, "The Black Revolutionary Woman," *Black Panther*, September 28, 1968, 11; "Women in the Struggle," *Triple Jeopardy*, September–October 1971, 8l. For analysis of these debates, see Ashley D. Farmer, *Remaking Black Power: How Black Women Transformed an Era* (Chapel Hill: University of North Carolina Press, 2017).

4. Scot Brown, *Fighting for US: Maulana Karenga, the US Organization, and Black Cultural Nationalism* (New York: New York University Press, 2003); Komozi Woodard, *A Nation within a Nation: Amiri Baraka (LeRoi Jones) and Black Power Politics* (Chapel Hill: University of North Carolina Press, 1999); Michael Simanga, *Amiri Baraka and the Congress of African People: History and Memory* (New York: Palgrave Macmillan, 2015); Kwasi Konadu, *A View from the East: Black Cultural Nationalism and Education in New York City* (Syracuse, N.Y.: Syracuse University Press, 2009).

5. E. Frances White, "Africa on My Mind: Gender, Counter Discourse, and African American Nationalism," *Journal of Women's History* 2 (Spring 1990): 75; Gwendolyn Patton, "Black People and the Victorian Ethos," in Bambara, *The Black Woman*, 143–48; Tiamoyo Karenga and Chimbuko Tembo, "Kawaida Womanism: African Ways of Being Woman in the World," *Western Journal of Black Studies* 36, no. 1 (2012): 33–47.

6. Floyd W. Hayes III and Judson L. Jefferies, "US Does Not Stand for United Slaves!," in *Black Power: In the Belly of the Beast*, edited by Judson Jefferies (Urbana: University of Illinois, 2006), 74.

7. Douglas Flamming, *Bound for Freedom: Black Los Angeles in Jim Crow America* (Berkeley: University of California Press, 2005); Josh Sides, *L.A. City Limits: African American Los Angeles from the Great Depression to the Present* (Berkeley: University of California Press, 2006).

8. "Watts Brothers Tell of Incident That Triggered Riot," *Los Angeles Sentinel*, September 9, 1965.

9. Imamu Clyde Halisi, ed., *Kitabu: Beginning Concepts in Kawaida* (Los Angeles: Saidi, 1971), 3; Brown, *Fighting for US*, 38.

10. Hayes and Jefferies, "US Does Not Stand for United Slaves!," 74; Clay Carson, "A Talk with Ron Karenga: Watts Black Nationalist," *Los Angeles Free Press*, September 2, 1966, 12.

11. "An Interview with Hakim Jamal," *Long Beach Free Press*, September–October 1, 1969, 6; Brown, *Fighting for US*, 39.

12. Carson, "A Talk with Ron Karenga," 12.

13. Halisi, *Kitabu*, 20.

14. Daniel Patrick Moynihan, *The Negro Family: A Case for National Action* (Washington, D.C.: US Department of Labor, Office of Policy Planning and Research, 1965); Frances Beal, "Double Jeopardy: To Be Black and Female," in Bambara, *The Black Woman*, 109–22; White, "Africa on My Mind," 73–97.

15. Hayes and Jefferies, "US Does Not Stand for United Slaves!," 78; "L.A.P.D. Raids US Headquarters," *Los Angeles Sentinel*, January 1, 1970; "Karenga Wife to Sue Cops," *Los Angeles Sentinel*, February 1, 1968.

16. "Brothers Arraigned in UCLA Slayings," *Los Angeles Times*, January 24, 1969.

17. Karenga, "Us, Kawaida, and the Black Liberation Movement in the 1960s: Culture, Knowledge, and Struggle," in *Engines of the Black Power Movement: Essays on the Influence of Civil Rights Actions, Arts, and Islam*, edited by James Conyers (Jefferson, N.C.: McFarland, 2007), 124–25.

18. Malaikas, "View from the Womans' [*sic*] Side of the Circle," *Harambee*, April 25, 1969, 4.

19. Malaikas, "View from the Womans' [*sic*] Side of the Circle."

20. Malaikas, "View from the Womans' [*sic*] Side of the Circle."

21. Malaikas, "View from the Womans' [*sic*] Side of the Circle."

22. Karenga, "Us, Kawaida, and the Black Liberation Movement," 126.

23. Maulana Karenga, "A Strategy for Struggle: Turning Weakness into Strength," *Black Scholar* 5, no. 3 (1971): 8–21.

24. Brown, *Fighting for US*, 125.

25. Scot Brown, "'To Unbrainwash an Entire People': Malcolm X, Cultural Nationalism, and the US Organization in the Era of Black Power," in *Malcolm X: A Historical Reader*, edited by James L. Conyers Jr. and Andrew P. Smallwood (Durham, N.C.: Carolina Academic Press, 2008), 144.

26. Robert Curvin, *Inside Newark: Decline, Rebellion, and the Search for Transformation* (New Brunswick, N.J.: Rutgers University Press, 2014), 36, 46–47.

27. Amiri Baraka, *The Autobiography of LeRoi Jones* (New York: Lawrence Hill Books, 1997), 331; Audreen Buffalo, "A Revolutionary Life Together: Amina and Amiri Talk Frankly about Their Marriage," *Essence*, May 1985, 84, 86; Woodard, *A Nation within a Nation*, 65–66.

28. "From Congress of African People to Revolutionary Communist League," *Unity and Struggle*, June 1976, 2; Russell Rickford, *We Are an African People: Independent Education, Black Power, and the Radical Imagination* (New York: Oxford University Press, 2016), 138.

29. Baraka, *The Autobiography of LeRoi Jones*, 358.

30. Baraka, *The Autobiography of LeRoi Jones*, 350–58.

31. Woodard, *A Nation within a Nation*, 88.

32. Sisters of Black Culture, *Black Woman's Role in the Revolution* (Newark, N.J.: Jihad, 1969), 2.

33. Baraka, *The Autobiography of LeRoi Jones*, 385.

34. "African Women Working and Studying toward Nationalism," Reel 2, Baraka Papers; Komozi Woodard, "It's Nation Time in Newark: Amiri Baraka and the Black Power Experiments in Newark, New Jersey," in *Freedom North: Black Freedom Struggles outside the South, 1940–1980*, edited by Jeanne Theoharis and Komozi Woodard (New York: Palgrave Macmillan, 2003), 299.

35. Woodard, *A Nation within a Nation*, 123.

36. Baraka, *The Autobiography of LeRoi Jones*, 403.

37. Woodard, *A Nation within a Nation*, 160–69, 171–72.

38. Baraka, *The Autobiography of LeRoi Jones*, 307.

39. Woodard, "It's Nation Time in Newark," 299.

40. Mumininas of the Committee for Unified NewArk, "Mwanamke Mwananchi."

41. Mumininas of the Committee for Unified NewArk, "Mwanamke Mwananchi."

42. Mumininas of the Committee for Unified NewArk, "Mwanamke Mwananchi."

43. Mumininas of the Committee for Unified NewArk, "Mwanamke Mwananchi."

44. For more on the Pan-African resurgence, see Rickford, *We Are an African People*.

45. Woodard, *A Nation within a Nation*, 161.

46. Simanga, *Amiri Baraka*, 86–90.

47. Bibi Amina Baraka, "On Afrikan Women," *Black NewArk*, August 1973, 2.

48. Baraka, "On Afrikan Women."

49. "CAP Afrikan Women's Conference . . . Will be Held in Newark—July 74," *Black NewArk*, January–February 1974, 3.

50. "CAP Afrikan Women's Conference . . . Will be Held in Newark—July 74," 3.

51. "Forum Planned by Black Women," *New York Times*, June 29, 1974.

52. "African Women's Confab Attracts Large Gathering," *Philadelphia Tribune*, July 27, 1974.

53. "African Women Unite," *Unity and Struggle*, August 1974, 11.

54. "African Women Unite," 11; Simanga, *Amiri Baraka*, 85–86.

55. Amiri Baraka, "The Meaning and Development of Revolutionary Kawaida," Reel 2, Baraka Papers.

56. Amiri Baraka, "The Organizing Meeting of the Black Women's United Front," in *Black Women's United Front: Congress of Afrikan People on the Woman Question: Position Paper and Speeches from Meeting Held in Detroit, Michigan, January 25, 1975*, Box 15, Folder: Black Women's United Front, Printed Ephemera Collection on Organizations, Robert F. Wagner Labor Archives, Tamiment Library, New York University.

57. Amiri Baraka, "Revolutionary Party, Revolutionary Ideology," Reel 2, Baraka Papers.

58. "Black Women's United Front: Black Women Struggle for Democratic Rights," *Unity and Struggle*, October 1, 1975, 4–6.

59. "BWUF Meets in Detroit," *Unity and Struggle*, June 1, 1975, 6.

60. Simanga, *Amiri Baraka*, 121.

Part IV

✦

Black Radicalism

Introduction

Robin D. G. Kelley

If studying the black radical tradition teaches us anything, it is that mass movements, insurrections, flight, and small acts of resistance emerged out of collective thought and critical analysis. Viewing black freedom struggles through a domination/resistance dialectic obscures the dialectic operating *within* insurgent communities. Aggregations of people with shared and divergent experiences shaped by class, gender, generation, language, spirituality, and national and ethnic identities wrestled with ideas, rethought inherited categories, debated strategies and tactics, and struggled over how to imagine liberation: as subjects, fugitives, citizens, sovereigns, or something entirely different.[1] In other words, their struggles for freedom entailed an internal struggle over the meaning of freedom.

The black intellectual traditions discussed in this book, particularly in this section, generally stand against the Western liberal tradition of political philosophy derived from Hobbes and others, that understands freedom as the right of the individual to do what *he* wishes, as long as it is lawful under the state. This "negative" liberty or freedom places a premium on the right to own property (including human beings), to accumulate wealth, to defend property by arms, mobility, expression, and political participation. Black struggles conceived of freedom in more expansive and radical terms. Freedom pivoted around the *collective* well-being of a people. It meant the right to a fully realized life, justice, authentic democracy, the abolition of all forms of bondage and exploitation. Whereas few black rebels believed that freedom was granted by the state in the form of law or proclamation or policy, the vast majority knew that freedom is hard-fought and transformative, that it is a participatory process that demands new ways of thinking and being.

The three essays by Christopher Bonner, Greg Childs, and Russell Rickford deepen our understanding of the dynamic process by which black people conceived of, and enacted, freedom, as well as the constraints they faced as rebels—and we continue to confront as historians. Although they range widely across time, space, and subject matter—from the eighteenth to the late twentieth century, from North America and Brazil to the Caribbean, from slavery, antislavery, and the law to Black Power—each essay breaks out of the domination/resistance dialectic to explore the internal dynamics of movements seeking liberation within and against the constraints of particular legal and state regimes.

Christopher Bonner's "Runaways, Rescuers, and the Politics of Breaking the Law" uses the dramatic cases of William Dixon (New York) and Adam Crosswhite (Michigan), free black men who escaped from slavery only to be apprehended by slave catchers, jailed, and presumably tried for the crime of stealing themselves. But they preserved their freedom, not by the courts but through mass "rescue," militant collective uprisings capable of challenging police authority and whisking them to freedom. These rescues served as a kind of political theater where ideas are not just being put into practice but are created. They drew people, including white bystanders, into a local and national discourse about slavery, freedom, and justice who otherwise had been silent or "neutral." In other words, Bonner shows us that these intense moments of public discord are also moments of public discourse.

In interrogating these cases and the legal ramifications, Bonner asks, "What do we learn about people and the communities in which they live when we see collective uprisings and individual acts of lawbreaking as political acts?" For Bonner these rescues and the legal cases that follow were both products and objects of black intellectual work. They reveal that even as communities shared a common belief in the injustice of slavery and racism, they differed over how best to secure justice and personal security and overturn human bondage. He writes that these rescues represent people who "embraced the possibility of equality embedded in the nation's founding language while simultaneously" resisting racist laws.

The evidence he presents, however, suggests that these were not two prongs of a single strategy but rather a point of contention within the resistance movement. There were those who simply did not believe the government "embraced" egalitarian ideas because it did not practice them. Behind the veil of unity Bonner exposes a pointed struggle between a black elite who believed that the system would ultimately work in their favor with proper pressure, and a portion of the masses who believed the system *did work*: to uphold slavery and racial subjugation. After all, these rescues occurred during the period of the 1830s and 1840s, when so-called free black men who owned property were being disfranchised as propertyless white men were guaranteed the vote.[2] This was the era after Nat Turner's rebellion, when laws constraining black life and movement proliferated. In other words, the foundations for this incredibly repressive regime had already been established a decade or two before the passage of the Fugitive Slave Act of 1850.

Finally, Bonner's work compels us to interrogate the very term *lawbreaking*. First, we must never forget that Africans were the *victims* of a crime whose conception of what is right, just, and humane was born not only in struggle but outside the bounds of Western civilization. So as the framers, the abolitionists, the liberal jurists, the Republicans debated over whether the Constitution defined enslaved Africans as property or persons held in service, the Africans themselves answered, *Neither*. Prince Hall's 1777 petition for liberty based on the Declaration of Independence argued that Africans were human beings, "unjustly dragged, by the cruel hand of Power," and victims of a crime, stolen "in Violation of the Laws of Nature & of Nation & in defiance of all the tender feelings of humanity, brought hither to be sold like beasts of burden, & like them condemned to slavery for Life."[3] In other words, what the rescues, along with the slave mutinies on the *Amistad* (1839) and the *Creole* (1841), reveal is that the discourse on slavery as a violation of natural rights wasn't just an abstract conversation by jurists and court philosophers but was *forced upon the nation by the actions of the enslaved and free black people themselves*. Second, we must also bear in mind that these acts of "lawbreaking" occurred during and immediately after the era of Jacksonian democracy—a period characterized by the rise of a mass press, political parties, *mob violence as a modality of political behavior*, and *a president who did not respect the rule of law*. Andrew Jackson was famous for violating the Constitution and legal rulings, particularly when he ignored a Supreme Court ruling protecting Cherokee sovereignty, pushed through the Indian Removal Act of 1830, and singularly nullified treaties with indigenous peoples in the Southeast. So what does *lawbreaking* mean when the president is one of the biggest lawbreakers?

Greg Childs's "Conspiracies, Seditions, Rebellions: Concepts and Categories in the Study of Slave Resistance" asks different but related questions: When enslaved people and their allies are convicted and punished for "conspiring" to rebel, how do we know the charges are true? Under what laws are conspirators charged? What is the legal threshold when the evidence consists mainly of words rather than weapons, gossip rather than guns? And, perhaps most important, how have the archives and our approach to evidence of slave conspiracies occluded our vision of the entire spectrum of resistance and the inner dynamics of struggle? Childs suggests that historians have looked at conspiracies through too narrow a lens, constrained, as it were, by a domination/resistance dialectic. The categories of resistance generated by this dialectic produce a coherence or unity that may not exist, except in the terrified imaginations of the ruling classes. What we miss, then, are all of the other acts of resistance that fall under different names. Pursuing these other categories, he argues, can give us "a fuller picture of the intellectual history of black communities under slavery . . . [and] point us to debates between and among people of African descent regarding questions of freedom and politics."

The problem is both methodological and conceptual. Until quite recently historians have focused their energies on either proving or disproving whether the conspiracies were true. Consequently they failed to take into account the specific legal regimes in which the alleged conspiracies occurred. "Rather than question what the meaning of conspiracy was in a given imperial or national framework," Childs writes, "historians often attempt to derive the veracity of a reported conspiracy through a set of qualifying questions that purport to bring us closer to understanding whether or not a real rebellion was being planned."[4] By not paying attention to local, national, or colonial legal cultures and codes, historians assume that the only question that matters is whether there is sufficient evidence of a real revolt in the offing. The specific context is papered over by a universal theory of the smoking gun. Childs argues that this not only forecloses a range of struggles taking place, but it completely ignores how the state is defining conspiracy. The legal threshold for prosecuting conspiracies in eighteenth-century societies was much lower than today, so just talk or rumors of talk could constitute sedition—a very serious offense. The flip side, of course, is that a studied consideration of what it means to commit a seditious act helps us see how and why some of the acts of enslaved and free Africans were not always hidden but direct and out in the open. As Childs's examination of the 1798 "conspiracy" in Bahia shows, the organizers at first met secretly to discuss and draft their list of grievances and then openly posted their demands backed by the threat of an uprising. By seeking evidence of a planned slave revolt, we not only collapse the discrete legal categories of sedition and conspiracy but risk losing the broader story of political mobilization against colonial power. In this instance, in order to round up rebels, guns and plans are not necessary when words are sufficient—words that articulate precisely what people are openly demanding.

Sedition is a category of immense importance if we wish to deepen our understanding of the intellectual history of black communities in struggle. Antisedition laws target ideas, spoken or written, that are regarded by the state to be subversive. Sedition is about talking, mobilizing, drawing potential allies into possible actions, but in the context of black Atlantic slave regimes it is about enslaved and free African people spreading dissident information. As Childs puts it, such seditious acts provide a window into the creation of "black publics." Here I'm reminded of the late Stephanie Camp, who spent the better part of her tragically short life thinking about what enslaved political culture looks like and what it means to engage in acts of sedition. In her book, *Closer to Freedom: Enslaved Women and Everyday Resistance in the Plantation South*, she tells the story of an enslaved woman named California, who not only possessed abolitionist literature but displayed it on the walls of her slave cabin, in utter defiance of her master. Her act was significant precisely because the enslaved had no right to privacy, no semblance of privacy. Their dwellings were constantly surveilled due to the threat of conspiracy, which is why the enslaved always had to "steal away" to create safe spaces for worship, conversation, and conviviality beyond the panoptic view of the plantation regime.[5] Camp did not take these instances to be exceptional but rather indicative of what might have been the prevailing sentiments, evidence of the circulation of abolitionist literature among the enslaved, and the beginnings what, by the late 1850s, would become a rupture, accelerating black resistance to slavery. In many ways Childs is asking that we do the same for the entire Western hemisphere. In other words, we ought to stop looking for weapons and instead listen—not just for the plans but for the possibilities, the prayers, the dreams.

But as Russell Rickford demonstrates in his sobering account, "African American Expats, Guyana, and the Pan-African Ideal in the 1970s," utopian dreams can become nightmares. Although a century and a half separates Rickford's essay from the other two, they all share a recurring theme of seeking the promised land, either by fighting to transform the country they are in or seeking sovereignty and freedom elsewhere. Although neither Bonner nor Childs makes emigration a central question, they both know that it was always present among the insurgent communities they discuss. But this is where the parallels end. The ex-pats were not maroons, though there were a few genuine fugitives escaping the American repressive state apparatus. Guyana was a sovereign nation in the postcolonial era, about to enter the storm of neoliberal globalization and debt. It was also supposed to be a kind of radical haven for black leftists and Pan-Africanists looking for a regime friendly to anti-imperialist movements, expatriate black nationalists, political refugees, and the like. Guyana, after all, was a self-declared socialist state, first under Cheddi Jagan and later Forbes Burnham. And Guyana was the third radical black nationalist utopia in fifteen years, following Kwame Nkrumah's Ghana and Julius Nyerere's Tanzania.[6]

Rickford skillfully introduces the reader to Guyana through the rose-colored glasses of the novelist Julian Mayfield, the artist-writers Tom and Muriel Feelings, the essayist Ann F. Cook, and other prominent ex-pats. Then suddenly the story pivots, revealing what a few expatriates soon discovered: that there is a darker side to the story. President Burnham was not what he seemed. He was tyrannical and undemocratic and held power with tacit support from the United States and other imperialist powers. Sovereignty certainly allowed Guyana to open its doors to black political exiles from around the world, but it also meant that Burnham had his own state apparatus, and he used it against his enemies. This is not what the Pan-African utopia was supposed to look like, and yet the story of Guyana is highly instructive for historians wishing to deepen their understanding of transnational and diasporic black movements. What his account reveals is the degree to which romance and realism were the thesis and antithesis that generated, in dialectical fashion, a kind of synthesis of representations of blackness, of tensions between home and exile, nation and diaspora. Rickford challenges our entire conception of a diasporan identity grounded in memory and instead reveals a dynamic process of identification rooted in time and space (history and geography) and the circulation of ideas. Guyana represents just one of many untold stories that "illustrate black America's romance with the modern nation-state, its yearning for a viable counterforce to US imperialism, and the tragic collision of those two ideals."

Tragic or not, such internal tensions and contradictions constitute a central feature of black intellectual history. Whether we're talking about debates over how best to liberate enslaved people, strategies to spread dissident ideas and foment revolution, or fights between warring political factions over the future of the modern nation-state, it is within these dynamic moments that we find dreams of liberation in their most incipient form.

Notes

1. For a brilliant yet often overlooked treatment of the multiple tendencies in the struggles against slavery and beyond, see Cedric J. Robinson, *Black Movements in America* (New York: Routledge, 1997), in addition to his better-known work, *Black Marxism: The Making of the Black Radical Tradition* (Chapel Hill: University of North Carolina Press, 2000).

2. See Joel Olsen, *The Abolition of White Democracy* (Minneapolis: University of Minnesota Press, 2004), 42–44.

3. Prince Hall's petition has been reprinted many times and circulates widely on the internet. One of its first appearances in popular form is in William C. Nell, *The Colored Patriots of the American Revolution* (Boston: Robert F. Wallcut, 1855), 47. I cite this edition to suggest that the recovery of Hall's analysis shaped black political discourse during the antislavery struggles of the 1850s.

4. One of the exceptions Childs cites is Aisha K. Finch, *Rethinking Slave Rebellion in Cuba: La Escalera and the Insurgencies of 1841–1844* (Chapel Hill: University of North Carolina Press, 2015). Although Childs does not say so, I suspect that Finch was able to move beyond the question of veracity precisely because she focused on gender and women, the most invisible agents in a slave revolt that had been virtually rendered invisible. In trying to unravel the mystery of why one of the biggest slave revolts in Caribbean history virtually disappeared from public memory, she discovered evidence of what she calls "the hidden labor of rebellion," labor often performed by women who too often are rendered invisible or depicted as helpless victims. In other words, the very architecture of revolt was built on vast networks of people, built over years, across a wide terrain. The idea of a rebellion as a single event renders women and their labors illegible. Finch not only rethinks slave rebellion—she rethinks leadership, gender, time, space, memory, and the archive itself.

5. Stephanie M. H. Camp, *Closer to Freedom: Enslaved Women and Everyday Resistance in the Plantation South* (Chapel Hill: University of North Carolina Press, 2004), chapter 4.

6. See Kevin Gaines, *American Africans in Ghana: Black Expatriates and the Civil Rights Era* (Chapel Hill: University of North Carolina Press, 2006); Seth M. Markle, *A Motorcycle on Hell Run: Tanzania, Black Power, and the Uncertain Future of Pan-Africanism, 1964–1974* (Lansing: Michigan State University Press, 2017); Fanon Che Wilkins, "'In the Belly of the Beast': Black Power, Anti-Imperialism, and the African Liberation Solidarity Movement, 1968–1987," Ph.D. diss., New York University, 2001.

Runaways, Rescuers, and the Politics of Breaking the Law

Christopher Bonner

William Dixon did not want to spend another night in a dank, crumbling cell in Bridewell Prison. But on the afternoon of April 12, 1837, inside a courtroom at New York City Hall, Judge Richard Riker announced that he had not yet decided whether Dixon was free, as the prisoner so vehemently claimed. Two sheriffs approached the African American defendant and prepared to escort him to the nearby jail. Dixon had been arrested the previous week by a group of slave catchers who claimed that he was a fugitive from Maryland. As the sheriffs led Dixon downstairs and toward the doors of City Hall, he would have looked through the large windows that lined the front of the building and had a clear view of the massive crowd waiting outside.[1]

City Hall stands today, as it did on that spring afternoon, in the middle of an eight-acre park carved out of lower Manhattan's irregular blocks. On April 12, as Dixon sat in the courtroom, more than one thousand African Americans congregated in that park. The sheriffs escorting Dixon out of City Hall were apparently unconcerned about the crowd. Just after 3 o'clock they led Dixon through the front doors and the people in the park surged toward the captive. Several attacked the sheriffs with wooden clubs. A woman pulled a knife from beneath her dress and passed it to Dixon, who, in his surprise, stood by for a few minutes while a thousand strangers fought to seize his freedom. When he overcame his shock, Dixon fled toward Broadway to seek shelter in the busy city streets. The crowd continued to struggle with authorities. A judge ran out from City Hall to support the sheriffs, but "a strapping negro wench" grabbed him in a chokehold, and a group of young black men "pretty well pummeled him, and tore the coat completely off his back." Meanwhile Dixon ran north along Broadway. A man on horseback tried to stop him, but Dixon's new escort—several black men armed with clubs—protected the fleeing prisoner. Perhaps tired from running or concerned that he should take cover, Dixon hid in a coal cellar on Duane Street, just a few blocks from City Hall Park, and his protectors dispersed. But his freedom lasted only a few hours; that evening a witness led authorities to the cellar, and Dixon was finally returned to Bridewell.[2]

Dixon's case reveals some of the ways that black people confronted fugitive slave legislation in the antebellum United States. Dixon was the captive of a legal system designed to preserve black slavery; measures like the Fugitive Slave Law of 1793 empowered individuals to cross state lines to pursue runaway property. That legal system, combined with the value of bound labor to the national economy, meant that black northerners like Dixon lived in a precarious freedom. In the face of that tenuous status black activists publicly denounced the injustice of slavery and the institution's legal foundations. Dixon's rescue was one such statement. The men and women who liberated him took part in an act of lawbreaking that constituted a kind of insurgent politics—black activists directly challenged the governing structures of the slaveholding republic. The rescue was one of many that took place in cases of alleged fugitives in the antebellum North. We can hear echoes of Dixon's claims to freedom and of his rescuers' footsteps in the case of Adam Crosswhite, a fugitive slave liberated twice in Michigan in 1848. Separated by a decade, these incidents come together through the rescuers who declared to lawmakers that they were unwilling to comply with the legal instruments that upheld slavery. Dixon, Crosswhite, and the dozens of women and men who came to their aid are part of a larger story of African Americans breaking the law in an effort to change it, to force it into alignment with a vision of justice rooted in racial equality.

Exploring the politics of lawbreaking helps us to understand more fully the work free black people did to transform their marginalized status in the nineteenth century.[3] Along with Dixon and Crosswhite we can include less familiar characters in the story of antebellum black politics. Further, their rescues and legal cases highlight the breadth and complexity of black intellectual work. African Americans decided together to break the law in these rescues because of a shared belief in the injustice of slavery and of the laws governing black freedom. They developed ideas that would promote black personal security and they put those ideas into practice, bringing their theories about law and justice to bear in specific acts in pursuit of freedom. Violent public protests had the potential to reach wide audiences and push for tangible legal change.

Dixon's and Crosswhite's rescuers were part of a black intellectual tradition that embraced the possibility of equality embedded in the nation's founding language while simultaneously denouncing, resisting, and working to dismantle the racially biased laws of state and federal governments. Black protest of the antebellum period blended profound anger at the denial of black peoples' rights and freedom with a radical hope that the nation might one day create just, egalitarian legal structures. Black political thinkers were acutely aware of the gap between the nation's expressed ideals and its realities, and they were invested in work that they believed would narrow that gap. In the 1850s, after federal fugitive slave legislation codified slave catchers' access to black bodies, Frederick Douglass declared that "the only way to make the [law] a dead letter is to make half a dozen or more dead kidnappers."[4] But by that time thousands of lesser-known black people had long promoted lawbreaking through politicized public displays that turned their ideas into actions. By looking at lawbreaking as politics we can craft a black intellectual history that includes a broad population, takes seriously a wide range of behaviors, and considers how that thought work might produce tangible change.

A diverse black intellectual community transformed Dixon's and Crosswhite's lives. Black Americans broke the law in order to dismantle a system designed to preserve racial slavery and to lay foundations for structures that would protect freedom. Dixon, Crosswhite, and their rescuers represent black thought in radical practice, ideas deployed to redefine the terms of legal and social belonging in the nation. Discussions of who belonged were critical in a republic, a form of government designed to empower and represent a community of people. At its creation white men dominated the nation's governing processes, and in the decades after the founding black politics sparked turmoil and change as activists fought to end slavery and to secure access to formal political power. When state legislatures ratified the Constitution in 1789, the nation was not yet fully formed, and Americans would struggle for decades to determine who belonged in the nation, who "the people" were that the Constitution empowered. Thus through nineteenth-century black politics, particularly in antebellum fugitive controversies, we can tell an alternative story of the long creation of the American republic.

The Rescuers of William Dixon

On April 4, 1837, the slave catcher A. G. Ridgeley arrested William Dixon, likely near Dixon's home on the Bowery in lower Manhattan. Dr. Walter Allender of Baltimore had hired Ridgeley to pursue a fugitive slave called Jacob Ellis, or "Allender's Jake," who had run away in 1832. Ridgeley brought the man he called "Jake" before Judge Richard Riker of New York City, a token of a successful manhunt. But the black man protested, "calling himself Wm. Dixon" and repeatedly asserting that he was "a freeman." It was after Dixon's testimony on April 12, the second day of his hearing, that black New Yorkers liberated him from City Hall Park.[5]

While kidnapping posed a persistent threat, it is difficult to know precisely why so many African Americans chose to liberate Dixon on that afternoon. In 1840 about sixteen thousand black people lived in New York City, so a crowd of several thousand was certainly possible. And black New Yorkers had a history of protecting freedom, represented in the New York Committee of Vigilance (NYCV), founded in 1835, to pursue "practical abolition" in the form of legal protections against kidnapping and aid for fugitives. It is possible that Dixon's rescue, like the NYCV, emerged from a sense that both kidnapping and enslavement were fundamental dangers demanding concerted response.[6]

Dixon's case and rescue became a focal point for the *Colored American*, a newspaper that the black minister Samuel Cornish had launched weeks before Dixon's arrest. Editors like Cornish simultaneously worked to ensure that African Americans could live in the United States and to improve the conditions of that life. The arrest of a man who said he was free was thus a central concern for Cornish and his readers. Cornish, who was among the leaders of the NYCV, credited the action of April 12 to a "brother Editor" who had called for public displays of outrage after Dixon's arrest. Cornish did not name that editor or his paper but reprinted portions of his message, including the anonymous editor's dream of "twenty, nay fifty thousand persons present" to witness—perhaps to oversee—the hearings of alleged fugitives. The editor continued, "This business of gentleman kidnapping ought to rouse the entire city." Ultimately the linked convictions that Dixon ought to have a fair hearing and that Judge Riker was not fit to provide it drove black people to action. The black women and men who gathered at City Hall protested Dixon's arrest, the pernicious, pervasive danger of kidnapping, and the ideologies and legal structures by which they were presumed enslaved and constantly threatened with bondage.[7] Dixon's status had massive stakes for all black New Yorkers.

Cornish condemned the mob action in an editorial that reveals important details about the people who rescued Dixon. He worried that by briefly liberating Dixon, "the Thoughtless part of our Colored Citizens" placed a new obstacle in the path of the "eminent lawyers" working to secure Dixon's freedom. Protecting black freedom through legal change, he argued, required that people show respect for the legal system. Cornish presented himself as an ideal black citizen, one who understood the law and, even in the face of an imminent threat, used available legal channels in pursuit of protection. He was especially upset that women had violated social norms by taking part in the violence, and instructed "their husbands to keep them at home . . . and find some better occupation for them." Cornish thus reveals the gendered limitations of his politics as he points to women's prominent roles in Dixon's rescue. Part of the power of street politics was that it provided spaces for black women to speak out in public. Rescuing Dixon appealed to women like the one who gave Dixon a knife because traditional political venues excluded them and also, perhaps, because prominent black men like Cornish tried to reinforce that marginalization. The woman who handed Dixon the knife stood on the front lines of the City Hall mob. She embraced a critical role in that rescue, and the promiscuous audience who joined her did not stand in the way of her radical protest act.[8]

As a whole, Cornish seemed to believe that the mob action limited the legal potential of Dixon's case. Black Americans were confronting a "REPUBLICAN *Slave* system" and therefore needed to change the law in pursuit of liberation. The NYCV lawyers argued that Dixon should have a jury trial, which they said was the right of any accused free man. They presented that argument as a simple request, but they and Cornish understood that it could establish a transformative precedent. A jury trial for Dixon would have shifted the state toward a presumption of black freedom. Securing that trial could be a critical first step in dismantling the slaveholding republic. Cornish thus embraced the conservative standards of respectability as part of the truly radical project of working to make the law protect black freedom. In truth, Dixon's rescuers also worked toward the goal of legal reform that was so important to Cornish. They violently, publicly declared that they would not accept legal processes that could produce black enslavement. But Cornish worried that a forcible liberation would not change the systemic problems that constantly threatened black freedom.

Vigilance had proven its ability to free individuals temporarily. But Cornish looked for African Americans to have real voices inside courtrooms, a center of formal legal power; he imagined a world in which prison rescues and vigilance work as a whole would be obsolete. He pushed for that change with a deft rhetorical move near the end of his comments on the riot, asking white lawmakers to reserve "pardon and clemency . . . in behalf of the ignorant part of our colored citizens."[9] This was an appeal for a new relationship, positioning African Americans within the community of citizens though they had openly broken the law. As Cornish explained it, the mob action had taken place only because black Americans doubted that they could secure their freedom through the law. No citizen should harbor such doubts. Cornish here showed that he understood why people broke the law and offered an explanation to others who may also have disagreed with the mob action. And so while Cornish exulted in the potential of the law to protect black freedom he implied that New Yorkers might continue to see mobs so long as the legal system denied African Americans substantive access.[10] Lawbreaking, he explained, resulted from a broken justice system, which bolstered his plea for legal reform. African Americans broke the law because those in power refused to listen when they spoke in other ways.

Relying on courts and lawyers proved fruitful in July 1837, when Judge Riker granted Dixon the writ *de homine replegiando*. The writ released Dixon on bail, provided that if called he would return to court at a later date for a jury trial. This was a surprising turn for Riker, known as a friend to slave catchers. But Riker had heard from several witnesses who testified to Dixon's freedom, and he decided that he lacked sufficient evidence to send the prisoner south. The writ *de homine replegiando* allowed Dixon to return to life in New York in a freedom made tenuous by the possibility of future legal proceedings, but all the same a life outside of southern bondage. Further, Dixon could defend his precarious freedom before a jury should Dr. Allender continue to press his claim. It seemed that Cornish and Dixon and his representatives in the NYCV had been right to rely on the law in pursuit of black freedom.[11]

The Rescues of Adam Crosswhite

Across the free states in the late 1830s, lawmakers and activists conveyed the increasing urgency of black personal security. New Jersey and Connecticut passed laws that provided jury trials for alleged fugitives in 1837 and 1838, respectively. Residents of Pennsylvania and Ohio petitioned for similar change. Farther west, black activists in Michigan declared "that persons claimed as fugitives from Slavery, ought to have the right of trial by Jury before being consigned to hopeless bondage." In these northern states, black Americans expressed a shared vision of how the law should work—their demands for specific legal change were also broader calls for governments to defend freedom rather than slavery.[12] These concerns emerged within the interconnected geography of antebellum black protest. The daily lives, the political concerns, and the dreams of African Americans in places like New York, Detroit, and Cleveland developed through the movement and exchange of people and ideas. Those interactions built a protest community that spanned the free states. The sense of urgency of the late 1830s would persist into the 1840s, spurred in particular by the Supreme Court case *Prigg v. Pennsylvania*, which concerned a Maryland slave catcher's attempt to apprehend an alleged fugitive in Pennsylvania. The Court's decision left open the door for northern states to pass personal liberty laws and encouraged an interracial antislavery community to deny any obligation to help capture alleged fugitives.

In 1847 and 1848 Adam Crosswhite called that community into action to counter an imminent threat to his family's freedom. Crosswhite, his wife, and their four children had fled slavery in Kentucky in 1843, running from their owner Francis Giltner and making a new home in Marshall, Michigan, about a hundred miles west of Detroit. Marshall would have been inviting because of its active abolitionist community, but ironically it is possible that the family's owner tracked them down by targeting antislavery centers in search of the fugitives.[13] Giltner sent his grandson Francis Troutman in search of the Crosswhites, and by January 1847 Troutman had located the family and gone in pursuit with a handful of slave catchers and a local sheriff named Harvey Dickson. The language of the subsequent court records produces a kind of civility in the ensuing encounter that obscures tension and fear yet also conveys the Marshall community's political and legal consciousness. On the morning of January 27, 1847, the slave catchers approached the Crosswhite home. Crosswhite saw them coming, and he and his eldest son tried to flee, but some of Troutman's men caught them and brought them back to the house. Troutman declared his intent to arrest the family as fugitives, prompting Crosswhite to take steps to ensure a fair hearing in court. The fugitive convinced the slave catchers to allow him to leave the house "to consult counsel," which he did, accompanied by Sheriff Dickson. In their absence dozens of black and white townspeople materialized in and around the house. When Crosswhite returned, a number of these townspeople threatened and attempted to fight off the slave catchers. James Smith, a black man "with a club raised, approached within five or six feet" of Troutman and "threatened to smash out his brains," but Dickson held him back.

The crowd outside the house grew to more than a hundred, keen on preventing the arrest. William Parker, a black neighbor, proclaimed that he was willing to risk his life to prevent the Crosswhites being taken to court. Alongside these threats the crowd took on some of the more genteel forms of antebellum politics, offering resolutions of their intent to resist the capture. White abolitionists were among the most vocal of those present, including Charles Gorham, who resolved "that these Kentuckians shall not take the Crosswhite family by virtue of physical, moral, or legal force." That call met with "general acclamation [and] much noise." Ultimately the activists prevented the arrest simply by expressing their willingness and exhibiting their capacity to break the law. Sheriff Dickson felt unable to control the crowd; Troutman gave him a signed warrant to arrest the fugitives, but Dickson refused to execute it. Convinced that a few slave catchers were no match for the antislavery mob, the sheriff persuaded Troutman that attempting an arrest would be dangerous and fruitless. The following day Gorham encountered Troutman in a Marshall courthouse and informed him simply, "Your negroes are gone." Overnight, abolitionists had ushered the Crosswhites east toward the Detroit River, where they crossed into a more secure freedom in Canada.

An interracial antislavery coalition broke the law to free the Crosswhite family for a number of reasons, chief among them the simple fact that the Crosswhites were fugitive slaves. Again Marshall's abolitionist community and proximity to Canada would have attracted fugitives. It seems likely that some of the Crosswhites' black defenders had previously freed themselves, and so it would have been important for those townspeople to show their willingness to fight for black liberty. Parker's claim that he would risk his life to protect the Crosswhites might also have been a claim that he would risk his life to ensure his own freedom.

The black and white crowd that gathered around the Crosswhite residence resisted the slave catchers because of a legal philosophy that convinced them of the righteousness of that act. Gorham had denied that Troutman could seize the Crosswhites even through the exercise of "legal force." The assembled crowd, composed largely of Crosswhite's black neighbors, agreed. According to later testimony, Gorham declared "that public sentiment was above the law." As they had in rescuing Dixon, black and white northerners in the antebellum period chose to resist laws that upheld slavery because they saw slavery as unjust. David Ruggles, a leading figure in black vigilance work in New York, had sketched this legal philosophy in 1843, writing in opposition to activists who framed the right to trial by jury as the ultimate protection of black freedom. "The existence of a jury trial law," Ruggles wrote in January 1843, "conceding to slavery the right to incarcerate humanity as a chattel personal, is at variance with my notion of equal rights, the Declaration of American Independence, the laws of Nature, and of the living God." A jury trial law meant that a black person could be sent into slavery by force of law and was therefore a tacit endorsement of slavery as a legitimate institution. The notion of an unjust enslavement that the law intended to prevent acknowledged that enslavement could be just for certain individuals.[14] Ruggles believed in the law but opposed manifestations of it that stood outside his vision of justice. The same idea might have motivated Dixon's rescuers and the Crosswhites' defenders—the very act of bringing the family before a judge to decide their fate would be a miscarriage of justice, regardless of the hearing's outcome. But in this philosophy black activists differed from abolitionists who rejected the Constitution and the nation's formal politics. These women and men were concerned that slavery was a corruption of the potential for justice within American legal systems; they held on to the possibility that they could break down embedded injustices and rebuild the law in a way that would protect free black lives.[15]

After the Crosswhites escaped, their owner Francis Giltner pressed charges against Gorham and two other white abolitionists who had aided the family of fugitives. The case seemed clear; it had been established and celebrated that abolitionists had rescued the Crosswhites and moved them to Canada. Defense lawyers argued that Gorham and his colleagues had not been active agents of that rescue, that they had not physically taken the Crosswhites out of Troutman's hands or led the family out of the country. The presiding judge rejected that legalese; if any man, he said, "by words or actions . . . encouraged others to make the rescue, he is responsible." The court found Gorham and his colleagues liable and ordered them to pay $4,500 in damages.[16]

While there may have been little doubt about the outcome of the case, there was surely some surprise when Adam Crosswhite appeared in the courtroom to testify. Presumably Gorham's lawyers had called him to deny that the white townsmen had been the driving force or the decisive presence in his family's rescue. Crosswhite stepped to the stand to testify, in effect, against his owner. He could do little but tell the truth: he was "born in Kentucky, the slave of his own father," and, in his significantly vague phrasing, "came to this State in 1843." Acknowledging his status in the presence of his owner and the men who had been hired to reclaim him placed Crosswhite in imminent danger, and so when he finished giving his testimony black Michiganders sprang into action. As the fugitive stepped down, "a rush was made to the door with Mr. Crossw[h]ite, by the colored citizens, who soon conveyed him across the Detroit River into Canada."[17] One year after abolitionists whisked Crosswhite away from his rural home, black activists liberated him again, this time from inside a US District Courthouse in Detroit.

As they had been after the first rescue, Michigan activists were explicit about the reasons they so brazenly broke the law. The day after Crosswhite's court appearance, a group met in Detroit's City Hall to declare in writing the ideas about slavery, freedom, and the law that they had embodied in each of the two rescues. They agreed to a series of resolutions, which they later had printed in antislavery newspapers, denouncing the decision in favor of Giltner as a restriction of "the rights and liberties of the citizens of the free state of

Michigan." Though protest tactics had flouted legal structures, particularly in the second rescue, the activists said that the law had an ultimate, definitive influence in American life. By acknowledging Giltner's claims the court had "deprived us of all protection and security in our lives." "Many of us have worn the galling chains of slavery," they continued; legally, many might still have belonged to other people.[18] Their appeal for legal protection demanded a fundamental reorganization of law in the slaveholding republic. It is not clear whether some or all of those meeting in Detroit had aided the Crosswhites, but they positioned themselves as facing the same threats from slave catchers and northern lawmakers, and they declared themselves willing to do the same work as the rescuers, refusing to "submit tamely to be converted into goods and chattels." The Crosswhites' rescuers had put into practice David Ruggles's ideas that legal slavery ought to be an impossibility. And the Detroit activists outlined a similar ideology: "Live or die, sink or swim, we will never be taken back into slavery." They expressed a wish "to be a peaceable and sober portion of the community" and proclaimed their willingness to "abide by the constitution and laws of this and all other states," provided they "recognize no slavery within their borders." That selective obedience was central to the ideas that motivated and energized the Crosswhites' rescuers. The statement produced in Detroit helps us to understand the rescuers' intellectual work, developing ideas that produced acts of lawbreaking with particular political meanings.[19] Black activists embraced traditional paths to legal change while at the same time rejecting and intentionally violating statutes that preserved human bondage. Despite their implicit embrace of lawbreaking, the Detroit meeting concluded with a resolution to petition the US Congress to repeal the Fugitive Slave Law of 1793. That was a call to eliminate the foundation of American law on property in people.[20] Recognizing that activists flouted the law while also appealing for legal change helps us to see that lawbreaking was a targeted political act in pursuit of a well-defined vision of justice. Black people argued that one need not obey all of the law in order to seek change through it. Lawbreaking as politics was about violating laws in an attack on unjust legal structures, the set of statutes designed to perpetuate the exclusion and oppression of black people, free and enslaved. Public displays of lawbreaking conveyed opposition to specific restrictions and also to the system's underlying impulses. Lawbreaking thus expressed public sentiment and threatened persistent, potentially violent challenges to enforcement in the slaveholding republic. For African Americans, breaking the law allowed them to seek and secure freedom in the United States and to work to make freedom more accessible and less precarious. Breaking the law was a multifaceted project of shifting the legal terrain of black and American life in the nineteenth century and moving toward a more secure, attainable freedom for African Americans.

Ultimately that politics had the opposite effect. Lawbreaking is fundamentally destabilizing, and so it would have struck legislators, interested in stability and control, and slave owners, interested in profits and power, as egregious and dangerous. In response to antislavery lawbreaking, southern legislators demanded stricter regulations, culminating in the Fugitive Slave Act of 1850. That federal law not only empowered but also obligated all people in the United States to uphold rights to human property in an effort to stabilize the peculiar institution. It was a direct response to antislavery vigilance and violence and it included a definitive statement on the people's obligation. "All good citizens," the law proclaimed, "are hereby commanded to aid in the prompt and efficient execution of this law."[21] For black and white activists, imbued with an ideology built around pursuing freedom and justice, the Fugitive Slave Act served as another example of why exactly they should break the law in their politics. At Shiloh Church in New York City in October 1850, a black man stood before the crowd and pledged to protect his family, to "send [a slave catcher] to hell before he shall accomplish his mission." His pledge met boisterous cheers from the crowd.[22]

Our Troubled Pasts

Adam Crosswhite's liberation echoed the tones of William Dixon's rescue from the steps of City Hall a decade earlier. Perhaps the most remarkable tie between their stories is that both men ended up free, far from a given for African Americans, especially after direct encounters with legal efforts to send them into bondage. Fundamentally black Americans broke the law because they understood that most of the law was designed to enslave them. But Dixon benefited tremendously from the work of the legal team organized by the NYCV. During his 1837 hearing Dixon's counsel called several witnesses to testify to his freedom. A white ship's captain said that he had employed Dixon occasionally since 1831. A black barber came north from Philadelphia to testify that he had known Dixon as a free man for fifteen years. Dr. Allender, the alleged slave owner, had a much more difficult case. Because the slave called Jake had run away in 1832, none of Allender's witnesses could say that they had seen the man for at least five years. They then had to prove that they could identify one of Baltimore's twenty thousand free and enslaved African Americans. Dixon waited in Bridewell Prison for months before he learned that Judge Riker had agreed to grant him bail.[23]

After Dixon's release his uncertainty about whether he might be called back to court, or possibly arrested or kidnapped, added tension to his daily encounters in New York City. Perhaps no single encounter was more frightening than a chance meeting with a runaway slave from Maryland. In his second autobiography, *My Bondage and My Freedom*, Frederick Douglass described his arrival in New York hours after he escaped slavery in Baltimore in 1839. Feeling lost and lonely as he wandered the streets in his newfound freedom, Douglass was overjoyed to see a black man he remembered from Baltimore as Allender's Jake. "I knew Jake well," Douglass wrote. He had heard that Allender had hired slave catchers but was glad to see that Jake appeared to be thriving in freedom. Jake was less than pleased. He silenced Douglass, declared, "I am 'William Dixon,' in New York!," and left the recent runaway alone in the street.[24]

Douglass's account allows us to see that Dixon's case was in fact a series of acts of lawbreaking. For Jake himself, it might have been a simple matter of wanting freedom. Again and again he declared himself "a freeman." He performed freedom in the courtroom and on the streets, using his voice in an effort to change the fact that he was legally enslaved. A fugitive called Jake appears to have known that the legal landscape of New York might be favorable to his efforts, that he could lie in court, transforming himself into a free man named William Dixon.

Douglass's story also requires us to think more broadly about who was breaking the law. Who knew the truth of Allender's Jake? The mob that rescued Dixon did so because they understood that the law sided with slave owners. Regardless of whether they knew Dixon was Jake, they knew that there were limits to the justice available to a black person, and they rescued him in protest of those limits. When they broke the law the rioters declared that they would not acquiesce to a marginal legal status, that they would resist anything that stood in the way of clear, strong safeguards of their freedom.

Perhaps more surprising, Dixon and his defense team broke the law repeatedly, brazenly, in a courtroom inside New York City Hall. In that lawbreaking they helped the case move toward a legal precedent that would safeguard black freedom. Activists created the character of William Dixon and worked to get a judge like Richard Riker to grant him a writ of *de homine replegiando*. State law allowed for a jury trial through the writ, but Riker had shown reluctance to grant it in the past. In September 1836 black New Yorkers had protested what they saw as a legalized system of kidnapping under Riker's influence. Citing a number of people who had recently been seized and removed south, they argued, "The people of color can expect no protection from the laws as at present administered." They appointed a committee to appeal to Riker directly but also made plans for the interim. "While we, the people of color," they said, "are deprived of that *bulwark of liberty*, a trial by jury, it is in vain to look for justice in the courts of law."[25]

The NYCV and Jake's lawyers built a case, gathered witnesses, and constructed the character of William Dixon, a freeman, seeking a writ of *de homine replegiando* for a hearing before a jury. These proceedings might have been designed as a sort of test case: if Judge Riker granted the writ, it would establish a precedent securing for alleged fugitives one avenue to a jury trial. It would have been a high-stakes test—a man's freedom hung in the balance— but perhaps Jake and his counsel agreed that breaking the law, becoming William Dixon, was his best opportunity to find freedom. And for all his condemnation of the collective rescue, it is possible that Samuel Cornish, a leader in the NYCV, also knew the truth about Allender's Jake. In fact he might have denounced the City Hall mob in print because of his knowledge. Perhaps Cornish was eager to have Dixon's fate decided in court because he had helped design a case with so much legal potential. Cornish could have seen the indoor lawbreaking as far more transformative and valuable than that which took place in City Hall Park. There are many ways to see the logic behind transforming a fugitive into a free man, especially in pursuit of legal protections. But whether or not the case was designed as such, Jake's perjury was part of the process of determining how black people would be treated in New York courts when slave catchers claimed them as fugitives. He and his attorneys and their witnesses broke the law inside a courtroom, using a set of formal legal processes in a way that could have fundamentally changed black life in New York.

Allender's Jake and Adam Crosswhite and the people who rescued them, in and outside of courtrooms, all stepped outside the bonds of the law in pursuit of individual freedom and a more collective liberation for black Americans. This has remained a central aspect of black freedom struggles in the United States, as people grapple with the question of how to confront injustices that are embedded in old, enduring legal and social structures. In August 2015 St. Louis County police officers shot an eighteen-year-old African American, Tyrone Harris Jr., during protests in memory of Michael Brown, an unarmed black man whom a Missouri police officer had killed in 2014. The *Washington Post* described Harris as a young man with a "troubled past."[26] That phrase, so often reserved for those deemed to be on the wrong side of the law, obscures long and complex histories of individuals, groups, and nations. It frames arrest, incarceration, or violent death as the logical ends of a person's own ill-advised choices. And it conceals the ways American governments and people have marginalized and oppressed large segments of the US population. In recent years we have seen a series of public protests, often violent, in response to police killings of African Americans, and at times in direct, immediate response to acts of police brutality. Commentary on these protests, especially as they emerged in Baltimore, Maryland, and Ferguson, Missouri, has often taken the shape of simple condemnations of that protest and violence. Too often people ignore or obscure the histories, long and short, that have led African Americans to seek violent, collective political forms, histories of economic and legal marginalization that leave people in search of a way to be heard. As we reflect on the many manifestations of African American politics in our world, we would do well to think about antebellum cases of fugitive slaves and the acts of lawbreaking those cases produced. We should think about riots as uprisings, about violence as protest, and about lawbreaking as politics. We should explore the ideas embodied in individual and collective political expressions. What do we learn about people and the communities in which they live when we see collective uprisings and individual acts of lawbreaking as political acts? Why might marginalized peoples choose these avenues to political expression? How are these acts organized, and what do they look like in practice? What are the legal philosophies that produce and are represented in public acts of lawbreaking? Exploring the expansive forms of black politics in the nineteenth century allows us to see how people have tried to dismantle legal and social structures and to consider breaking laws as part of the work of breaking down barriers to equality, work that can continue to bring the United States closer to justice.

Notes

1. For contemporary coverage of Dixon's case and the surrounding mob action, see "Kidnapping in New-York," *Liberator* (Boston), April 21, 1837; and in the *Colored American* (New York): "The Slave Case," April 29, 1837; "On Monday, John Davis . . . ," May 27, 1837; "After a Long . . . ," July 8, 1837, "Dixon Meeting," July 15, 1837. The New-York Historical Society site New-York Divided has compiled a collection of evidence that forms a narrative of the controversy. See http://www.nydivided.org/popup/People/WilliamDixon.php.

2. "Tremendous Riot in the Park," *Liberator* (Boston), April 21, 1837.

3. The stories of these men and their rescuers contribute to scholarship on direct, collective abolitionism and black politics in relation to American law. See Graham Russel Gao Hodges, *David Ruggles: A Radical Black Abolitionist and the Underground Railroad in New York City* (Chapel Hill: University of North Carolina Press, 2010); Eric Foner, *Gateway to Freedom: The Hidden History of the Underground Railroad* (New York: Norton, 2015); Steven Kantrowitz, *More than Freedom: Fighting for Black Citizenship in a White Republic* (New York: Penguin Press, 2013); Andrew K. Diemer, *The Politics of Black Citizenship: Free African-Americans in the Mid-Atlantic Borderland, 1817–1863* (Athens: University of Georgia Press, 2016); Kate Masur, *An Example for All the Land: Emancipation and the Struggle for Equality in Washington, D.C.* (Chapel Hill: University of North Carolina Press, 2010).

4. "From the N.Y. Tribune: National Free Soil Convention," *Frederick Douglass' Paper* (Rochester, N.Y.), August 20, 1852.

5. "More Slave Trouble," *Herald* (New York City), April 12, 1837; "Kidnapping in New-York," *Liberator* (Boston), April 21, 1837. On Riker's politics, see Hodges, *David Ruggles*, 61–64.

6. *First Annual Report of the New York Committee of Vigilance* (1837), 13, Historical Society of Pennsylvania, Philadelphia; Hodges, *David Ruggles*, 84–94. On black New York, see Leslie Alexander, *African or American? Black Identity and Political Activism in New York City, 1784–1861* (Urbana: University of Illinois Press, 2008); Leslie Harris, *In the Shadow of Slavery: African Americans in New York City, 1626–1863* (Chicago: University of Chicago Press, 2002).

7. "Dickson's Trial," *Colored American* (New York), April 29, 1837. My use of "mob" reflects the work of Paul Gilje, who shows that mob action was a central aspect of popular politics in the early American republic. Gilje, *The Road to Mobocracy: Popular Disorder in New York City, 1763–1834* (Chapel Hill: University of North Carolina Press, 1987). On early American street politics, see

Simon P. Newman, *Parades and the Politics of the Street: Festive Culture in the Early American Republic* (Philadelphia: University of Pennsylvania Press, 1999); David Waldstreicher, *In the Midst of Perpetual Fetes: The Making of American Nationalism, 1776–1820* (Chapel Hill: University of North Carolina Press, 1997).

8. "To the Thoughtless Part of Our Colored Citizens," *Colored American* (New York), April 15, 1837. On gender and respectability in black politics, see Patrick Rael, *Black Identity and Black Protest in the Antebellum North* (Chapel Hill: University of North Carolina Press, 2002), esp. chapter 4.

9. "To the Thoughtless Part of Our Colored Citizens."

10. "To the Thoughtless Part of our Colored Citizens." In the aftermath of the riot, Cornish corrected a *New York Times* editorial that described a parade of the Clarkson Benevolent Society as a public protest against Dixon's apprehension. "Base Slander," *Colored American* (New York), April 29, 1837. In national conventions during the early 1830s, black activists repeatedly advised against public processions because of their concern with respectability but also because of the increasing problem of racially motivated mob violence in struggles over public space. See "Minutes and Proceedings of the Second Annual Convention . . . 1832," 27, and "Minutes and Proceedings of the First Annual Convention . . . 1831," in Howard Holman Bell, ed., *Minutes of the Proceedings of the National Negro Conventions, 1830–1864* (New York: Arno Press, 1969). On the turn from mobbing to race riots, see Gilje, *The Road to Mobocracy*, chapters 5 and 6.

11. *Herald* (New York City), April 19, 1837; *Liberator* (Boston), April 21, 1837; Thomas D. Morris, *Free Men All: The Personal Liberty Laws of the North, 1780–1861* (Baltimore: Johns Hopkins University Press, 1974), 11. Dixon's counsel would have directed the writ *de homine replegiando* to a sheriff, paid a bond, and declared before a judge that the accused would return for a hearing when called.

12. Samuel Cornish helped knit together this news and the communities involved in the pages of his *Colored American*. See "Ohio Legislature," February 17, 1838; "Fugitive Slaves" and "Connecticut Coming Round," June 16, 1838; "From the Michigan Observer: A Bright Spot," August 18, 1838; "Public Meeting in Philadelphia," January 30, 1841; "Legislature," May 11, 1839; "A Voice from New Haven," August 1, 1840; and "Thomas C. Brown," July 15, 1837. Morris, *Free Men All* offers an extensive overview of legal struggles regarding fugitives, slavery, and federalism in the mid-nineteenth century.

13. This narrative of the Crosswhite affair comes from *Giltner v. Gorham*, 4 McLean, 402; 6 West. Law J. 49 (Circuit Court, D. Michigan, 1848). See also Roy E. Finkenbine, "A Beacon of Liberty on the Great Lakes: Race Slavery and the Law in Antebellum Michigan," in *The History of Michigan Law*, edited by Paul Finkelman and Martin Hershock (Athens: Ohio University Press, 2006), 83–107.

14. "Inalienable Rights," *Liberator* (Boston), February 10, 1843. On the antislavery concept of a "higher law" and its applications, see Morris, *Free Men All*; David Brion Davis, "The Emergence of Immediatism in British and American Antislavery Thought," *Mississippi Valley Historical Review* 49, no. 2 (1962): 209–30; David Brion Davis, *Inhuman Bondage: The Rise and Fall of Slavery in the New World* (New York: Oxford University Press, 2008).

15. William Lloyd Garrison was the leading advocate of the idea that the US Constitution was fundamentally, irreparably corrupt. See W. Caleb McDaniel,

The Problem of Democracy in the Age of Slavery: Garrisonian Abolitionists and Transatlantic Reform (Baton Rouge: Louisiana State University Press, 2013).

16. Finkenbine, "A Beacon of Liberty," 90.

17. "Detroit, December 6, 1848," *North Star* (Rochester, N.Y.), December 15, 1848.

18. "Public Meeting of the Citizens of Detroit," *North Star* (Rochester, N.Y.), December 29, 1848.

19. "Public Meeting of the Citizens of Detroit."

20. "Public Meeting of the Citizens of Detroit." See also "From the Model Worker: Crosswhite Case," *North Star* (Rochester, N.Y.), April 7, 1849.

21. Morris, *Free Men All*, 145–47; Margot Minardi, *Making Slavery History: Abolitionism and the Politics of Memory in Massachusetts* (New York: Oxford University Press, 2010), 135.

22. "Meetings of the Colored Citizens of New York," *North Star* (Rochester, N.Y.), October 24, 1850.

23. Leonard P. Curry, *The Free Black in Urban America, 1800–1850: The Shadow of the Dream* (Chicago: University of Chicago Press, 1981), 245; *Herald* (New York City), April 19, 1837; *Liberator* (Boston), April 21, 1837; Morris, *Free Men All*, 11.

24. Douglass guessed that Dixon was worried Douglass "might be a party to a second attempt to recapture him." Frederick Douglass, *My Bondage and My Freedom* (New York: Miller, Orton, and Mulligan, 1855), 337–38.

25. "From the Emancipator: City Recorder—Kidnapping—and Free People of Color in New-York," *National Enquirer*, October 15, 1836.

26. *Washington Post*, August 10, 2015.

Conspiracies, Seditions, Rebellions
Concepts and Categories in the Study of Slave Resistance

Gregory Childs

Secrecy and criminal intent. These two concepts define our modern under-standing of *conspiracy* more than anything else. For historians of resistance, our interest in studying and trying to understand the significance of conspir-acies has often rested in part on our belief that archival research and recon-struction are tools best suited to interrogating the secrets of insurgents and officials. Yet the very thing that draws us to study conspiracies also creates a problem for our presupposition about the archive. If an event is alleged to have happened in secret before it was punished publicly, how can we be certain that it actually happened? How much stock can we put in words imputed to subjects under duress? These, among other questions, confront the historian with a demand for something more than just gossip, something more than just words said about another.

However, The problem of the category of conspiracy goes beyond the efforts of historians to reconstruct and narrate the past. There is also the ques-tion of whether those who lived through the event in question only behaved conspiratorially or whether their actions and the way they or other observers narrated the event went beyond this categorization. Yet this sensitivity to ways that agents produced history through both their social actions and their efforts to organize and make sense of their historical moment—what Michel-Rolph Trouillot famously referred to as the "full historicism" of an event—is often missing from the ways we approach our interrogations of conspiracies.[1] Accordingly we rarely take notice of the other forms and names of resistance that are being told to us in the same documents that contain alleged evidence of a conspiracy.

These other names of resistance are many, from *sedition* to *protest, lam-poon, conjuration*, and more. Yet shifting our focus to the different names that were frequently used to describe and define a single, supposedly unified politi-cal event is not merely an exercise in semantics or discourse analysis. What is at stake in this gesture, rather, is a fuller picture of the intellectual history of black communities under slavery. Following the different names of resistance thus can point us to debates between and among people of African descent regarding questions of freedom and politics. This exercise also reveals that those in power were often aware that the movements they aimed to repress were not static but dynamic, growing from conspiratorial assemblages into other modes of insurgent expression.

This chapter applies this concern with listening for the different names of resistance in incidents that we have come to regard as conspiracies. As a historian of the African diaspora in Latin America and the Caribbean, I draw primarily on examples and historiographies related to this region of the Americas. More specifically, in this chapter I focus almost exclusively on conspiracies against slavery in Cuba and Brazil from the end of the eighteenth century through the first half of the nineteenth. In the first section I focus on the limits that historians confront when we stick to probing secrets of an alleged conspiracy to ascertain if it was indeed real. In addition to encountering gaps in archival evidence that might provide more proof of the guilt or innocence of alleged conspirators, I argue that historians' attempts to prove or disprove the veracity of conspiracies are often divorced from any account of the legal cultures in which these movements took place. Rather than question what the meaning of conspiracy was in a given imperial or national framework, historians often attempt to derive the veracity of a reported conspiracy through a set of qualifying questions that purport to bring us closer to understanding whether or not a real rebellion was being planned. Among these questions are inquiries about access to guns, foreign aid, and whether or not clear, undisputed leadership of the movement can be identified. What often gets overlooked in asking these questions, however, is that enslaved and free people of color lived in regimes where speaking ill of the crown was enough in itself to warrant death, that they would likely be charged with multiple categories of crime and not just one, and that these were known facts to the majority of the population. We therefore miss the historical importance of legal cultures and accordingly end up studying incidents labeled conspiracy largely according to our own contemporary criteria and without appreciation for the fact that insurgent activity can exist across multiple categories or in regimes where the meaning of conspiracy is quite different from our own.[2] Furthermore this oversight keeps us from taking account of and reckoning with moments when conspirators have attempted to communicate elements of their clandestine plot to broader publics.

The second section thus moves from the constriction encountered in our conceptions of conspiracy and toward the challenge of thinking through cases of conspiracy that were also categorized as sedition, a crime that was defined in seventeenth-, eighteenth-, and nineteenth-century legal codes as publicly encouraging disloyalty to crown or nation. The case example for this is the Tailors' Conspiracy, an alleged plot to overthrow slavery, racism, Portuguese rule, and low wages that was discovered in 1798 in the city of Bahia, Brazil. This movement was organized and carried out by more than thirty free or freed people, along with the participation of over one dozen enslaved people and several whites. Though long understood as a conspiracy, the movement and the subsequent rebellion were announced to residents of the city through handwritten bulletins posted in prominent locations around Bahia. This section thus takes up the preceding section's call to think more carefully about how resistance movements of the late eighteenth and early nineteenth century enter the archive through legal cultures that we cannot assume to be transparent and whose punitive measures we cannot assume people of African descent to have been wholly unaware of. Retracing how enslaved and free insurgents moved between holding conspiratorial meetings and disseminating seditious writing helps us see the need to approach cases categorized as conspiracy with enough patience and discernment to take seriously the categorization and to see how such a categorization overshadows and draws critical attention away from other practices of resistance that were purposeful, meaningful, and indicative of the growth of black political thought during the Age of Revolution.

Conspiracy and the Historiographical Imagination

The historical literature on slavery in the Americas continues to grow at an impressive and expansive rate. Over the past twenty years new approaches to some traditional questions have encouraged historians to reevaluate many concepts that were once understood to be clearly defined categories of analysis. For example, before the burst of studies in the late 1980s and early 1990s that focused on the postemancipation era, we assumed we inherently knew what the concept of freedom meant.[3] Likewise, until the publication of several recent works on the development of the African diaspora and the Black Atlantic, we simply assumed that the flow of cultural transmission between Africa and the Americas was unidirectional: from the old world to the new. We now know that this flow was at least bidirectional, with African-descended people, cultural products, and ideas from the new world circulating in and transforming the old.[4]

In the field of Latin American and Caribbean history, studies of slave conspiracies—that is, conspiracies to rebel against slavery organized by or in the name of the enslaved—have also recently undergone reevaluations. For example, a number of scholars have revisited a string of rebellions that took place in 1812 Havana—known as the Aponte Rebellion or the Conspiracy of Aponte—to interrogate whether these were isolated events or were organized in a conspiratorial manner by a single leader. In reconsidering this important question, scholars such as Matt Childs, Sibylle Fischer, Stephan Palmié, and Ada Ferrer have stepped back from focusing exclusively on whether the free colored soldier José Antonio Aponte masterminded a conspiracy and have begun to interrogate the notebooks and writings of this individual as well. As a result the era of Aponte is no longer considered only a time of insurgent activity but is also seen as a time of intellectual growth for free and enslaved peoples in Cuba.[5] Similarly several historians have pushed us to rethink the

1844 Conspiracy of the Ladder (La Escalera) in Cuba. This event—so named due to the fact that numerous suspects were tied to ladders and tortured while being interrogated—has long been understood as an urban movement, and the question of whether or not it was organized and instigated by white abolitionists has been extensively debated. This memory of torture has not only provided a nomenclature for the 1844 movement but within historical scholarship has also rendered it unique, isolated, and too traumatic to be linked to Afro-Cuban political thought and activism in the second half of the nineteenth century. Recent works by Aisha Finch and Michele Reid-Vazquez on this movement, however, have demonstrated, respectively, that a significant portion of those who organized insurgent activity leading up to La Escalera came from the rural countryside of Cuba, and that those who survived the repression continued to contribute to intellectual life in Cuba and the wider Atlantic world.[6]

If these recent historiographical trends are any indication, then, we are well on our way to writing more robust intellectual histories of the Black Atlantic during the Age of Revolution, not simply demonstrating the rebellious capacity of people of African descent. However, there have still been relatively few serious attempts to understand the idea of conspiracy within the legal cultures of the late eighteenth and early nineteenth centuries.[7] And this is not related just to studies of conspiracies that took place in Latin America and the Caribbean. Whether the discussion is about the discovery of a plot to rebel against slavery at the town of Second Creek, Mississippi, during the Civil War or about the aforementioned discovery of a supposed plot to destroy slavery across all of Cuba in 1812 Havana, surprisingly little is ever said about how the legal category of conspiracy is applied and what it means in a particular legal culture.[8] Rather we often proceed with our studies by interrogating the veracity of an alleged plot to rebel, and thus often proceed to give an account of black political life without defining or questioning how the alleged plotters' actions or discourses might have been measured according to legal practice. We thus give very little attention to terminologies and legal codes that colonial courts operate within, often choosing to focus on interrogation records and black agency as though these things existed outside of such codes. This way of conceptualizing black politics of resistance is not stated outright so much as it is suggested by the principal question that animates all studies of slave conspiracies: whether the accused individuals actually were intending to start a rebellion or were the unfortunate scapegoats in a drama of white fear and paranoia over the possibility of black resistance.

To put the problem more simply, the principal question in studies of slave conspiracies up until now has been whether or not the supposed plot to rebel was real or was a figment of the white imagination (or a figment of the imagination of the historian in the archives). To get at this question an entire subset of qualifying questions has been developed, and behind each of these qualifying questions there seems to lie the assumption that every affirmative answer moves us one step closer to being able to say "Yes, the supposed conspiracy was in fact real." In particular there are three questions that seem to demand attention in studies of slave conspiracies: Did the suspected conspirators have access to guns? Can we identify a chain of command or a set of leaders? and Were the individuals in question seeking some form of foreign aid? Let us begin by looking at one of these questions, namely whether or not the participants of the movement had access to and intended to use guns to launch their uprising.

In historiographies devoted to the study of conspiracies to rebel against slavery, the question of whether or not the suspected conspirators had acquired firearms or had ready access to guns looms large. For example, in the case of the Denmark Vesey Conspiracy against slavery that took place in Charleston, South Carolina, in 1822, it has been argued that it was and was not a real conspiracy, and the presence or absence of firearms continues to be one of the key features of the argument. Most recently the historian Michael Johnson, who concludes that there was no real conspiracy on the part of Vesey and his associates and that the only real conspiracy in Charleston in 1822 was the mock trial and fatal punishments administered by racist white judges, argues that since "the court could not find any guns secreted away by the conspirators," and that even though some slaves testified that they had seen a gun but had no luck trying to discharge it, we can safely assume that Vesey and company did not have access to firearms, and thus were not really plotting a violent rebellion.[9] In her marvelous study of slave resistance in midnineteenth-century Cuba, Aisha Finch writes that "one of the long-standing arguments against the existence" of the Conspiracy of La Escalera in 1844 "is that such a stockpile of weapons was never found."[10] Most studies of the Tailors' Conspiracy of 1798 have been no different in this regard. Luis Henrique Dias Tavares, who has contributed several important works on the subject, states plainly that the captain of the free black militia seriously considered joining the movement before denouncing it, and that his contribution to the uprising would have been firearms and a cavalry of men from his regiment.[11] The implication is that since organizers and leaders of the movement were in fact trying to secure a stash of guns when the arrests and interrogations began, the men were serious about revolting and sacking the city.

Yet as Finch demonstrates, linking the realness of a plot to rebel to the presence of or access to firearms is suspect primarily because it discounts all other types of weaponry and styles of warfare that dispossessed groups of people make use of. Thus fire, building tools, sticks, cudgels, and poisons are characterized as premodern, ineffective, and not seriously worth considering.[12] Mimi Sheller demonstrates this point in her analysis of the Piquet Rebellion and the subsequent "piquettiste movements" in Haiti in 1844–68.[13] I would merely add to these astute observations that the continued appeal to the presence or absence of weapons in general rests on a contemporary understanding about the law and evidence. That is, if there is no hard evidence to show culpability, one is innocent until proven guilty. This is most evident in the Vesey case. Even though no firearms were found, the judges asserted that this was no proof of innocence. On the contrary, they argued that a few of the suspected men were just better at hiding arms than investigators were at discovering them. Johnson deals with this dilemma in a few sentences, treating these statements as hearsay evidence and never questioning to what degree both the black men and their white interrogators would have understood this logic.[14]

If identifying the veracity of a conspiracy is a process of stacking up affirmative responses to qualifying questions, then when the answers to more than one of the qualifying questions is negative, we move one step in the opposite direction, toward debunking the idea that anything revolutionary took place. In short, we begin to characterize the event in question not as a conspiracy but as an example of "loose talk" that was exploited by paranoid white officials. The idea of loose talk is that when people get upset or drunk they might speak out of turn or say the wrong thing to the wrong person, but such occasions cannot be considered proof of rebellious activity. This is exactly the argument that Johnson makes in his treatment of the Denmark Vesey Conspiracy. Similarly historians have doubted that participants of the 1798 movement in Bahia were truly committed to racial egalitarianism, the abolition of slavery, and actual rebellion due to the supposed absence of weapons but also the fact that one of the freed leaders of the movement rented slaves and did not invite them to participate in the planned uprising. The claims of the entire movement to be against slavery thus become colored as nothing more than idealistic words espoused by overzealous individuals.[15]

The central problem in the idea of loose talk is not that historians raise doubts about the sincerity of historical actors to follow through on their words. Indeed the sincerity of the claims is not what is at stake. In fact the real dilemma that engulfs the notion of loose talk is that the sincerity of speech takes precedence over the *operation* of speech in a colonial, imperial, or national setting where slavery is legal and prevalent. To characterize talk against slavery, the state, or the king as merely loose talk seems to be a direct effect of living in a contemporary society that operates (at least in theory) under the premise that there is something called "free speech." Yet there was no such concept, and imperial subjects and slaves knew this. Slanderous and seditious words often led to court cases or death in the Americas in the eighteenth and nineteenth century.[16] This same point has been elucidated in the debate surrounding Johnson's assessment of the Denmark Vesey Conspiracy.[17]

Yet the concern that some historians show toward distinguishing loose talk from actual conspiracy stems from the widest held assumption about the concept of black political life in colonial slave regimes: that persons of African descent could plan and organize only in secret. This is an assumption that undergirds all of the qualifying questions that have been discussed thus far, and furthermore brings us back to the original point, that conspiracies were defined as clandestine plots and confederations. How, then, can we avoid this circular problem of secrecy that seems to structure every utterance or analysis of resistance by persons of African descent?

Seditions within Conspiracies or Conspiracies within Seditions

One answer to the question may be found in the meaning of the term *sedition*, particularly in cases where that term shows up alongside *conspiracy* in official records. While the historical literature on conspiracy continues to be preoccupied with readymade lines of inquiry such as leadership, ammunition, and foreign aid, the concept of sedition provides a framework for thinking about resistance by African-descended persons that has little in common with such concerns. The doctrine of sedition was employed by nearly all western European monarchies to categorize rebellious movements that either intended to physically harm the person of the king and his family or publicly encouraged a lack of confidence and disloyalty toward the throne and its public officials. It is a political crime that in its current understanding dates back to the fifteenth and sixteenth centuries, with the transformations introduced by the development and diffusion of the printing press and the Protestant Reformation.[18] The word *seditio* existed in Roman law, but for much of the history of the Roman Empire there was no precise legal definition attached to the word. Thus a fair amount of political libel and slander of officials and the emperor was tolerated. As Roger Manning observes, "It was assumed that any person who assailed the emperor's name was either drunk, insane, or beneath contempt." Officials were given instructions to burn any inflammatory papers and simply report the case to the emperor, "who could alone decide punishment."[19]

After the Reformation and the advent of the printing press, though, a period that perhaps not coincidentally also saw the rise of Absolutism across Europe, the spread of seditious libel and defamation of the king became a serious concern. This perception of sedition as a threat was not due solely to the growth of literacy, however. It was due in large part to a cross-fertilization between literate and nonliterate cultures. While the press could make an author famous through circulation, that popularity was often directly related to an author's ability to engage with and express his or her thoughts in popular forms of verse and satire.[20]

Thus a common culture of royal critique developed between upper and lower strata of colonial and homeland populations in seventeenth- and eighteenth-century Europe. And it must be mentioned that not all such critiques called for the end of monarchy; most in fact did not. But public calls for reform could easily escalate into public cries to depose or even execute a particular monarch. Hence in times of political turmoil absolute heads of state and their public officials came down hard on cases of defamation and libel, giving very little quarter to the notion that seditious talk could be explained away by the presence of alcohol, insanity, or low-ranking birth.[21] From the seventeenth century onward neither loose talk nor drunken talk would have been a sufficient excuse to exonerate one found guilty of sedition.

Thus while conspiracies against slavery have been broadly conceived as a process of plotting in secret to rebel violently and unlawfully against the status quo, sedition has encompassed something much more specific: a public threat or call for disobedience against the ruling regime. Indeed for metropolitan and colonial officials in the Portuguese Empire the unifying element of sedition was not rebellion but any form of contesting royal authority that was promoted publicly or that was first done in secret and then subsequently either discovered by public officials or promulgated by disaffected individuals. This could be as simple as talking in a tavern or writing private letters that contained seditious content, and as complex as plotting, attempting, and trying to publicly secure support for an uprising.

Historians of revolutionary America are most familiar with the concept of sedition through the Alien and Sedition Acts of 1798. These bills were signed into law by President John Adams in an effort to curb public criticism of the federal government by opposing parties and to check the growth of immigration. Sedition, then, is linked in American historiography to the growth of party politics and is consequently centered on the political actions, xenophobia, and struggles for power between white men of varying political persuasions. By contrast, the absence of established or growing political parties in late eighteenth- and early nineteenth-century Latin America meant that sedition was not employed to such a degree in high politics. Instead seditious subjects could be and were identified across all ranks and classes of society, and as the Age of Revolution intensified in the 1780s and 1790s, reported incidents of sedition increased significantly.

For example, a plot to assassinate the king of Portugal in 1758 resulted in the charge of sedition and execution of one prominent family of nobles, as well as their Jesuit confessor. Their crime was not simply attacking the king's coach in broad daylight, but in also publicly questioning his authority to rule.[22] Later, in 1789, a conspiracy in the Brazilian captaincy of Minas Gerais was halted and one of the participants was hanged and torn to pieces. The aims of this movement were for independence from Brazil, an idea that had grown and been discussed by several elite white men who often met in cafés and who also spread their ideas through poetry. Once again their crime was not only plotting to rebel but also publicly disseminating their disloyal ideas to others.[23] Finally, there was the 1798 movement in Bahia that, although referred to as the Tailors' Conspiracy, was in fact also classified by authorities as a case of sedition. As stated earlier, this movement was announced in handwritten bulletins posted around the city of Bahia that called for an end to slavery, racism, Portuguese rule in Bahia, and unfair wages for artisans and soldiers. While the participants of this movement were likewise charged with plotting rebellion and attempting to spread their ideas to the public, the repression of this movement was decidedly different due to the fact that those who were arrested were almost exclusively people of African descent. Thus one of the more important reasons to reexamine the Tailors' Conspiracy is that, contrary to the understanding we have of sedition in US history, it reveals sedition as a crime that was not just reserved for elite politics.

In calling for this attention to the importance of sedition, I do not intend to argue that the 1798 movement in Bahia was not a conspiracy to rebel against slavery. Yet in brushing past the category of sedition and focusing our entire investigations around our own questions regarding what constitutes a real conspiracy we close off other possible conceptions and discourses of contesting authority. We also ignore the public component of many events, choosing instead to look for skullduggery and secret rendezvous even when the challenges to royal authority were postulated in broad daylight. For example, what does it mean that participants of the 1798 event posted their demands, their critiques, and the call for an end to Portuguese rule in public places around the city? What significance can we attach to the public nature of the event, and what does it tell us about resistance and the idea of the public in eighteenth-century Brazil? Here we will need to look briefly at some of the documents from the trial, specifically the content of the handbills that revealed some of the key demands and grievances of the movement.

When the captain of the black militia, Joaquim Jose de Santana, reported to the office of Doctor Judge Francisco Sabino Alvares da Costa Pinto on August 28, 1798, he came armed with incriminating testimony about an insurgent movement that had been announced in the city of Bahia two weeks earlier, on August 12. Santana testified that he had been invited to help lead the assault on the city by a free tailor of color named João de Deus do Nascimento.[24] He had told his superiors in the military about this invitation, and they in turned commanded him to keep the information secret, attend the meetings he was invited to, and operate as a spy for the colonial administration. He had carried out his orders for more than a week and now was coming to give his testimony to the judge.

A few hours after Santana came forward, a freed blacksmith and doorman by the name of Joaquim José da Veiga also came to tell the High Court judge that the mastermind behind the plot was João de Deus do Nascimento.[25] In subsequent accounts relayed by others who were arrested as a result of these initial denunciations, it was clear that many secret meetings to discuss politics had taken place at João de Deus's house. Secret meetings took place in the homes of other participants as well, most of them tailors or artisans of some sort. Thus the case for classifying this movement as a conspiracy turned in part on the fact that regardless of whether it could be proved that they had intended to rebel, the evidence overwhelmingly suggested that they met in secret to discuss topics that were deemed subversive and disloyal to the crown.

Yet this discovery of secret meetings through denunciations came two weeks after the planned uprising had already been announced to the city. On

August 12 residents of Bahia had awoken to discover numerous handwritten bulletins posted in the most public plazas and church fronts announcing a "coming revolution." The bulletins also contained denunciations of racism, slavery, and Portuguese rule and made a promise that in the aftermath of the revolution "blacks and browns who live scorned and abandoned will all be equal, having no difference, only having liberty, equality, and fraternity." Thus the first step for authorities was not discovering or hearing about secret plots to rebel or searching for evidence of guns and clear leadership, but rather a seditious attempt to persuade the populace of Bahia to join a campaign against Portuguese rule.

The public proclamations and demands demonstrated to colonial officials that what might have begun in secret, closed meetings could become the basis for a more diffuse public movement against crown authority. In stating that colonial officials were concerned about the movement serving as a basis for a broader public culture of dissent, I do not simply mean that they were concerned about a rebellion planned in secret turning into a rebellion played out in public. Here we must pause and think not just about rebellion but about the fear that people of African descent meeting in secret to talk politics could serve as a model for other groups and other members of society to congregate for similar purposes. A public culture of debate and discussion about any and all political grievances had just as much if not more potential to topple and undo colonialism as a physical uprising against slavery and racism. The charge of sedition thus was leveled at both the public dissemination of writings and the potentiality for greater public discussion of politics that was signaled by secret meetings to talk politics.

Let us actually dwell for a moment on the appearance of the handwritten bulletins across the city to understand this problem more concretely. Though numerous handwritten bulletins appeared in Salvador da Bahia on August 12, only eleven of them survived the processes of discovery and confiscation to be preserved in the archives. One bulletin charged the king of Portugal and his ministers with despotism and unworthiness to rule.[26] Another bulletin declared the time had come for the people of Salvador "to revive from the abyss of slavery, in order to raise forth the Sacred Flag of Liberty." This piece of paper stated in unambiguous terms that a "projected revolt" was being planned and counted more than six hundred individuals as either supporters or participants.[27] Another set of papers called for regular pay for soldiers and for a more equitable share of agricultural capital to be redistributed to cultivators of the land. Finally, more than one *pasquinade* threatened death to all priests who attempted to derail the "liberty and good of the people."[28]

In light of how much discussion had been happening clandestinely prior to the appearance of the bulletins, we must consider how political debate between those who attended meetings likely shaped the appearance of different kinds of handbills that were plastered across the public spaces of the city. In other words, some may have simply wanted to rebel and end everything about Portuguese rule; hence the simple announcement of a coming rebellion. Others may have been more focused on winning public support by airing specific grievances, such as fair pay. Those who were committed to these aspects of the movement did not attempt to gauge the level of support for their actions only through hidden transcripts and recruiting people to hidden meetings but also through discussions and meetings in well-known places and public proclamations against the crown and its ministers. For the High Court judges and the governor of Salvador, then, this was not just about putting down a potential rebellion but also about warning future would-be critics about what would happen if they attempted to publicly disseminate antimonarchical, antihierarchical, or antireligious politics to the people of the city. The 1798 movement in Bahia must thus be understood as both a case of sedition and a case of conspiring to rebel. It was not one or the other, and only by thinking through diasporic political movements in ways that grapple with the full scope of the political and legal cultures that such movements were enmeshed in can we begin to think more concretely about how to write histories of black political and intellectual life under Western colonialism.

The case I have been making for the importance of sedition in Bahia extends beyond the geographical borders of Brazil. Sedition was also linked to black political activity in early nineteenth-century Cuba. For example, the movement associated with José Antonio Aponte was also catalogued and indexed as an example of sedition. Whereas the Bahian case revolved around the appearance of handwritten bulletins across the city, Aponte's movement was characterized by the discovery of a somewhat infamous notebook he had compiled. Between the covers of this book Aponte had inserted a hand-drawn map of the Nile River, drawings of black armies fighting white ones, even a black soldier holding the still-dripping head of a decapitated white soldier, images of the Spanish king Carlos III and an "Abyssinian" king, and of Toussaint Louverture, Jean-Jacques Dessalines, and Henri Christophe. The discovery of this notebook was all the evidence governing authorities needed to declare Aponte the singular leader of an islandwide conspiracy that linked at least five rebellions together into a massive war against slavery.

Historians still debate whether or not Aponte was the mastermind behind a conspiracy to coordinate rebellions across the colony.[29] Historians, literary scholars, and anthropologists also continue to debate what the collection of images that Aponte created could have symbolized to himself and to others who saw the book. Yet for the purposes of this chapter, I am not as interested in the images as I am in why Aponte did not deny ownership of the book. If Aponte had no compunction about admitting showing the book to others, is it because others were involved in the making of the book from its earliest stages? Was the famed book a project that included an array of viewpoints and ideas that had been compiled by Aponte, though not necessarily created by him? Though the act of compiling such a work would still remain an impressive feat, considering the Aponte rebellion in this light allows us to entertain the idea of a more dynamic political imagination for Afro-Cubans in the early nineteenth century.

What I am suggesting for Aponte is not out of keeping with Spanish imperial politics in Cuba. Cases of sedition and public *infidencia* (disloyalty) were not uncommon in early nineteenth-century Cuba. As early as 1780 cases of sedition appear in the register of political disorders.[30] In 1824 and 1827 officials in Trinidad and Havana were trying to identify the author of various handwritten seditious bulletins that had been discovered.[31] In 1826 in Santiago de Cuba the problem confronting authorities was a "French Negro (negro frances)" by the name of Salvador la Frontaigne who was suspected of publicly inciting enslaved blacks to "proclaim liberty."[32]

There is much at stake in delving deeper into these incidents and considering the meaning of conspiracy and sedition in these cases. For starters, such an approach offers a way to think about black politics under slavery and colonialism without the inquiry being structured so strongly by the question of singularity or exceptionality. If scenarios of open discussion and debate among black individuals played a significant part in the creation of knowledge books like that produced by Aponte and in the demands that appeared in handwritten bulletins in Bahia in 1798, then what we are talking about are not merely the ideas and organizational capacity of exceptional individuals but the ideas and organizational capacities of multiple individuals of African descent, both common and not so common, that moved throughout the spaces of Latin America and the Caribbean publicly trading and sharing dissident information and ideas. Considering such formulations may thus be a significant avenue for opening up further investigations into the construction of black publics.

Notes

1. Michel-Rolph Trouillot, *Silencing the Past: Power and the Production of History* (Boston: Beacon Press, 1995), 24.

2. For example, in nineteenth-century Jamaica it was enough to simply be accused of imagining the death of a white person to be charged with the capital crime of criminal conspiracy. Plans to follow through on the fantasy were not necessary to legally convict an enslaved or free black person of this crime. I am thankful to Vincent Brown for this reminder. See Brown, *The Reaper's Garden: Death and Power in the World of Atlantic Slavery* (Cambridge, Mass.: Harvard University Press, 2008), 3.

3. See, among others, Frederick Cooper, Rebecca J. Scott, and Thomas Holt, *Beyond Slavery: Explorations of Race, Labor, and Citizenship in Postemancipation Societies* (Chapel Hill: University of North Carolina Press, 2000); Thavolia Glymph,

Out of the House of Bondage: The Transformation of the Plantation Household (Cambridge, UK: Cambridge University Press, 2008); Laurent Dubois, *Avengers of the New World: The Story of the Haitian Revolution* (Cambridge, Mass.: Harvard University Press, 2004); Ada Ferrer, *Insurgent Cuba: Race, Nation, and Revolution, 1868–1898* (Chapel Hill: University of North Carolina Press, 1999); Mimi Sheller, *Democracy after Slavery: Black Publics and Peasant Radicalism in Haiti and Jamaica* (Gainesville: University of Florida Press, 2000).

4. J. Lorand Matory, *Black Atlantic Religion: Tradition, Transnationalism, and Matriarchy in the Afro-Brazilian Candomble* (Princeton, N.J.: Princeton University Press, 2005); Brent Hayes Edwards, *The Practice of Diaspora: Literature, Translation, and the Rise of Black Internationalism* (Cambridge, Mass.: Harvard University Press, 2003).

5. Matt D. Childs, *The 1812 Aponte Rebellion in Cuba and the Struggle against Atlantic Slavery* (Chapel Hill: University of North Carolina Press, 2006); Sibylle Fischer, *Modernity Disavowed: Haiti and the Cultures of Slavery in the Age of Revolution* (Durham, N.C.: Duke University Press, 2004); Stephan Palmié, *Wizards and Scientists: Explorations in Afro-Cuban Modernity and Tradition* (Durham, N.C.: Duke University Press, 2002); Ada Ferrer, *Freedom's Mirror: Cuba and Haiti in the Age of Revolution* (Cambridge, UK: Cambridge University Press, 2014).

6. Aisha K. Finch, *Rethinking Slave Rebellion in Cuba: La Escalera and the Insurgencies of 1841–1844* (Chapel Hill: University of North Carolina Press, 2015); Michele Reid-Vazquez, *The Year of the Lash: Free People of Color in Cuba and the Nineteenth-Century Atlantic World* (Athens: University of Georgia Press, 2011).

7. One notable exception in this regard is Thomas J. Davis, "Conspiracy and Credibility: Look Who's Talking, about What: Law Talk and Loose Talk," in "Forum: The Making of a Slave Conspiracy, Volume II," special issue, *William and Mary Quarterly*, third series, 59, no. 1 (2002): 167–74.

8. Winthrop D. Jordan, *Tumult and Silence at Second Creek: An Inquiry into a Civil War Slave Conspiracy* (Baton Rouge: Louisiana State University Press, 1992); Childs, *The 1812 Aponte Rebellion*; Fischer, *Modernity Disavowed*; Palmié, *Wizards and Scientists*.

9. Michael P. Johnson, "Denmark Vesey and His Co-Conspirators," *William and Mary Quarterly* 58, no. 4 (2001): 957–58.

10. Finch, *Rethinking Slave Rebellion*, 193–95. The argument was considered so strong a piece of evidence against the existence of the conspiracy that Robert Paquette, who attempted to show that the Conspiracy of La Escalera was real, goes about trying to prove the existence of the plot without ever really answering the question of whether or not Cuban slaves had access to weapons. He instead focuses on British abolitionists who were present in Cuba, whom he thinks had contact with Cuban conspirators and whom he believes had access to guns. See Paquette, *Sugar Is Made with Blood: The Conspiracy of La Escalera and the Conflict between Empires over Slavery in Cuba* (Middletown, Conn.: Wesleyan University Press, 1990).

11. Luis Henrique Dias Tavares, *História da sedição intentada na Bahia em 1798: A conspiração dos alfaiates* (São Paulo: Livraria Pioneira Editora, 1975), 52–53. See also Tavares, *Da sedição de 1798 à revolta de 1824 na Bahia* (Salvador: Editora UFBA, 2003).

12. Finch, *Rethinking Slave Rebellion*, 273–86.

13. Sheller, *Democracy after Slavery*, 111–42.

14. Johnson, "Denmark Vesey and His Co-Conspirators," 958.

15. Hendrik Kraay, *Race, State, and Armed Forces in Independence-Era Brazil: Bahia, 1790s–1840s* (Stanford: Stanford University Press, 2001), 61–81; Stuart E. Schwartz, *Sugar Plantations in the Formation of Brazilian Society: Bahia, 1550-1835*, (Cambridge, UK: Cambridge University Press, 1985), 476–79.

16. See Lyman L. Johnson and Sonya Lipsett-Rivera, eds., *The Faces of Honor: Sex, Shame, and Violence in Colonial Latin America* (Albuquerque: University of New Mexico Press, 1998).

17. Davis, "Conspiracy and Credibility," 153–58.

18. On origins of sedition as a political crime, see Roger B. Manning, "The Origins of the Doctrine of Sedition," *Albion: A Quarterly Journal concerned with British Studies* 12, no. 2 (1980): 99–121.

19. Manning, "The Origins of the Doctrine of Sedition," 114.

20. On this cross-fertilization between literate and nonliterate cultures in forms of public defamation of the crown, see Kathleen Wilson, *The Sense of the People: Politics, Culture, and Imperialism in England, 1715–1785* (Cambridge, UK: Cambridge University Press,1998), especially 84–136. On the same phenomenon in the eighteenth-century Portuguese Empire, see Kenneth R. Maxwell, *Conflicts and Conspiracies: Brazil and Portugal 1750–1808* (New York: Routledge, 2004), 103–4; Fischer, speaking of the Conspiracy of La Escalera, contends that Plácido wrote poems that attempted to mimic the form of popular verse games that would have been played that embarrassed the Creole elite of Cuba and thus led to his being rejected as a poet (*Modernity Disavowed*, 84–86).

21. See J. H. M. Salmon, "Venality of Office and Popular Sedition in Seventeenth-Century France: A Review of a Controversy," *Past & Present*, no. 37 (July 1967): 21–43; Timothy Tackett, "Conspiracy in a Time of Revolution: French Elites and the Origins of the Terror, 1789–1792," *American Historical Review* 105, no. 3 (2000): 691–713; James P. Martin, "When Repression Is Democratic and Constitutional: The Federalist Theory of Representation and the Sedition Act of 1798," *University of Chicago Law Review* 66, no. 1 (1999): 117–82.

22. Kenneth R. Maxwell, *Pombal, Paradox of the Enlightenment* (Cambridge, UK: Cambridge University Press, 1995), 69–86.

23. Maxwell, *Conflicts and Conspiracies*.

24. "Denuncia publica jurada e necessaria que dâ o Capitão do Regimento Auxiliar dos homens pretos Joaquim José de Santa Anna," Autos de Devassas de Conspiração dos Alfaiates (hereafter cited as ADCA), vol. 1, 287–90, Arquivo Publico do Estado da Bahia.

25. "Denuncia publica jurada e necessaria que dâ Joaquim Joze da Veiga . . . ," ADCA, vol.1, 283–86.

26. "Aviso ao Povo Bahinense," ADCA, vol. 1, 33.

27. "Avizo," ADCA, vol. 1, 33.

28. "Prélo," ADCA, vol. 1, 34.

29. For example, Stephan Palmié casts some doubt on this possibility, while Ada Ferrer suggests Aponte was likely a leader of the rebellion. See Palmié, *Wizards and Scientists*; Ferrer, *Freedom's Mirror*.

30. "Previniendo se publique mañosamente la inquietud y sedicion del Pueblo de Londres," 23 Junio 1780, Arq. Assuntos Políticos, Num. de Orden 102, Legajo 2, Archivo Nacional de Cuba (hereafter cited as ANC).

31. "Sedición," 1824, Arq. Assuntos Políticos, Num. de Orden 13, Legajo 28, ANC; "Sedición," 1827, Arq. Assuntos Políticos, Num. de Orden 20, Legajo 32, ANC.

32. "Procedimento contra Salvador Lafrontaigne, negro frances, y otras negros eslavos de esta ciudad sobre sedicion (Santiago de Cuba)," 23 Marzo 1826, Arq. Assuntos Políticos, Num. de Orden 16, Legajo 31, ANC.

African American Expats, Guyana, and the Pan-African Ideal in the 1970s

Russell Rickford

> Ultimately, those wishing to preserve the postwar liberal order within the United States as the center of the solar system shared a focus with those who looked to the revolutions in Asia and Africa for the key to global emancipation. All embraced the nation-state as the measure of progress and searched for power within its frameworks of possibility.
>
> —Brenda Gayle Plummer, *In Search of Power: African Americans in the Era of Decolonization, 1956–1974*

During the early to mid-1970s a host of progressive and radical African American activists, artists, writers, and refugees from racial oppression in the United States came to regard the Caribbean nation of Guyana as a kind of sanctuary from unraveling mass movements back home. Guyana's image as a Pan-African and socialist mecca for the Americas was highly improbable. The poor, sparsely populated country—the only English-speaking nation in South America—is no bigger than England, with a dense equatorial forest that forces the vast majority of its inhabitants to reside near its narrow coastline. When the former British colony gained its independence in 1966, few North Americans even knew the country existed. Guyana attracted practically no tourism and was frequently confused with either Ghana or Guinea. Yet beginning in 1970 the hope of US Pan-Africanists for the establishment of a socialist "land base" in the Western hemisphere came to rest briefly on the obscure nation.[1]

The appeal of Guyana for African American dissidents stemmed from the particular blend of black nationalism, Pan-Africanism, optimism, and despair that marked the later stages of the Black Power movement in North America. Fascination with the Caribbean country also reflected much older impulses, including the desire to flee the decadence and racism of the United States, an ambition that had long shaped black nationalist and leftist politics.[2] The stream of influential African American visitors who passed through Guyana in the early 1970s, and the handful of black American expats who settled there during this period, were not just looking to escape harsh economic and political realities in the United States. They were also engaged in a search for fulfillment—a quest for immersive blackness, self-government, and true social belonging that mirrored the aspirations of many African Americans who had never even heard of Guyana.

However, the black left utopia of the English-speaking Caribbean proved short-lived. The Guyanese state—a self-proclaimed cooperative socialist republic—degenerated rapidly over the course of the 1970s, highlighting both the insidious nature of neocolonial domination and the political limitations of the Pan-African ideal. The brief, troubled history of African American expatriation in postcolonial Guyana deserves further examination, as does the country's role in the radical imaginary of the post–civil rights era. Such lesser-known currents of transnationalism illustrate black America's romance with the modern nation-state, its yearning for a viable counterforce to US imperialism, and the tragic collision of those two ideals.

Studying contemporary African American engagement with Guyana expands our knowledge of the intricate relationships that political actors forged across the black diaspora. A host of scholars have underscored the transnational dimensions of postwar black political culture.[3] They have shown conclusively that participants in the civil rights and Black Power movements never confined themselves to domestic concerns. Crossing national boundaries during the era of decolonization proved intellectually and politically generative for a wide array of African Americans.

At the same time, the pursuit of diasporic visions was often fraught. International encounters enabled African Americans to construct expansive political networks and cultural identities. But venturing abroad also exposed myriad conflicts—including tensions between race and class and between the state and civil society—in new and unfamiliar environments. By tracing the complexities and paradoxes of global exchange, this essay addresses a theme that must continue to occupy serious students of transnational blackness.

This chapter is designed to contribute to a larger rethinking of African American intellectual history. We need more consideration of the underexplored sites and paradigms of black knowledge production. This means not simply chronicling the ideas that propelled African American dissidents overseas but also situating those ideas within alternative political frameworks that refused to equate democracy with Western liberalism. Far more than alienation animated black expatriation in the postcolonial era. African Americans who sought a path beyond capitalism and US global hegemony produced a rich tapestry of thought. Their forays into the Third World, even when abortive, were not just futile detours. Rather they were manifestations of intellectual endeavor and affirmations of the relentless drive for human dignity.

Guyana has long-standing traditions of black internationalism. The Harlem Renaissance writer Eric D. Walrond, the négritude movement founder Leon

Damas, and T. Ras Makonnen, a convener of the Fifth Pan-African Congress at Manchester, England, in 1945, were all eminent race men of Guyanese descent.[4] The country's identity as a Pan-Africanist stronghold of the 1970s, however, reflected more contemporary developments. One factor was the internationalization of black struggle within and beyond the United States. Over the course of the 1960s mass African American insurgencies ruptured the cold war parochialism that had constrained black political culture after World War II. Members of the civil rights and Black Power movements drew explicit connections between liberation movements abroad and domestic battles for freedom. By the late 1960s the resurgence of radical internationalism had led to a revival of Pan-Africanism as a major tendency in African American thought. For a wide spectrum of activists, the interconnection of black struggles around the globe reemerged as an essential social and political precept.[5]

Critical questions arose about how African Americans should define their relationship to the nonwhite world. While some radicals promoted multiracial Third Worldism as an answer to Western imperialism, others emphasized "blackness" itself as the crucial foundation for global solidarity. Nor was it clear how the principles of black nationalism and internationalism were to be reconciled. Was black America a subjugated nation that should forge diplomatic ties primarily with formal states and governments? Or were political and cultural relations between oppressed masses of people—that is, nonstate actors—to serve as principal bases of Pan-African unity?

Even as such debates continued, the demoralizing decline of 1960s social movements reinforced the desire of some African American activists and cultural figures to escape "Babylon" (the United States). The early 1970s witnessed a variety of grassroots struggles by women, Native Americans, Latinos, workers, and African Americans throughout the United States. However, the fundamental social transformation that many militants had envisioned in the late 1960s had not come to pass. Indeed the forces of counterrevolution, from Nixon and the New Right to the violent apparatuses of state repression, had grown in organization and power, while many of the most dynamic elements of the black liberation movement had foundered. Political demobilization accompanied economic retrenchment and social disarray. Battered by deindustrialization, automation, and cutbacks in social spending, great portions of the black masses were reduced to a surplus labor force, a permanent and seemingly expendable caste.[6]

By the dawn of the 1970s some African American intellectuals and activists had concluded that they would have to venture overseas on a long-term basis to see far-reaching social change in their lifetime. The rebirth of emigrationist sentiment was often cast as a product of disillusionment. Theorists who argued that African American power bases must be developed on the African continent or in other parts of the diaspora rather than in deteriorating American metropolises were accused of defeatism and of abandoning the struggle in the heart of global capitalism. For Pan-Africanists who favored some form of political emigration, however, resettlement overseas seemed to offer a promising means of individual and collective regeneration. Here was an opportunity to help build developing nations rather than agitating endlessly for civil and human rights that never seemed to fully materialize. Expatriation meant transcending the militant rhetoric of the 1960s and actually *living* one's commitment to transnational blackness. It meant purging Western-cultivated tendencies and adopting a whole new "value system" beyond the vulgarity of American materialism. It meant joining the ranks of a racial majority rather than remaining a member of a marginalized US "minority." It meant contributing one's talents to a society bristling with postcolonial hope.[7]

In the early to mid-1960s, Ghana had been the premier site of black American political emigration. After the 1966 coup that ousted Ghanaian leader Kwame Nkrumah, Tanzania emerged as the primary destination of Pan-African sojourners from throughout the black world. An assortment of African American intellectuals and professionals—including Bob and Janet Moses of the Student Nonviolent Coordinating Committee, the anti-imperialist crusader Mae Mallory, and other veterans of the liberation struggle—relocated to the East African country, which had dedicated itself to *Ujamaa*, a variety of "African socialism," under the leadership of the philosopher-statesman Julius Nyerere. The Pan African Skills Project, a New York City–based organization devoted to sending African American technicians abroad to participate in nation-building projects, placed the vast majority of its recruits in Tanzania, which was widely regarded as the most progressive black nation and the most promising setting for African American "repatriation" to the Mother Continent.[8]

After 1970, however, a less distant locale began filtering into the consciousness of some black American internationalists. Airfare to Guyana, a Caribbean nation of three-quarters of a million people perched on the northeastern shoulder of the South American continent, was cheaper than a transatlantic flight to Africa. And unlike Tanzania, where the official language was Kiswahili, Guyana presented no language barrier. The Caribbean country, moreover, appeared to be essentially "black"; its inhabitants consisted primarily of descendants of African slavery and Indian indenture. (The latter group was slightly more populous than the former.) During the long prelude to Guyana's negotiated independence in 1966, at least one black American leftist, New York City's Una Mulzac, had settled briefly there, determined to aid the revolution by working for the People's Progressive Party (PPP) under Cheddi Jagan, the Indo-Guyanese Marxist and father of the anticolonial struggle.[9] However, Guyana's rise in the African American radical imagination did not occur until 1970. And then it was two of Jagan's political rivals, Eusi Kwayana and Forbes Burnham, who engineered the ascent.

Kwayana (born Sidney King) was Guyana's Malcolm X, an indefatigable Pan-Africanist sworn to eliminate the psychological vestiges of colonialism by nurturing a potent black consciousness in a notoriously color-conscious land. Kwayana was founder and head of the African Society for Cultural Relations with Independent Africa (ASCRIA), a grassroots organization that had launched a "cultural revolution" in 1968 to raise awareness of and pride in Guyana's African heritage. Like Burnham, a longtime politician of African descent, Kwayana had once been a prominent member of Jagan's leftist PPP, the largely Indo-Guyanese formation that had led the fight against British rule. However, both Burnham and Kwayana had split with Jagan. With the assistance of Western forces who feared Jagan's revolutionary socialism and close ties to Moscow, the more moderate Burnham had emerged as prime minister of independent Guyana. Kwayana, meanwhile, had allied with Burnham's People's National Congress (PNC) and embarked on a crusade to foster a Black Power renaissance in the Caribbean nation.[10]

Toward that end Kwayana organized a Seminar of Pan Africanist and Black Revolutionary Nationalists in Georgetown, Guyana's capital, in 1970. Many of the prominent African American Pan-Africanists of the day attended the gathering, including Owusu Sadaukai (born Howard Fuller, head of North Carolina's Malcolm X Liberation University), Jitu Weusi (born Leslie Campbell, a Brooklyn activist), and Tom Feelings, a celebrated artist who had lived and worked in Nkrumah's Ghana. One of the summit's aims was to establish a Pan-African secretariat to coordinate hemispheric efforts in support of ongoing struggles against European settler-colonialism and white minority rule in southern Africa and the Portuguese territories. The conference, which coincided with Guyana's official self-designation as a cooperative socialist republic, heralded the emergence of the Caribbean nation as a locus of Pan-Africanist activity. Burnham used the occasion of the gathering to present Guyana to foreign visitors as a stalwart supporter of African liberation, as a dedicated member of the community of nonaligned nations, and as a revolutionary country striving to forge a path of autonomy from the Great Powers while elevating its citizens to a position of dignity. The objective, Burnham explained, was to "make the little man a real man."[11]

In the wake of the 1970 seminar, awareness of Guyana among African American internationalists grew, as did the country's reputation as a bastion of progressive blackness. Some North American observers began to regard the former colony as a proxy Africa, a black Zion nestled in the Western hemisphere. The claim rested on a firm cultural foundation. Guyanese society was awash with African influences—from "queh-queh" wedding celebrations to the rituals of Obeah priests. Cuffy, an enslaved African who had led an eighteenth-century rebellion in the local region of Berbice, had been declared a national hero. ASCRIA members, including a growing segment of black workers and college students, actively promoted the adoption of African names and the recitation of creole proverbs. Word of the African renaissance soon reached American shores. In summer 1970 a Durham, North Carolina, Pan-Africanist who had died tragically in the United States was buried on

Guyanese soil in a ceremony that combined Swahili and Yoruba traditions. The young man had long expressed the desire to be laid to rest in a land populated by African people.[12]

Guyana's efforts to follow a socialist course of development further enhanced its reputation among American radicals of all colors. Burnham had nationalized portions of the bauxite industry. He had identified cooperative enterprises, particularly agricultural ventures, as the means by which Guyana would combat capitalist exploitation and pursue self-reliance. (The nation, he vowed, would "feed, clothe, and house itself" by 1976.) Because Guyana's early Amerindian and African inhabitants were said to have relied on similar forms of cooperative production, even this economic strategy was steeped in the mystique of cultural reclamation. Here was a South American nation seemingly rising from African roots. For African Americans, who were dealing with a virtual economic catastrophe back home, Guyana's co-op movement seemed to represent a bold but practical answer to the scarcity and unemployment so evident in many of their own communities. *Black Journal*, the popular American television program, focused on Guyanese cooperatives when it profiled the country in 1971. One major African American newspaper hailed the birth of the Caribbean nation's cooperative system as a "quiet revolution."[13]

Burnham also appeared to be moving leftward in the area of foreign policy. During the early 1970s the leader embraced socialist bloc states, expressed solidarity with Palestinians, and made financial contributions to guerrilla forces in Southern Africa. Yet it was Guyana's status as a legal haven that truly endeared the country to African American dissidents. In 1970 Burnham officially invited political refugees from South Africa, the United States, and other troubled parts of the black world to settle in Guyana. This was a significant gesture at a time of intense state repression of black American militants. Burnham burnished his revolutionary credentials by explicitly offering asylum to those African Americans who, in his words, found life in the United States "intolerable and a contradiction of human dignity." Skilled émigrés with advanced technological training were especially welcome in the developing nation. Guyana could not match American salaries; black Americans were not to arrive "starry-eyed and believing this is the millennium or this is a utopia." What the country *could* provide, Burnham maintained, was self-respect. "Here the black man is a full man," the leader declared in a 1973 interview. "There ain't no white boss 'round here, in social terms, political terms, or economic terms."[14]

Of course some of the black American ideologues who lived in Guyana for extended periods beginning in the early 1970s were drawn as much to the country's fertile soil and lush vegetation as they were to its promise of political sanctuary. An exotic ecological haven, Guyana represented the ultimate "back to the land" experiment at a time when many US environmentalists, counterculturalists, and black militants were searching for radical alternatives to the consumerism and decadence of industrialized societies. ASCRIA had long urged Afro-Guyanese "Turn back to the land!" as a way to revive agrarian roots and achieve economic self-sufficiency. Similar motives drove the dozens of African American naturalists who settled in Guyana's rugged interior and established government-subsidized cooperative farms. The practice was actively encouraged by Burnham's PNC, which was looking to populate and develop the nation's vast rainforest while deterring territorial encroachment by Venezuela, a hostile neighbor to the west. A contingent of Brooklyn Pan-Africanists who had been visiting Guyana since 1970 to study cooperatives and participate in self-help projects eventually secured three hundred acres in the interior. For these and other "pioneers," farming the Guyanese hinterland offered a way to "restructure [their] lives," establish an independent source of income, and escape the concrete jungle of the American ghetto.[15]

Most African Americans who spent any length of time in Guyana during the 1970s were somehow connected to cooperative farming and the dream of settling the interior. However, even those expats who remained in urban areas near the country's low-lying coastline shared some of the outlooks and aspirations of their agrarian counterparts. All "Afros" (as African Americans expats who dwelled in Guyana during the 1970s called themselves) were seeking refuge from Western imperialism and white supremacy. They were hardly overawed by the domestic social progress made by African Americans during the 1960s. In their view, neither the advent of formal legal equality nor the burgeoning ranks of black elected officials in the United States signaled genuine empowerment—not when the land, the means of production, and the monopoly of violence remained in the hands of the white American establishment. By contrast, the Guyanese power structure was largely black, and the society was replete with African images with which one's children could identify. Here in the "land of many waters," Afros believed, African Americans could start anew and contribute meaningfully to the construction of an infant nation.[16]

A small and eclectic group of educators and activist-intellectuals accepted the challenge. Though a procession of black American dignitaries passed through Guyana during this period—everyone from the black consciousness singer Odetta to the historian John Henrik Clarke and the Nation of Islam's Louis Farrakhan—the number of long-term, politically oriented African American settlers never exceeded a few dozen. Most of the expats were ideologues of one kind or another. They possessed some education and skill, though one or two were itinerants who had had "to jive their way through the white man's world" simply to survive. Several were bohemian artists (sculptors, painters, filmmakers, and photographers) who wished to make a nonwhite society their muse. These and other Afros had arrived in Guyana seeking a sense of dignity and self-determination that they felt had eluded them their entire lives.[17]

A few were fleeing prison sentences as well. Herman Ferguson, a one-time Malcolm X aide and member of the Revolutionary Action Movement, absconded to Guyana in 1970 after he was convicted of the politically dubious charge of conspiring to kill moderate civil rights leaders. Joined by his African American spouse, Iyaluua, he assumed the name Paul Adams and spent the next nineteen years in the country, working for the government and eventually rising to the rank of lieutenant colonel in the Guyanese Defense Force. Another fugitive, David Hill, followed a somewhat different trajectory. A civil rights and Black Power leader from Cleveland who was charged with extortion in connection with political protests against white-owned McDonald's franchises, Hill made his way to Guyana in 1972, rechristened himself Rabbi Edward Emmanuel Washington, and proceeded to construct a powerful black nationalist cult (the House of Israel) whose members allegedly served as violent enforcers for the ruling PNC.[18]

While many black American expats found employment in the Burnham administration, some clustered around Kwayana and ASCRIA. Among them was Ann F. Cook, a black nationalist writer from Georgia who had traveled to several African countries in the early 1960s before discovering Guyana on a 1968 tour of Latin America. The Afro-Guyanese, Cook found, bore the deep psychological scars of slavery and colonial brutality. Yet thanks to an incipient black consciousness movement, some were striving to "rid themselves of this self-hatred." Deeply impressed with what she saw as a vital struggle for mental liberation, Cook returned to Guyana in 1970, determined to help forge cultural and political ties between African Americans and Afro-Caribbeans. Eventually she married Eusi Kwayana and became Tchaiko Kwayana. Working alongside a handful of Pan-Africanists from the United States and South Africa, she taught disadvantaged children at a cooperative high school in the village of Buxton while helping to operate ASCRIA's ideological institute.[19]

Like Tchaiko Kwayana, some Guyana Afros were seasoned internationalists who had lived overseas in the past. The artist Tom Feelings and the writer Julian Mayfield, both of whom took jobs with the PNC government, were alumni of Ghana's African American expat community. After the fall of Nkrumah in 1966, Feelings feared that the black world had lost an irreplaceable power base. His grief abated, however, when he discovered that "the pendulum of history . . . had moved across the Atlantic Ocean and come to rest over the co-operative Republic of Guyana." In 1971 he and his spouse, Muriel Feelings, a writer and onetime member of Malcolm X's Organization of Afro American Unity, moved to Guyana with their infant son to begin working for the Ministry of Education. The pair were to help produce a new series of multiethnic textbooks designed to replace the Eurocentric school primers of the colonial era, thus hastening the end of "foreign control" of the minds of the country's children.[20]

The move to Guyana offered Tom Feelings an exhilarating opportunity to help develop a positive black ideology from the ground up. It was futile, he believed, to attempt to "build an Africa" in the United States, a land "where there are 180 million white people to our 40 million, where the struggle can only be for a 'job' and for 'equality.'" In Guyana Feelings no longer felt obliged to function "under somebody else's white terms." Coming to the South American nation enabled him to participate freely in a movement "to link up the minds and bodies of black people all over this world." Here was a chance to continue the left Pan-Africanist project that the Ghana Afros had begun in the 1960s. Guyana was to be a spiritual "middle passage"; Feelings planned to make his contribution there before resettling on the Mother Continent with his family. "My heart is with the Black people of America," he wrote during the Guyana sojourn, "but my soul is in Africa."[21]

Mayfield was equally taken with Guyana, which he saw as a nation on the move, a nation striving to control its destiny in bold defiance of the developed world. He was especially impressed with Guyana's status as the only place on Earth "where a black minority controls the government." Perhaps even more than some of his fellow émigrés, he seemed to equate nation-building with the formal exercise of state power. Mayfield had served as an aide to Nkrumah between 1962 and 1966. It was in Ghana that he met Eusi Kwayana, who had convinced him of Guyana's value as a matrix of black self-determination. Mayfield had returned to the United States after the dissolution of Nkrumah's regime. In 1971, however, he had moved to Guyana ("highly trained nationals are at a premium," he later observed) to work as a communications officer in the Ministry of Information and Culture. Within a year he had been promoted to senior special political assistant to the prime minister, a job that enabled him to serve as political strategist, PNC propagandist, and liaison between Burnham and the many stateside black Americans—from journalists to political refugees—who were eager to behold "this 83,000 square miles of untold wealth called Guyana."[22]

Mayfield believed his adopted country was embarking on a genuine socialist mission, but he had no illusion that the task would be easy. The Guyanese people, he concluded, had yet to shed the psychic fetters of colonialism. The brainwashing of the country's African-descended population had been especially severe. "In all things that truly matter the highest standard is nearly always British," he lamented. Mayfield doubted that most Guyanese nationals possessed the willpower or temperament to transform their homeland from a backwater ex-colony to a beacon of the nonaligned world. That kind of discipline required "the psychology of war." It required both the dogged pursuit of national interest and the elimination of cultural attitudes that had been inbred for generations.[23]

Mayfield therefore was happy to be working for Burnham. The prime minister was a wily politician, a man afflicted with none of the sentimentality that Mayfield saw as an obstacle to the modernizing crusade so desperately needed throughout the Third World. Though Mayfield had been present in Ghana as Nkrumah's government had degenerated into a vulgar personality cult, the African American writer was not the least concerned that Guyana was also, in effect, a one-party state (Jagan's official role as opposition leader notwithstanding). What Guyana needed more than vigorous parliamentary debate was a leader who could govern with a firm hand. In the final analysis, Mayfield concluded, Burnham was exceptionally qualified to perform the rugged duties of leadership. Furthermore, in the context of a polarized society in which Indians and black people appeared to compete bitterly for almost every available political and economic resource, Mayfield was not at all sorry that the chief executive was unabashedly "a man of Africa." Content with his job and his new life, the advisor to the prime minister decided that he would make Guyana a permanent home and perhaps even try his hand at farming on the East Bank.[24]

Not for the first time, however, the African American dream of a distant promised land proved illusory. The contradictions of the Caribbean Zion were soon revealed. Guyana's Afros encountered some of the usual difficulties experienced by black American émigrés to the Third World. The expats, for example, faced resentment from an indigenous middle class that regarded them as competitors for professional jobs. Other problems proved more significant. Among them was the tendency of African American sojourners to import definitions of *blackness* and *Pan-Africanism* that failed to fully capture the dynamics of class and power in a nonwhite, postcolonial society. Many of the expats also clung to inflated notions about the pace and scope of change that could be achieved in a poor, Third World country. Even more ominously, political rifts began to appear within their ranks. It was not long before the Guyana Afros found themselves divided between PNC loyalists (based largely in Georgetown) and supporters of ASCRIA (headquartered in Buxton).

At issue was Burnham's legitimacy. Despite Guyana's positive image among much of the black American intelligentsia, troubling questions had lingered over the office of the chief executive. In the 1950s and 1960s Americans who were even vaguely aware of Guyana knew that the country's leader before independence, the leftist Jagan, had been sidelined by British military intervention and CIA intrigue. The ascent of Burnham, an erstwhile Jagan protégé, to the country's highest political station reeked of opportunism, if not counterrevolutionary maneuvering. In the early aftermath of Guyana's 1966 independence, progressive US publications had derided Burnham as a neocolonial stooge. Some North American observers continued to regard Guyana as more or less a US client state. Even as Burnham shifted to the left in the late 1960s, reports surfaced of the growing corruption and authoritarianism of his regime.[25]

Those allegations gained traction after ASCRIA defected from the PNC in the early 1970s. The Pan-Africanist organization's support for Burnham had helped bolster Guyana's profile among African American politicos. By 1972, however, Kwayana and other ASCRIA members had begun denouncing

Burnham as an agent of "feudal-capitalism," the system by which multinational sugar companies maintained control of the best coastal land in the country. Kwayana, who had long accused Jagan of practicing a crude brand of racial politics, now charged that Burnham too had fomented racial strife as a means of consolidating his political base. More damaging for Burnham's international reputation, the ASCRIA leader wrote a series of articles for *Black Scholar* and other progressive publications in which he condemned the prime minister as a faux Marxist and a defender of the interests of foreign capital and the Guyanese petit bourgeoisie. Meanwhile the influential *Muhammad Speaks*, a major source of African American knowledge about the black world, warned of Guyana's "false prestige" as a stronghold of Third World socialism.[26]

The specter of neocolonial intrigue and the dispute between Kwayana and Burnham ruptured Guyana's aura of Pan-African unity. The Afros found themselves embroiled in a political battle whose historical dynamics they as newcomers could not fully comprehend. Fearing the disintegration of their tiny expat community, Feelings and Mayfield attempted to mount an intervention. In late 1972 they asked Kwayana to meet privately with Burnham to discuss a possible detente. The conflict between the two principal Afro-Guyanese nationalists, they argued, represented a tragic feud that threatened to divide the country's black population on the eve of a national election. Kwayana, however, insisted that reconciliation was impossible. In his view Burnham was "playing games with the idea of the cooperative revolution," an offense that required principled opposition from the grassroots. Feelings and Mayfield then sought to broker a truce between the ASCRIA Afros and those in the PNC. But the schism could not be suppressed. Each side envisioned itself as the true agent of revolutionary Pan-Africanism and as an adversary of bourgeois opportunism.[27]

Any lingering notion of Guyana as a New Jerusalem—and of the Afros as a cohesive body—evaporated in early 1973, when Burnham abruptly deported two African American intellectuals. Mamadou Lumumba and Shango Umoja, of the revolutionary nationalist journal *Soulbook*, based in the San Francisco Bay Area, had lived in the country as schoolteachers and officials of the Pan African Secretariat, having been granted permanent residence by the government. As Burnham and Kwayana drifted apart, however, the pair of Afros had sided with Kwayana. Then ASCRIA had escalated its campaign of agitation, initiating a squatters movement by calling on poor Afro- and Indo-Guyanese to participate in a seizure of unused land monopolized by the large sugar estates. After this provocation Burnham appears to have decided that those expats most openly aligned with his political foes were no longer welcome in the republic (despite the assurances of Feelings that no Afro posed a serious threat to his administration). Thus in the early hours of January 31, 1973, Lumumba and Umoja were apprehended by soldiers, bundled onto a flight bound for New York City, and whisked out of the country.[28]

Upon arriving stateside, the deportees wasted no time in preparing a coun-
terassault. Dispatching essays to several Caribbean and African American
publications, the pair launched a major effort to end what they saw as the
misguided romance between black American internationalists and the Guyanese state. Burnham's promise of political asylum to freedom fighters from
throughout the diaspora, they asserted, was "pure legal fiction." The ejection
of African American refugees (Lumumba and Umoja were, in a sense, voluntary exiles, as opposed to those who had fled formal legal prosecution in the
United States) was an example of modern-day "slave trading" and another
indication of the prime minister's "willingness to work hand-in-hand with US
imperialism to destroy Pan-African revolutionaries and uproot black liberation movements." Kwayana echoed the charges in another flurry of articles,
dismissing PNC leaders as parasitic elites and maintaining that any black
American who received formal political asylum in Guyana was "here with
the consent of Nixon."[29]

Those Afros still employed by the Guyanese government were aghast. In
their view, the Lumumba-Umoja diatribes were sophomoric and cynical, a
case of "blacker than thou" grandstanding born of frustration and shame. By
accusing Burnham of collusion with Western imperialism, the deportees and
their allies had endeavored not only to discredit the prime minister and his
administration but also to impugn the whole project of Pan-African internationalism in the Caribbean. If Lumumba and Umoja were victims, the Georgetown Afros insisted, they were victims of their own naïveté. As several of the
expats observed, all sovereign governments reserve the right to expel any alien
deemed undesirable. A guest enjoying the hospitality of a friendly government
is obliged to conduct himself or herself in such a manner that his or her host is
not compelled to withdraw the invitation. Instead Lumumba and Umoja had
violated the first rule of expatriation: *Steer clear of local politics*. The outcome
of such indiscretion should have been predictable.

Small countries, Mayfield noted in a *Black Scholar* essay about the Lumumba-
Umoja affair, "have enough problems already without importing them from
abroad." What the deportees had not recognized, the Burnham aide asserted,
was that "in Guyana they were dealing with a sovereign government and not
some college or NAACP-type situation in the United States." Indeed Lumumba
and Umoja had exhibited not just ignorance but extreme hubris. By presuming
to tell Guyanese how their country should be run, they had demonstrated that
black folks were no more immune to "Great American chauvinism" than were
any of their compatriots.[30]

Feelings shared Mayfield's indignation. He was especially incensed at charges,
leveled by ASCRIA and other opposition groups, that Burnham had cooperated
with US authorities to return to the land of their oppression two vulnerable
political refugees. In truth, Feelings declared in a published essay, the Guyanese
government had never failed to assist "any brother or sister from the States"
who, in good faith, requested sanctuary and/or employment. Despite Lumumba

and Umoja's self-serving rhetoric, Feelings pointed out, a number of devoted African American activists remained in Guyana, where, "without fuss or fanfare," they continued to work diligently "to help build a self-reliant nation."[31]

Feelings, however, was willing to concede that some accusations of PNC corruption might be credible. He himself had glimpsed signs of impropriety. By contrast, Mayfield remained unwavering in his support of the ruling party and its charismatic leader. The advisor to the prime minister continued to view his boss as a devoted nationalist who was prepared to act decisively to protect the interests of his beleaguered homeland. Burnham, Mayfield argued in an unpublished manuscript, was struggling valiantly to reduce Guyana's dependency on foreign powers. The squatters movement launched by Kwayana and company, a stunt clearly designed to embarrass the government, had occurred just as the prime minister was actively negotiating with Bookers, the largest sugar concern in the country, over the question of surplus land. Burnham's problem was not corruption, Mayfield insisted. His problem was the recklessness of opposition groups and the recalcitrance of a citizenry that too often lacked the drive and vision to do what needed to be done: wean themselves of colonial sensibilities; settle and develop the interior; and, with the harvest of ten thousand cooperatives, fashion a flourishing and self-sufficient republic.

The Lumumba-Umoja affair eventually faded from the headlines. The damage, however, was done. The Afros remained bitterly divided. Relations between African American supporters of ASCRIA and backers of the PNC grew so acrimonious that Mayfield, fearing violence, asked Burnham for special permission to carry a concealed pistol. The expatriate project that had begun with great promise was dissolving in discord and disillusionment. The Pan-African ideal that had brought the Afros to Guyana was vanishing like a mirage. Some of the exiles wondered whether they would ever see the new society for which they had labored. "We can move to other countries," Feelings noted sadly, "but some of us still carry the shackles in our heads."[32]

Around this time Feelings began to intimate that his future in Guyana was uncertain. For the moment, however, Mayfield stayed the course. He continued to serve as Burnham's advisor and as a stalwart defender of the administration. There were practical reasons for doing so. The aide to the prime minister was well employed by local standards. He had married a Guyanese national, and he still hoped to carve a fruitful life for himself in the Caribbean. Beyond these circumstances lay the simple reality that Mayfield *believed* in Burnham—both as the politician best equipped to usher Guyana into the postcolonial future and, perhaps more important, as the embodiment of the genuine black power and autonomy that had proved so elusive back in the United States.

It was absurd, Mayfield reasoned, to blame Guyana's chief executive for economic woes that stemmed in part from fluctuations in the international price of bauxite, sugar, and rice. Nor would the African American writer accept characterizations of Burnham as an emerging dictator—not while Washington itself continued to demonstrate its violent disregard for the sovereignty and democratic will of foreign nations (most recently in Southeast Asia and Allende's Chile). The fact was that Burnham was *necessary*. He was a bulwark against the rise to political power of the Indo-Guyanese, an event that would surely mean the loss of one of the very few black land bases in the hemisphere. For many US Pan-Africanists this was an unthinkable scenario. Whatever its shortcomings may have been, the Black Arts writer Marvin X observed in a 1973 letter to *Muhammad Speaks*, the Guyanese government had taken the extraordinary step of opening its doors to just about any African American refugee who came calling. "Where in the western hemisphere can a Black man go?" the essayist wondered aloud. "Except for Guyana, where can you go and be among Black/English speaking people?"[33]

Yet visions of Guyana as a vital political frontier could not mask the brutal realities of the Burnham regime. During the first half of the 1970s, conditions deteriorated rapidly in the Caribbean nation. Despite the PNC's Marxist-Leninist rhetoric, the ruling party pursued a form of cronyism and state capitalism that severely exacerbated the country's poverty and instability. Government officials used the nationalization of industry to enrich themselves while much of the citizenry faced chronic food shortages and soaring unemployment. Meanwhile Burnham transformed the society into a virtual police state, violently suppressing political dissent and labor unrest and committing widespread election fraud. Crime, racial enmity, and social alienation intensified amid the growing repression.[34]

In 1974, with Guyana's progressive international image faltering, Feelings and Mayfield finally left the Caribbean country for good and returned to the United States. Both men had mundane reasons for heading back to what Mayfield called "the hell hole." Feelings hoped to start a major new art project and recover from the dissolution of his marriage. Mayfield had been advised that he required medical treatment that needed to be administered in the United States. Both men said they missed a distinctly African American sense of community and camaraderie. But their departures from South America were tellingly abrupt. The Pan-African initiative in Guyana had collapsed.[35]

The heyday of African American internationalist activity in Guyana had been brief but instructive. More than any other factor, it was the seductive appeal of the nation-state that both drew black Americans to Guyana and doomed the Pan-Africanist mission they pursued. Like many black emigrationists before them, the Afros had left the United States seeking not just a haven from white supremacy but also a base of power and a counterweight to Western imperialism. The black-controlled nation-state appeared to be the essential mechanism of self-determination. Viewing the exercise of state power as the fulfillment of racial destiny, many of the Afros had failed to examine thoroughly the internal dynamics of Guyanese society.

The idea that an enlightened political elite—aided by a like-minded cadre of skilled expats—could construct a just civilization on the ashes of colonialism camouflaged the reality of the PNC as a bureaucratic middle-class formation devoted primarily to private capital accumulation. As the historian and activist Walter Rodney, one of Guyana's most eloquent dissidents, later noted, the neocolonial politics of the Burnham regime derived largely from "the consolidation of the petty bourgeoisie as a class around the state." The venality and statism of nationalist leaders led to a sharp decline in the living standards of the peasantry and working class. Ultimately the façade of revolutionary socialism and the politics of racial chauvinism facilitated the neocolonial penetration of the society by international finance capital.[36]

What blinded some Guyana Afros to these circumstances—at least temporarily—was, in a sense, their Americanness. Many of the expats had brought to the Caribbean the privileges and frustrations of a tenuous African American educated class. They had arrived with a profound awareness of the relative political powerlessness of African Americans and the severe limitations on both their social mobility and their larger sense of individual and professional fulfillment. Combined with personal ambition, their yearning for refuge and for a genuine alternative to social marginality in the United States deepened their political and emotional investment in the practice of formal power. As Kwayana himself observed (not unsympathetically) in 1973, "You [African Americans] need contacts abroad. You need anything that gives you a little more dignity than you are enjoying in the white man's plantation."[37]

The expatriate experience in Guyana thus might be seen as a rather painful episode in the evolution of contemporary black internationalism. Indeed for some African American Pan-Africanists, the 1970s was a period of rapid analytical maturation. Close examination of the political economy of the English-speaking Caribbean, especially in the wake of the region's Black Power revolts, led to greater awareness of the nature of neocolonial domination of the Third World. International conferences within and beyond the United States and exposure to opposition groups in Guyana, Trinidad, Barbados, Jamaica, and Grenada deepened the understanding of some activist-intellectuals of the ways in which ruling elites had helped convert the Caribbean into "a hunting ground for finance capital." Neither populist rhetoric nor limited nationalization of resources, African American progressives learned, could guarantee social justice in the long term. Creating the new society, at home and abroad, required qualitative changes in relations of power and production and in the lives of the peasantry and/or working class.[38]

Those who learned such lessons realized that the quest for freedom in the postcolonial era would be even more complicated than the struggle for independence had been—a particularly useful insight for black Americans as they grappled with the social contradictions of the "postsegregation" years. Any viable campaign of black internationalism had to confront the ravages of monopoly capitalism in the metropolitan countries while remaining rooted in the material circumstances of the masses of the Global South. Even as their awareness deep-ened, some African American thinkers continued to look abroad for alternative social bases. Convinced that they would never achieve full human dignity in the land of their residence, they remained confident in the ability of black people to build a better world somewhere else. As Feelings wrote shortly after his Guyana sojourn, "America is not a do or die place for me. I could leave again."[39]

Notes

1. The epigraph to this chapter is from Brenda Gayle Plummer, *In Search of Power: African Americans in the Era of Decolonization, 1956–1974* (New York: Cambridge, 2013), 19; Jane Kramer, "Letter from Guyana," *New Yorker*, September 16, 1974, 100; "Guyana—Traveling a Revisionist Road?," *African World*, May 27, 1972; Julian Mayfield, "Stumping Berbice with Forbes Burnham," unpublished manuscript, Box 32, Folder 7, Julian Mayfield Papers, Schomburg Center, New York (hereafter cited at JMP, SC).

2. James T. Campbell, *Middle Passages: African American Journeys to Africa, 1787–2005* (New York: Penguin, 2006).

3. See, for example, Nikhil Pal Singh, *Black Is a Country: Race and the Unfinished Struggle for Democracy* (Cambridge, Mass.: Harvard University Press, 2004); Roderick D. Bush, *The End of White World Supremacy: Black Internationalism and the Problem of the Color Line* (Philadelphia: Temple University Press, 2009); Kevin K. Gaines, *American Africans in Ghana: Black Expatriates and the Civil Rights Era* (Chapel Hill: University of North Carolina Press, 2006); Penny M. Von Eschen, *Race against Empire: Black Americans and Anticolonialism, 1937–1957* (New York: Cornell University Press, 1997); Robeson Taj Frazier, *The East Is Black: Cold War China in the Black Radical Imagination* (Durham, N.C.: Duke University Press, 2015); Nico Slate, ed., *Black Power beyond Borders: The Global Dimensions of the Black Power Movement* (New York: Palgrave Macmillan, 2012); Gerald Horne, *Black Revolutionary: William Patterson and the Globalization of the African American Freedom Struggle* (Champaign: University of Illinois Press, 2013).

4. For a discussion of Guyanese and Caribbean contributions to Pan African politics, see Winston James, *Holding Aloft the Banner of Ethiopia: Caribbean Radicalism in Early Twentieth Century America* (London: Verso, 1998).

5. Fanon Che Wilkins, "'In the Belly of the Beast': Black Power, Anti-Imperialism, and the African Liberation Solidarity Movement, 1968–1987," Ph.D. diss., New York University, 2001; Russell Rickford, *We Are an African People: Independent Education, Black Power, and the Radical Imagination* (New York: Oxford University Press, 2016).

6. Manning Marable, "Black Nationalism in the 1970s: Through the Prism of Race and Class," *Socialist Review* 10 (1980): 57–108.

7. Nathan Hare, "Wherever We Are," *Black Scholar*, March 1971, 34; Daniel H. Watts, "The Third World," *Liberator*, October 1970; Courtland Cox, "Sixth Pan African Congress," *Africa*, September 1973; Tom Feelings, "A Letter from Tom Feelings to Julian Mayfield," *Black World*, August 1971; Tom Feelings,

handwritten notes for autobiography, n.d., Box 17, Tom Feelings Papers, Schomburg Center (hereafter cited as TFP, SC).

8. Gaines, *American Africans in Ghana*, 245–58; Seth M. Markle, "'We Are Not Tourists': The Black Power Movement and the Making of 'Socialist' Tanzania, 1960–1974," Ph.D. diss., New York University, 2011.

9. Clairmont Chung, *Walter Rodney: A Promise of Revolution* (New York: Monthly Review Press), 133.

10. Eusi Kwayana, *The Bauxite Strike and the Old Politics* (Georgetown, Guyana: Author, 1972); Arlene Torres and Norman E. Whitten Jr., eds., *Blackness in Latin America and the Caribbean: Eastern South America and the Caribbean* (Bloomington: Indiana University Press, 1998), 172–75.

11. Tom Feelings, autobiographical notes, Box 17, TFP, SC; "Guyana," *Black News*, March 21, 1970; "Guyana Welcomes African Americans and West Indians," *Black News*, July 23, 1970; "Guyana Conference on Pan Africanism," *Third World*, March 1970; Ann F. Cook, "Letters from Our Readers: All-Black Conference to Be Held in Guyana Soon," *Muhammad Speaks*, February 6, 1970.

12. "Guyana: A Growing Black Nation," *Black News*, April 15, 1973; "Black So. American Festival Set," *Afrika Must Unite*, March–April 1972; Eusi Kwayana, "Cultural Revolution in Guyana," *Soulbook*, Fall–Winter 1970; "Afro-Caribbean Liberation: Don't Grow Your Child with a Slave Name," *Third World*, March 1970; "Guyana Africans Bury North Carolina Freedom Fighter," *Liberation*, September 1970.

13. "Burnham of Guyana," unpublished manuscript, Box 15, Folder 8, JMP, SC; "Guyana Moves towards Self-Reliance," *SOBU Newsletter*, July 10, 1971; "Guyana Independence Day, February 23, 1971," *SOBU Newsletter*, February 20, 1971; "Guyana Nationalizes Bauxite," *SOBU Newsletter*, March 20, 1971; "Thoughts on Things within . . . at the Roots," *Guy News*, November 1971; "Socialism to Be Built on Co-operatives: CDE Burnham," *News from Guyana*, July 12, 1975; "Bona Fide Co-Operative Our Ideal," *The Pan African*, October 16, 1970; "New Self-Help Thrust in Guyana," *Chicago Defender*, September 18, 1971; "Credit Guyana Gains to Self Help," *Chicago Defender*, October 9, 1971.

14. Marvin X, "A Conversation with Forbes Burnham," *Black Scholar*, February 1973, 29.

15. "Guyana: Teachings of the Cultural Revolution," *Pan-African Journal*, Spring 1969; "Putting Your Muscle Where Your Mouth Is," *SOBU Newsletter*, October 31, 1970; "Uhuru Schule [*sic*] Inc. in Guyana," *News from Guyana*, September 8, 1973; "Americans Love Guyana's Self-Help," *News from Guyana*, August 11, 1973; "Guyanese Pioneers Are Face-Lifting Their Country," *Chicago Daily Defender*, February 6, 1973; Kasisi Jitu Weusi, "Return to the Soil Cooperative," *Black News*, September 1975; "A View on Guyana Deaths," *New York Amsterdam News*, December 2, 1979; Adeyemi Bandele, "Reflections of a Year in the Guyanese Interior," *Black News*, October 1977.

16. Tom Feelings, handwritten notes for autobiography, n.d., and Tom Feelings to Shirley Field-Ridley, July 20, 1971, Box 17, TFP, SC.

17. "Burnham of Guyana," unpublished manuscript, Box 15, Folder 8, JMP, SC; Herb Ottley, "Nation Time or Integration Time?," *Black World*, July 1971; "One Year Later," *Third World*, October 1970.

18. Herman Ferguson, *An Unlikely Warrior: Evolution of a Black Nationalist Revolutionary* (Holly Springs, N.C.: Ferguson-Swan, 2011), 215–26; Carey Winfrey, "A Second Guyana Cult Is Focus of Dispute," *New York Times*, November 22, 1978.

19. Ann F. Cook, "Black Pride? Some Contradictions," in *The Black Woman*, edited by Toni Cade (New York: Signet, 1970), 158–59; Ann F. Cook, "Guyana as Seen by an African-American," *Muhammad Speaks*, February 6, 1970; Mamadou Lumumba and Shango Umoja, "Ripped Off in Guyana," *Third World*, March 30, 1973.

20. Tom Feelings, "Guyana: Sanctuary or Slave Trader?," *Black News*, June 30, 1973, 9; transcript of April 1976 Tom Feelings speech to the Second National Conference of Afro-American Writers, Box 17, TFP, SC.

21. Feelings, "A Letter from Tom Feelings to Julian Mayfield," 30, 33; Feelings, handwritten notes for autobiography, n.d., Box 17, TFP, SC; Tom Feelings, *Black Pilgrimage* (New York: Lothrop, Lee & Shepard, 1972), 71. For an examination of Ghana's African American expat community during the cold war, see Gaines, *American Africans in Ghana*.

22. "Burnham of Guyana," unpublished manuscript, Box 15, Folder 8, JMP, SC; Julian Mayfield, "Political Refugees and the Politics of Guyana," *Black Scholar*, July–August 1973, 35.

23. "The Case for Television in Guyana," memo, Box 32, Folder 4, and "Burnham of Guyana," unpublished manuscript, Box 15, Folder 8 JMP, SC.

24. "The Case for Television in Guyana."

25. Feelings, handwritten notes for autobiography, n.d., Box 17, TFP, SC; Eusi Kwayana, "Politics in Guyana: Jaganism, Burnhamism and the People," *African World*, July 14, 1973; Selwyn Cudjoe, "Revolution in the West Indies," *Liberator*, August 1970; Marvin X to the editor of *Muhammad Speaks*, n.d., Box 32, Folder 3, JMP, SC; Peter Blauner, "The Fugitive," *New York*, August 7, 1989; Manning Marable, *African and Caribbean Politics* (London: Verso, 1987), 170–71; "Book Review: CIA Destroyed Guyana's Freedom," *SNCC Newsletter*, May 1967, 4; Cheddi Jagan, "The U.S.A. in South America," *Freedomways*, Winter 1968; Cheddi Jagan, "Former Prime Minister Vows to Break America's Iron Grip on Guyana," *Muhammad Speaks*, August 1, 1968.

26. Colin Collymore, "Division Holds Back Progress in Guyana," *Muhammad Speaks*, April 24, 1970; Eusi Kwayana, "Burnhamism, Jaganism, and the People of Guyana," *Black Scholar*, May–June 1973; Eusi Kwayana, "Burnhamism in Guyana," *African World*, August 11, 1973; Charles Watts Jr., "Guyana: What Is Glitter and What Is Gold in Burnham Rule?," *Muhammad Speaks*, April 14, 1972.

27. Tom Feelings to Forbes Burnham, n.d., Box 5, Folder 1, JMP, SC.

28. Lumumba and Umoja, "Ripped Off in Guyana," 11–13; Kwayana, "Burnhamism in Guyana," 12.

29. Lumumba and Umoja, "Ripped Off in Guyana"; Kwayana, "Burnhamism, Jaganism, and the People of Guyana," 40–46; "Eusi Kwayana Speaks," *Black News*, October 22, 1973; Kwayana, "Burnhamism in Guyana," 12; Eusi Kwayana, "Guyana Politics: Jaganism, Burnhamism and the People," *African World*, July 28, 1973.

30. Feelings, "Guyana: Sanctuary or Slave Trader?," 8–9; Mayfield, "Political Refugees and the Politics of Guyana," 33–34.

31. Tom Feelings to Eusi Kwayana, 1973, Box 4, TFP, SC; Feelings, "Guyana: Sanctuary or Slave Trader?," 9.

32. Julian Mayfield to Hon. L. F. S. Burnham, n.d., Box 7, Folder 3, JMP, SC; Feelings, handwritten notes for autobiography, n.d., Box 17, TFP, SC.

33. "Memo from Don Evans," Box 17, TFP, SC; Mayfield to Clarke, October 14, 1972, John Henrik Clarke Papers, Schomburg Center (hereafter cited as JHP, SC); "Burnham of Guyana," unpublished manuscript, Box 15, Folder 8, JMP, SC; Marvin X to the editor of *Muhammad Speaks*, n.d., Box 32, Folder 3, JMP, SC.

34. Marable, *African and Caribbean Politics*, 164–78; Kramer, "Letter from Guyana," 100–128; Cheddi Jagan, "Guyana at the Crossroads," *Black Scholar*, July–August 1974, 43–47.

35. Mayfield to Clarke, March 27, 1974, Box 6, Folder 2, JHC, SC; Committee for Democracy and Majority Rule in Guyana, flyer, Box 42, Folder 31, JHP, SC; Liz Gant interview with Willy Look Lai, "New Directions? Trinidad and the Caribbean," *Black World*, May 1974, 60–77.

36. "Rodney in Guyana," November 2, 1979 speech transcript, Box 42, Folder 41, JHP, SC; Walter Rodney, "Contemporary Political Trends in the English-Speaking Caribbean," *Black Scholar*, September 1975, 15–21.

37. "Eusi Kwayana Speaks," 26.

38. "Crucial Caribbean Issues Aired at Fisk," *African World*, December 1973; "Declaration of the Caribbean Unity Conference" and "The Organizations of the Caribbean Revolution," press releases, Box 5, Folder 71, JHP, SC.

39. Untitled notes, Box 17, TFP, SC.

CONTRIBUTORS

Keisha N. Blain teaches history at the University of Pittsburgh. She is the author of *Set the World on Fire: Black Nationalist Women and the Global Struggle for Freedom* (2018) and the coeditor of *Charleston Syllabus: Readings on Race, Racism, and Racial Violence* (2016).

Christopher Bonner is an assistant professor of history at the University of Maryland, College Park. He is currently completing a book manuscript titled *The Price of Citizenship*, which examines black activists' efforts to construct American citizenship before the passage of the Fourteenth Amendment.

Brandon R. Byrd is an assistant professor of history at Vanderbilt University. He is currently completing a book manuscript titled *The Black Republic: African Americans, Haiti, and the Rise of Radical Black Internationalism*, which focuses on the ways black intellectuals in the postemancipation United States conceptualized the link between Haitian independence and racial progress, civic inclusion, black self-determination, and eventually black liberation.

Christopher Cameron is an associate professor of history at the University of North Carolina at Charlotte. He is the author of *To Plead Our Own Cause: African Americans in Massachusetts and the Making of the Antislavery Movement* (2014).

Gregory Childs is an assistant professor in the Department of History at Brandeis University. He is currently completing a book titled *Seditious Spaces, Public Politics: Antiracism, Freedom, and Sedition in 1798 Bahia, Brazil*. It provides an in-depth examination of a late eighteenth-century movement known as the Tailors' Conspiracy.

Pero Gaglo Dagbovie is a professor of African American history and associate dean in the Graduate School at Michigan State University. His books include *Black History: "Old School" Black Historians and the Hip Hop Generation* (2006); *The Early Black History Movement, Carter G. Woodson, and Lorenzo Johnston Greene* (2007); *African American History Reconsidered* (2010); *Carter G. Woodson in Washington, D.C.: The Father of Black History* (2014); and *What Is African American History?* (2015).

Ashley D. Farmer is an assistant professor of history and African and African diaspora studies at the University of Texas at Austin. She is the author of *Remaking Black Power: How Black Women Transformed an Era* (2017), the first comprehensive study of black women's intellectual production and activism in the Black Power era.

Reena N. Goldthree is an assistant professor of African American studies at Princeton University. Her current book project, "Democracy Shall Be No Empty Romance: War and the Politics of Empire in the Greater Caribbean," examines how the crisis of World War I transformed Afro-Caribbeans' understanding of and engagements with the British Empire.

Robin D. G. Kelley is Distinguished Professor and Gary B. Nash Endowed Chair in US History at UCLA. He is the author of several books, including *Hammer and Hoe: Alabama Communists during the Great Depression* (1990); *Race Rebels: Culture, Politics, and the Black Working Class* (1996); *Freedom Dreams: The Black Radical Imagination* (2002); *Africa Speaks, America Answers! Modern Jazz in Revolutionary Times* (2012).

Ibram X. Kendi is a professor of history and international relations and the founding director of the Antiracist Research and Policy Center at American University. His second book, *Stamped from the Beginning: The Definitive History of Racist Ideas in America* (2016), won the 2016 National Book Award for Nonfiction and was a finalist for a National Book Critics Circle Award, an NAACP Image Award, and a Hurston/Wright Legacy Award.

LeRhonda S. Manigault-Bryant is an associate professor of Africana studies at Williams College. She is the author of *Talking to the Dead: Religion, Music, and Lived Memory among Gullah/Geechee Women* (2014) and the coauthor of *Womanist and Black Feminist Responses to Tyler Perry's Productions* (with Tamura A. Lomax and Carol B. Duncan, 2014).

Celeste Day Moore is an assistant professor of history at Hamilton College. She is currently completing a book manuscript, "Soundscapes of Liberation: Race, Music, and the Making of the Postwar Atlantic World," which reframes African American history within the commercial, political, and diasporic networks that composed the twentieth-century Atlantic world.

Guy Emerson Mount is a postdoctoral fellow and an instructor in the Department of History at the University of Chicago. He is currently working on a book manuscript based on his dissertation, "The Last Reconstruction: Slavery, Emancipation, and Empire in the Black Pacific." It is the first global history of emancipation to focus on the efforts of black activists and white politicians to colonize over five million African Americans in Hawai'i and the Philippines after the passage of the Thirteenth Amendment.

Russell Rickford is an associate professor of history at Cornell University. He is the author of *We Are an African People: Independent Education, Black Power, and the Radical Imagination* (2016) and the editor of *Beyond Boundaries: The Manning Marable Reader* (2011). His other publications include *Betty Shabazz: Surviving Malcolm X* (2005), the only major biography of Malcolm's late widow.

David Weinfeld is a visiting assistant professor of Judaic studies at Virginia Commonwealth University. His research interests include American Jewish history, intellectual history, and Black-Jewish relations. He is currently completing a book project titled "An American Friendship: Horace Kallen, Alain Locke, and the Development of Cultural Pluralism."

Judith Weisenfeld is the Agate Brown and George L. Collord Professor in the Department of Religion at Princeton University. She is the author of *New World A-Coming: Black Religion and Racial Identity during the Great Migration* (2017); *Hollywood Be Thy Name: African American Religion in American Film, 1929–1949* (2007); and *African American Women and Christian Activism: New York's Black YWCA, 1905–1945* (1998).

Michael O. West is a professor of sociology and Africana studies at Binghamton University (SUNY). His publications include *The Rise of an African Middle Class: Colonial Zimbabwe, 1898–1965* (2002); *From Toussaint to Tupac: The Black International since the Age of Revolution* (with William G. Martin and Fanon Che Wilkins, 2009); and *Out of One, Many Africas: Reconstructing the Study and Meaning of Africa* (with William G. Martin, 1999).

INDEX

AAIHS. *See* African American Intellectual History Society

Abbas. *See* 'Abdu'l-Bahá

'Abdu'l-Bahá ("Servant of Bahá"), 85–86, 88–90, 93

abolition/abolitionist movement, 5, 6, 12, 72, 143, 195–96, 198, 203, 207–8

Achille, Louis, 30, 34

activism, 6, 8–10, 12–13, 19–20, 59–73, 115, 175–88, 204, 207–13, 247. *See also* black activism

Adams, John, 224

Adams, Paul. *See* Ferguson, Herman

Adler, Felix, 87–88

affirmative action, 8

African American Intellectual History Society (AAIHS), 3

African diaspora, 3, 5, 7–8, 13–14, 30, 42, 45, 59–60, 125, 133, 141, 199, 218–19

African Society for Cultural Relations with Independent Africa (ASCRIA), 237–38, 240, 242–45

African Studies Association (ASA), 162

"African Woman," 12, 136, 175–80, 182, 183–85, 187–88

Afrikan Women's Conference (1974), 136, 186–87

Afro-American (newspaper), 30, 33

Age of Revolution, 13, 219–20, 224

agnosticism, 11, 99, 108

Akiba, Malaika, 182

Alain Locke Society, 95

Alexis, Alice Pierre, 64

Alexis, Pierre Nord, 64

Ali, Duse Mohamed, 7

Ali, Noble Drew, 99

Alien and Sedition Acts (1798), 224

Allen, Richard, 5

Allender's Jake. *See* Ellis, Jacob

Alliance Française, 34

American Dilemma, An (Myrdal), 161–62

American Philosophy Today and Tomorrow (Kallen), 83

American Revolution, 70

Amherst College, 27, 30

Amistad (1839), 197

Amsterdam News (newspaper), 32, 71, 110

Angelou, Maya, 118

antioccupation movement, 59–73

antislavery, 20, 195, 206–8, 210

apartheid, 21

Aponte, José Antonio, 219, 227

Aponte Rebellion, 219

Argudin, Pastor, 46

Armstrong Manual Training School, 85–86

ASA. *See* African Studies Association

ASCRIA. *See* African Society for Cultural Relations with Independent Africa

ASNLH. *See* Association for the Study of Negro Life and History

asphyxiation, 48–49

assimilation, 12, 21, 84, 93, 133–35; Black Power intellectuals and, 157–69; racial identity and, 47–49

Association for the Study of Negro Life and History (ASNLH), 28, 33

atheism, 11, 88, 99, 102–3, 108

Atlanta Compromise, 145, 147

Atlanta Exposition (1895), 19

Atlanta University, 9, 26, 33, 34

Atwood, Charlotte, 65–68, 71

Báb, the ("the gate," Siyyid Ali Muhammad), 85, 90

Baha'i faith, 10, 80, 83–96

Bahá'u'lláh ("Glory of God," Mirza Husayn-Ali), 85, 88, 93